DATE DUE

GOOD COMPANY

GOOD COMPANY

Business Success in the Worthiness Era

Laurie Bassi
Ed Frauenheim
Dan McMurrer
with Larry Costello

BK

Berrett–Koehler Publishers, Inc.
San Francisco
a BK Business book

Berrett-Koehler Publishers, Inc.
235 Montgomery Street, Suite 650
San Francisco, CA 94104-2916
Tel: (415) 288-0260   Fax: (415) 362-2512   www.bkconnection.com

Ordering Information
Quantity sales. Special discounts are available on quantity purchases by corporations, associations, and others. For details, contact the "Special Sales Department" at the Berrett-Koehler address above.
Individual sales. Berrett-Koehler publications are available through most bookstores. They can also be ordered directly from Berrett-Koehler: Tel: (800) 929-2929; Fax: (802) 864-7626; www .bkconnection.com
Orders for college textbook/course adoption use. Please contact Berrett-Koehler: Tel: (800) 929-2929; Fax: (802) 864-7626.
Orders by U.S. trade bookstores and wholesalers. Please contact Ingram Publisher Services, Tel: (800) 509-4887; Fax: (800) 838-1149; E-mail: customer.service@ingrampublisherservices .com; or visit www.ingrampublisherservices.com/Ordering for details about electronic ordering.

Berrett-Koehler and the BK logo are registered trademarks of Berrett-Koehler Publishers, Inc. Good Company Index is a trademark of McBassi & Company, Inc.

Printed in the United States of America

Berrett-Koehler books are printed on long-lasting acid-free paper. When it is available, we choose paper that has been manufactured by environmentally responsible processes. These may include using trees grown in sustainable forests, incorporating recycled paper, minimizing chlorine in bleaching, or recycling the energy produced at the paper mill.

Library of Congress Cataloging-in-Publication Data

Good company : business success in the worthiness era / Laurie Bassi ... [et al.]. — 1st ed.
     p.   cm.
   Includes bibliographical references and index.
   ISBN 978-1-60994-061-4 (hbk. : alk. paper)
   1. Corporations—Moral and ethical aspects. 2. Corporations—Social aspects.
3. Management—Moral and ethical aspects. 4. Management—Social aspects. 5. Business ethics. 6. Social responsibility of business. 7. Success in business—Moral and ethical aspects. I. Bassi, Laurie J. (Laurie Jo), 1954–
   HF5387.G656   2011
   658.4'08—dc23   2011017709

First Edition
16   15   14   13   12   11   10   9   8   7   6   5   4   3   2   1

COVER DESIGN: Irene Morris; INTERIOR DESIGN AND PRODUCTION: BookMatters; EDITING: BookMatters; INDEXER: Leonard Rosenbaum, PROOFING: Janet Reed Blake

Dedicated to all who are paving the way to
the Worthiness Era

CONTENTS

PREFACE

We're losing patience with bad companies.

Not just the four of us authors, but Americans generally. And people across the globe.

Fed up with Goldman Sachs's greed and sickened by BP's pollution. Tired of tainted food, tightfisted employers, and "corporate social responsibility" that is more marketing spin than true caring for our communities.

Society hasn't given up on capitalist corporations. We rely on companies for the basic necessities of food, clothing, and shelter, as well as modern conveniences like computers, air travel, and wireless connectivity. And we love the surprises they generate, from iPads and Wiis to Snuggies and even Silly Bandz.

But collectively we're setting a higher standard for businesses. We're beginning to make it more difficult for them to profit from pillage and plunder. A convergence of forces—economic, social, and political—is pushing businesses to be better to their employees, customers, and communities. In effect, people are demanding that companies in their lives be "good company."

We authors are big fans of Jim Collins and his influential 2001 book *Good to Great: Why Some Companies Make the Leap . . . and Others Don't*, which describes how companies can make the leap from good to great results. In *Good Company*, we focus on a fundamentally different concept of *good*: not as decent performance but as worthy behavior. And in the economic age that's emerging, companies cannot be great unless they are good.

We call this new chapter in our economic history the Worthiness Era.

In it, the reactive, halfhearted corporate responsibility efforts common today will increasingly ring hollow. Only thoroughly worthy companies that genuinely seek to do more than enrich a narrow set of shareholders and executives will thrive.

This a hopeful message. But it is not a softheaded one. A range of hard evidence points to this conclusion. Evidence from the stock market. From surveys of workers and consumers. From interviews with leaders of companies both big and small who agree a new economic era is at hand.

You may be skeptical. Amid a tepid recovery, after all, high unemployment is giving companies the upper hand with workers. And the world has just witnessed galling examples of corporate wrongdoing. Goldman Sachs bets against clients and exacerbates the Great Recession of 2008–2009 with its casino-like operations—then posts record profits. BP, with its "beyond petroleum" motto, fouls the Gulf of Mexico with a massive oil spill—but continues to rake in billions in revenue. It can look like the bad guys finish first.

But their days are numbered. The good guys have the wind in their sails. We took a tough-minded look at whether worthiness pays off with the Good Company Index, our ranking of the Fortune 100 (the 100 largest businesses on the Fortune 500 list of America's largest corporations) regarding their records as employers, sellers, and stewards of society and the planet. The results were clear. Companies in the same industry with higher scores on our index—that is, companies that have behaved better—had outperformed their peers in the stock market.

These "good" companies show the tremendous power of seeking win-win relationships with all their stakeholders—employees, customers, shareholders, and the communities where they do business. A business ethic of real reciprocity, in other words, reaps rich rewards.

The four of us authors couldn't be happier with this finding. We have made careers in business and journalism, fields that depend on dispassionate, coolheaded analysis. But of course we have our passions as well. In particular, we share a belief that workplaces, too often the sources of people's problems, can instead become solutions to those problems. As we worked to articulate this shared perspective, we came to understand the ways that being a good employer, being good to customers, and being a good steward are fundamentally connected. That understanding—and our commitment to better workplaces—set us on the quest that has culminated in this book.

For Laurie it all started when she was a young assistant professor of economics at Georgetown University in the mid-1980s. She found herself deeply moved by an interview she did in a steel mill with a worker who told her that he went home at the end of every day, "whupped, tired, and disgusted." That started Laurie thinking. What if that workplace could be changed, so that worker could come home more energized or could learn new skills at work? What would those changes mean for his ability to raise his children, to become more involved in their education, or to contribute more actively to his community? And what if that could be played out in millions of workplaces, touching hundreds of millions of lives?

As a result of that conversation, Laurie's research took a different turn. She focused her work on the relationship between corporations' workplace practices (especially those related to employee management and development) and business results. If she could identify what practices improve the bottom line while also enhancing the lives of employees, those would be practices that employers should want to pursue while simultaneously changing the workplace in a positive way.

Along the way, Laurie met and enrolled Dan (one of her graduate students at Georgetown), followed by Larry (an early client of the consulting firm that she and Dan founded), and finally Ed (a journalist who met Laurie and Dan while writing a profile of them).

We have written *Good Company* for leaders at all levels within organizations—from frontline employees up to the Board of Directors—who want to be better prepared to help shape the future of their organizations in positive ways. But the book is also written for all consumers and investors who seek to understand, benefit from, and contribute to the emergence of the Worthiness Era.

Good Company is divided into four parts, which can be read in sequence or separately. Part I outlines the forces that herald the beginning of the Worthiness Era. Chapter 1 provides a high-level overview of a convergence of forces—economic, social, and political—that is behind the "worthiness imperative," while Chapters 2 through 4 describe each of these forces in turn.

Part II focuses on quantifying the Worthiness Era from an organizational perspective. If you want to see evidence that good behavior will make or break firms in the near future, go to Chapter 5. If you want to jump right to our Good Company rankings of the Fortune 100, skip to Chapter 6. While the evidence and rankings in this part are focused primarily on large, publicly traded companies (because of data availability), the perspective is relevant for all organizations, including small businesses, privately held companies, and nonprofit organizations.

To get the very latest Good Company rankings, visit our Web site: www.goodcompanyindex.com. The site also offers additional features, including the ability to drill down into the data behind each company's rating.

Part III spells out the essential components of being a good company. For details about being a good employer, go to Chapter 7. More about developing a worthy relationship with customers and being a good steward can be found in Chapters 8 and 9, respectively.

In Part IV, Chapters 10 and 11 provide a glimpse into the future of worthiness, including how the concept dovetails with the rise of Asia as an economic power.

Work on *Good Company* began before the Great Recession. We were concerned, to be honest, that harsh economic times might reverse a nascent trend of more ethical economic behavior by consumers, workers, and investors. People could have focused strictly on selfish needs like low prices and quick, high returns. They could have lowered their standards and dealt a blow to the Worthiness Era. But by and large they didn't. Despite some personal sacrifice, people continued to make choices that were caring toward others and thoughtful about the planet's future. And as we complete this book in early 2011, all signs indicate those trends will strengthen in the years ahead.

In other words, people are keeping each other company better than they have in the past. That means we—all of us—no longer want to keep company with bad companies. And pretty soon we won't.

PART I The Worthiness Era

The Worthiness Imperative

The Home Depot didn't look bad on paper in early 2007. But online, the home improvement giant didn't look good. And the story of that disconnect gets at the heart of this book: we're entering an age when goodness matters for companies like never before.

In January 2007, Home Depot ousted an unpopular, highly paid CEO, Robert Nardelli. And although Nardelli's whopping $210 million severance package irked investors, the company signed a much more reasonable deal with his successor, Frank Blake.[1] The Nardelli-Blake transition earned Home Depot positive press.[2] And although Home Depot was suffering from the housing market decline, Blake announced a hopeful outlook in late February.

"The long-term fundamentals of our company are strong," Blake said, "and we believe we can improve our performance and grow at, or faster than, the market beyond 2007."[3] He also outlined investments for better employee engagement, improved product innovation, and tidier stores.

But one month later, this corporate giant—which in 2006 had ranked 14th in the Fortune 100—was beset by the consumer equivalent of a mosquito swarm. The trouble started with an essay by personal finance columnist Scott Burns at Web site *MSN Money*. In the article, Burns lamented that Home Depot no longer held an intimate place in his life.

Sixteen years ago, I sent my wife a love note. It went like this:

"Carolyn: I've gone to Our Store. Be back soon. Love, Scott."

We called Home Depot "our store" because we spent a lot of time there back in 1990. We're house freaks. . . . But I have a confession to make. I still love my wife, but we don't shop much at Home Depot anymore. Indeed, we generally try to avoid it and grieve for the loss.[4]

The reason Home Depot fell from his good graces, Burns wrote, is that the company shifted from serving customers well to abusing their time through skimpy staffing. "The result is that a once-iconic, wonderfully American store has become an aggravation rather than a blessing," he wrote.

MSN Money invited readers to share their own experiences with the "Big Orange Box." They did. By the thousands. Within the first week alone, some 4,700 comments were posted at the site.[5] The bulk of them told withering tales of unhelpful employees and unpleasant visits.

One longtime customer echoed the loss Burns felt because of Home Depot's decaying service. "I have been shopping at HD for 18 yrs. I used to go in and walk the aisles in the evening to relax and see new products," the reader commented. "I now dread a trip to HD for any reason. The place is filthy and in disarray. If you need help too bad."[6]

Amid all the lamenting and lambasting, Home Depot stepped into the fray—and in an unconventional way. Rather than have the firm publish a traditional press release, Frank Blake himself posted a comment directly on MSN's discussion board. Blake said the company was taking steps to improve its service and shopping experience and apologized for the disappointment.

"There's no way I can express how sorry I am for all of the stories you shared," Blake wrote. "I recognize that many of you were loyal and dedicated shoppers of The Home Depot.... And we let you down."[7]

The torrent of unflattering testimonials about Home Depot by everyday people and the fact that its CEO felt compelled to make a personal, direct appeal to customers speaks to a profound change under way in the business world today.

More and more, companies must be good to succeed. That is, they have to be good to their customers—as Home Depot wasn't a few years back—as well as good stewards of communities they touch and of the broader environment. And they must be good employers. Not just generous and caring, but smart about managing people effectively and able to inspire them—something that Home Depot apparently wasn't doing well at the outset of 2007.

In effect, people are choosing the companies in their lives in the same way they choose the guests they invite into their homes. Consumers, employees, and investors are demanding that companies be "good company." When Home Depot went from being a trusted companion to a "consistent abuser of its customers' time," for example, Scott Burns kicked it out of his life. He no longer considered Home Depot to be worthy of his business.

And he let the world know about it, prompting thousands of other people to give their two cents. That they all did so through an online give-and-take gets at the reasons goodness—or worthiness—is fast becoming an imperative.

Chief among the factors pushing companies to behave better are the rise of interactive Web 2.0 technologies and a corresponding culture of participation and disclosure, whereby millions of people are publishing their experiences and opinions online. Also forcing companies in the direction of worthiness is a growing global consciousness. Heightened appreciation of human interdependency—fueled by factors like international trade, travel, and concern about global climate change—is making people care more about how companies treat workers, customers, communities, and the environment.

Now more than ever, people are interested in and able to evaluate which companies are worthy of their business as customers, their best efforts as employees, and their capital as investors. In short, people have newfound power to reward and punish corporations for their actions, and they are doing so in a rising wave of "ethical" economic behavior.

Perhaps surprisingly, the Great Recession did not diminish people's desire to keep company with good companies. Buying sustainable products from high-road companies often costs more. But people, many of them making do on reduced income, have become more scrupulous about companies' morals in recent years. A 2009 study of 6,000 consumers globally found that 61 percent bought a brand that supports a good cause even if it wasn't the cheapest brand. What's more, 64 percent said they would recommend a brand that supports a good cause, up from 52 percent only a year earlier.[8]

It is as if the financial crisis slapped Americans and others in the face, opening their eyes to the materialism and me-firstism that have largely guided our culture and economy over the past three decades. People are holding themselves and the companies with which they do business to a higher standard. Greed is giving way to goodness.

As a result of heightened consumer ethics and of forces with roots deeper than the recent recession, we are entering a new economic age. We call it the Worthiness Era. In it, companies face mounting pressures to prove themselves worthy of their employees, customers, and investors. In order to do so, they must combine competitive savvy with a genuine desire to do more than maximize short-term profits or enrich a narrow circle of stakeholders. And then they must back up those good intentions with actions. It's an era based fundamentally on reciprocity. Put simply, companies must demonstrate they care about people and the planet if they are going to prosper.

In fact, the oft-heard aphorism that companies "can do well by doing good" requires an update. Companies will not be able to do well *unless* they do good. What has been a nice-to-have over the past decade or so is becoming a necessity.

"Companies that become catalysts for social change and respond to rising consumer expectations that they and their brands help make the world a better place will not only survive, but also thrive, in ways their competitors will not," says Mitch Markson, president of consumer marketing at public-relations firm Edelman.[9]

The idea that good behavior is becoming a requirement may seem far-fetched at the moment. After all, among the companies profiting during the recent downturn were financial services firms like Goldman Sachs, which bet against its own clients and whose trading practices arguably worsened the economic crisis.[10] And American workers have never been more "disposable," as a *Bloomberg Businessweek* cover story in early 2010 put it.[11] Many workers have had little choice but to settle for precarious or part-time jobs amid high unemployment, greater use of temporary labor, and continued offshoring.

Forces like these can slow the drive to better behavior. But even in a more free-agent economy, with work defined by contingent, impermanent arrangements, the world is changing in ways that ensure that worthy companies eventually will prevail. Whether they use employees or contractors to accomplish their mission, firms increasingly will have to respect, care for, and inspire workers. Failure to do so will translate into poor productivity, poor products, and a poor reputation in the eyes of workers, consumers, and investors.

Exactly how a company puts worthiness into effect will depend on its particular industry, workforce, and abilities. But it won't be enough to have piecemeal corporate social responsibility programs. Nor will *greenwashing*—the all-too-common practice of cloaking less-than-good environmental stewardship with eco-marketing—fool a public ever-more savvy about what true sustainability looks like. Increasingly, organizations will be judged on how thoroughly worthy they are.

Not many corporations receive a top grade on that test right now. We developed a measurement of worthiness based on multiple criteria associated with customer care, people management, and stewardship, which we call the Good Company Index. Our research shows that just two Fortune 100 firms—shipping titan FedEx and entertainment giant Disney—earned an A, thereby meeting our definition of a Good Company. Plenty of the largest companies are laggards, with grades of D or F.

If we are right about the dawning of a new era, such less-than-fully commendable companies may still be able to survive in the years ahead. But unless they shift to a course of real reciprocity with their stakeholders, they will not flourish. As Home Depot discovered in 2007, the business world is changing. Changing for good.

The Telltale Signs

Among the telltale signs that worthiness is becoming an imperative:

- In early 2011, the "trust barometer" study by public-relations firm Edelman found that only 46 percent of U.S. respondents trust business to do what is right.[12]

- Despite the recession, sales of "ethical" consumer products have been growing rapidly. The U.S. market for items marketed as green, natural, organic, humane, or the result of fair trade has grown annually in the high single- to low double-digits over a recent five-year period, to a projected $38 billion in 2009.[13]

- In 2010, nearly three out of four Americans said they are more likely to give their business to a company that has fair prices and supports a good cause than to a company that provides deep discounts but does not contribute to good causes.[14]

- A 2010 study found that 64 percent of global consumers believe it is no longer enough for corporations to give money; they must integrate good causes into their everyday business. The report also found that 72 percent expect corporations to take actions to preserve and sustain the environment.[15]

- Consumers in emerging markets—projected to be increasingly important customers for many of the worlds' biggest companies— are more willing than their developed-world counterparts to pay a premium for technology products marked as environmentally friendly. On average, 84 percent of consumers in China, India, Malaysia, and Singapore say they would accept a higher price for a green product, compared with 50 percent in the United States, Japan, France, and Germany.[16]

- Globally, 56 percent of people want a job that allows them to give back to society versus 44 percent who value personal achievement more.[17]

- As we emerge from the Great Recession, Americans' job satisfaction has fallen to a record low. Just 45 percent of Americans were satisfied with their jobs in 2009.[18] Dissatisfaction with employers extends to the executive suites. A 2010 study of senior executives worldwide found 41 percent to be dissatisfied in their current positions, and 70 percent to be looking for new career opportunities.[19]

- Investors are starting to vote with their dollars for sustainable companies. The value of assets linked to the Dow Jones Sustainability

Indexes—which list the most sustainable large public companies in the world—has grown from about $1.5 billion at the end of 2000 to more than $8 billion at the close of 2009.[20]

- There are increasing signs that worthiness pays off. For example, studies by McBassi & Company—Dan and Laurie's consulting firm—demonstrate that providing opportunities for employees to learn is a key to future business success. Companies that spend more heavily on employee development subsequently outperform peers in the stock market.[21]

- Firms on *Fortune*'s 100 Best Companies to Work For list consistently outperform the overall stock market.[22]

- Data from the Good Company Index also shows that goodness has its rewards. When we compared Fortune 100 firms within the same industry, we found that those firms that had higher scores on the Good Company Index performed better in the stock market than their counterparts over 1-, 3-, and 5-year periods.

"Social Responsibility" Isn't Good Enough

Genuine corporate social responsibility up to now has been an option. Many companies tackle good citizenship only partially if at all. They may hire chief sustainability officers, publish reports about their philanthropic activities, and retool corporate mottos. But even when such efforts are sincere, companies often do not comprehensively demonstrate decency to stakeholders.

In fact, much of the eco-friendliness found in the market today is phony. A recent study found that 98 percent of consumer products were "greenwashed" in some fashion, such as the use of irrelevant claims, undocumented statements, or false labels.[23]

BP's devastating oil leak in the Gulf of Mexico in 2010 underscores the point. About a decade earlier, the company long known as British Petroleum changed its name simply to "BP" and adopted the tagline "beyond petroleum."[24] The novel spin on the company's initials came with a new white, yellow, and green sunburst logo, all of which conveyed the sense that BP had moved past oil into renewable energy sources. But renewable energy efforts have remained marginal to BP. Less than 1.2 percent of the company's revenue came from alternative energy in 2009, and its investment in alternative energy that year amounted to about 6 percent of its overall capital spending.[25]

BP is not alone in showing limited interest in sustainability. The data behind the Dow Jones Sustainability Indexes reveals that a cramped version of social responsibility is common. In compiling the indexes, research firm Sustainable Asset Management (SAM) grades the world's largest publicly traded companies on sustainability criteria, including corporate codes of conduct, labor practices, and environmental performance. For 2009, the average sustainability score was 48.[26] That figure represented an improvement from 1999, when the average score was 27. But most companies have a long way to go to achieve the maximum score of 100.

Although firms by and large aren't there yet, they are pursuing worthiness with greater determination. SAM reported a shift in attitude from "reactive to proactive" in a 2009 report.

"Previously, the integration of sustainability into business processes was driven primarily by regulatory, corporate governance and compliance requirements," said the report, which reviewed 10 years of sustainability assessments. "Today, companies embrace corporate sustainability as a key source of competitive advantage."[27]

We see worthiness as the successor to corporate social responsibility as it has been known thus far. The very term *responsibility* carries a ring of reaction, of responding, of taking action only after being questioned. Worthiness, by contrast, conveys a sense of intrinsic virtue, of purposefulness, of doing the right thing without being asked.

Why is worthiness gaining ground now? Because of a convergence of forces, some that have been gathering strength for centuries and others that have taken shape just in the past few years. Taken together, these economic, social, and political factors amount to technology-fueled people power.

Above, we highlighted the most prominent of the trends. People increasingly have a global, empathic mindset, making them concerned about how their shopping, work, and investing decisions affect other people and the planet. The emergence of Facebook, Twitter, blogs, interactive Web sites, and feedback sites like Yelp have given workers, consumers, and investors powerful tools for holding an organization accountable. And people are doing so thanks to a culture of increasing participation and disclosure.

What's more, Web sites such as Amazon.com and Yelp allow visitors to view average ratings for products and services, and also enable people to rate particular comments and assess reviewers. These features help ensure that the "wisdom of the crowd" is indeed wise—that overall assessments are accurate and the most meaningful praise and criticism rise to the surface.

The flood of comments about Home Depot at *MSN Money* in 2007 did not include an overall summary rating, nor were they filtered to highlight the best comments. Still, the sheer number of responses—a total of 7,092 messages by 6,051 authors—signaled something more than the gripes of a few disgruntled shoppers.[28] They validated the original essay by Scott Burns and his point that Home Depot had become a "troubled and unloved company" by "short-staffing" its stores.

Indeed, the shoddy service claim was corroborated by formal customer service studies. From 2001 to 2005, Home Depot's customer satisfaction rating fell from 75 to 67, according to the American Customer Satisfaction Index, an economic indicator created at the University of Michigan.[29] During the same period, rival Lowe's service rating rose from 75 to 78.[30]

Home Depot's sagging customer service figures may explain why CEO Blake was so quick to respond to the critical cries at MSN. He likely saw them as genuine. And Blake not only admitted fault, but did so among the masses in a regular posting and in a highly personal fashion.

"I'd like to thank Scott—his column about our company was insightful and revealing," Blake wrote. "You can easily tell that it struck a nerve with me."[31]

The form and tone of Blake's apology fit with the times. A desire for authentic communication from companies—instead of legalistic platitudes delivered from on high—is another feature of the growing democratization of media and the related culture of self-revelation and interactivity.

But the factors promoting worthiness go beyond these very visible trends. Other forces include increased globalization of trade, which dates back hundreds of years but has hit a critical intensity in the last 20 years. Increasing globalization is putting a premium on good people management. So is consumer desire for holistic "experiences" and a broader public concern for more economic security—anxiety that has escalated over the past three decades and reached a peak in the recent recession.

Also in play are continued worries about environmental degradation and catastrophic climate change, the rise of the civic-minded Generation Y, growing regulatory pressures, mounting shareholder activism, and increased workplace democracy.

To be sure, countervailing forces exist. Among these is the way globalization can lead to a race to the bottom in terms of labor standards, the recent skepticism about global warming, and the emergence of the U.S. Tea Party movement, which calls for small government.

But there are limits to the low-wage global strategy and increasing signs that even in emerging economies, treating employees well is crucial to company success. What's more, Americans profess deeply held concerns for the environment that extend beyond global warming to issues including clean air and water—and such cares have been reinforced by the movement to reexamine the safety and wisdom of the U.S. food system.

Even if regulatory demands were to weaken, the worthiness imperative would remain strong. Market forces—consumer, worker, and investor actions—are the main engines moving companies to be good.

Companies themselves are pushing each other in the direction of worthiness. FedEx, for example, is setting higher standards for its network of more than 100,000 suppliers. Most of the paper in its printing centers comes from suppliers certified by the Forest Stewardship Council, meaning it has come from responsibly managed forests.[32] FedEx also has provided training in its leadership principles to some of its suppliers, helping those organizations to manage their people better.[33]

"We're like a lot of companies," says Mitch Jackson, vice president of environmental affairs and sustainability at FedEx. "We want to do business with good companies."[34]

The recent economic slowdown could have put the brakes on the shift to the Worthiness Era. Consumers, workers, and investors could have focused exclusively on selfish needs like low prices and quick, high returns. But the downturn did not derail the public's move toward more moral choices around money. The economic ethics that began to gather momentum prior to the recession continued as people questioned spending habits and investment priorities. *Time* magazine put its finger on this pulse in a late-2009 story, declaring the emergence of the "citizen consumer": "There is a new dimension to civic duty that is growing in America—it's the idea that we can serve not only by spending time in our communities and classrooms but by spending more responsibly." [35]

What Does *Worthiness* Mean?

What does *worthiness* mean more concretely? The foundations are a degree of business smarts and a purpose that goes beyond making money. The ability to earn profits in the marketplace against tough competition is the table stakes of the emerging economy. Companies also must reframe their fundamental aims to be about a wide circle of stakeholders rather than about merely enriching shareholders. Economist Milton Friedman's argument that the only social responsibility of business is to increase profits has become outdated, if it ever made sense. Instead, companies will have to put worthiness at their center.

Pledges to be a good corporate citizen or commitments to sustainability must be taken seriously throughout an organization. Companies may want to formalize such promises along the lines of B-Corporations, a growing group of firms that incorporate the interests of employees, consumers, the community, and the environment into their governing documents.[36]

Beyond business acumen and a worthy purpose, successful firms of the future will have three key features: worthiness as an employer, as a seller, and as a steward.

Worthiness as an employer means treating workers decently while striking the right balance between viewing people as a cost and an asset. It requires a revision of the arms-length, layoff-prone relationship with workers common over the past three decades. It involves heeding workers' growing desires for employment security and career development. But it is not a return to the employment-for-life mentality that held sway from the 1950s through the 1970s.

In fact, good employers will combine greater care for workers with a more rigorous, analytic approach to people management than is typical today. Through wise use of data—about interests, abilities, performance, and how these tie to overall goals—employers will set up employees to thrive. And leaders will foster an inspiring culture, in part through a compelling mission. More intelligently orchestrated and stirring workplaces, in turn, will translate into better business results.

Our notion of the good company expands on the concern for employees typically found in corporate social responsibility efforts. The corporate responsibility movement and its variants—such as the push for a "triple bottom line" that accounts for people, planet, and profits—have focused chiefly on fundamental worker rights such as freedom from forced labor, freedom to organize unions, and decent pay. Those are necessary elements. But for a firm to go beyond these basic rights to the point of optimizing employees' contributions and helping them feel more alive on the job, smart people management and an inspiring mission are required. Increasingly, people are seeking such a worthy employment experience.

Worthiness as a seller means seeking win-win exchanges with customers that leave both parties better off. This emphasis on reciprocity upends the caveat emptor standard that has governed commercial transactions for centuries. The philosophy of buyer beware presumes a zero-sum situation, where one party will get the better of the other in a purchase. It lends itself to a mindset of corporate greed versus common good and leads to practices like the skimpy customer service found at Home Depot a few years ago. But increasingly, the public is calling for a new sensibility—*Seller take care.*

Worthiness as a steward means caring for the environment and the communities a firm affects. It means limiting the ecological harm a company's operations inflict through pollution and energy consumption. But it extends past doing less damage to doing more good. To creatively helping solve environmental problems.

A firm that's a good steward also demonstrates deep concern for localities in which it operates. Concern for the people who buy from it, certainly, but also for those who live or work nearby. Community stewardship encompasses traditional philanthropy such as donations to hospitals. But it also includes more active engagement in communities. It means helping to solve social problems with skills or resources specific to the firm.

Worthiness as a seller and a steward both imply a long-term view as well as a degree of humility and restraint. As a worthy seller and steward, taking care of business means—to a much greater extent than is typical today—taking care of others.

That's not to say that companies have to be perfect to be good. In fact, the three primary examples we use in the book to illustrate worthiness as an employer, seller, and steward—Beth Israel Deaconess Hospital, American Express, and Seventh Generation—all have stumbled in some respects in recent years. But fueled by expansive purposes, such as Seventh Generation's mission to inspire a more conscious and sustainable world, the three have kept at it. Persistence, in other words, can make up for inevitable setbacks on the road to becoming a good company.

Worthiness is a blend of the old and the new. It builds on notions of fairness, responsibility, and stewardship found in ancient myths and the stories of all the world's great religions. In the context of more recent decades, it meshes the tighter bonds with employees found in the 1950s, 60s, and 70s with the focus on higher performance dominant since the 1980s.

Worthiness seeks to marry the best of smaller, family-owned businesses, which often embody good employee relations and a sense of community service, with the economic scale and clout of large publicly owned corporations.

Worthiness also represents a union of East and West. It takes the connectedness of people and environment central to Eastern religions and philosophy and fuses it with the power of individual initiative and the sense of progress fundamental to Western thinking.

The Good Company Index

The worthy company, then, starts with good intentions and puts those into practice as an employer, a seller, and a steward. Most companies aren't there yet. Most are somewhere along a continuum of worthiness. We have placed each of the Fortune 100 companies on the worthiness continuum, assigning a Good Company grade—from A to F—to each. To do so, we gathered data about company actions with respect to employers, customers, and the environment.

We did *not* judge particular industries to be inherently good or bad. Many industries (oil, financial services, entertainment) have generated vehement opposition from some segments of the population. We steered clear of all industry-based debates, opting instead for alternative criteria in assessing the goodness of companies: their record as employers, sellers, and stewards.

Our index is based largely on publicly available information. We considered *Fortune*'s list of the best companies to work for and *Newsweek*'s ranking of America's largest 500 firms on green criteria. We also tapped the Dow Jones Sustainability Index of the most sustainable large companies in the United States and the employee ratings of firms at Glassdoor .com. For data on customer service and experience, we drew on information from research firm wRatings.

Our index also accounts for other evidence of bad corporate behavior, such as egregious CEO pay and significant fines by regulatory agencies.

Finally, we asked the companies in the Fortune 100 about the extent to which they marshal their particular strengths to do good in the world.

We were looking for cases like the one in which IBM employees used their computer expertise to help coordinate relief efforts after the 2004 tsunami in South Asia.[37] To us, such practices are an important sign of a genuine commitment to a wide circle of stakeholders.

Among the publicly traded Fortune 100 firms, only Disney and FedEx got a grade of A, qualifying them as "Good" in early 2010. FedEx stood out as a good employer and steward on our index. The shipping titan made *Fortune*'s Best Companies to Work For in America from 2008 to 2010, and it is working to minimize its environmental impact through steps like the introduction of zero-emission electric delivery vehicles in the United Kingdom.[38] FedEx prides itself as being a sustainability leader and showed as much in 2007 by calling for the U.S. Government to set fuel-efficiency standards annually for medium- and heavy-duty vehicles.[39] Founder and CEO Fred Smith also was named by Forbes.com in 2010 as one of the seven most influential people in "clean tech."[40]

Disney earned points as an employer, seller, and steward, reflecting the way the entertainment giant has done such things as emphasize leadership training, deliver holistic "experiences" to customers at its theme parks, and hold "Environmentality Summits" focused on sustainability issues.[41]

Disney also is in step with the shift from "responsible" to something worthier. As of late 2010, the company was revamping its "Corporate Responsibility" efforts under the new name of "Corporate Citizenship."[42] A wording change means little by itself. But Disney by its actions is proving to be a good, well-rounded corporate citizen.

And its philosophy captures the way worthiness allows all of a company's stakeholders to win. "At The Walt Disney Company, we believe that being a good corporate citizen is not just the right thing to do; it also benefits our guests, our employees and our businesses," Disney's Web site states. "It makes the Company a desirable place to work, reinforces the attractiveness of our brands and products, and strengthens our bonds with consumers and neighbors in communities the world over."[43]

Still, both Disney and FedEx have room to improve. FedEx, for example, set up shop in a tax haven, effectively doing a disservice to the communities it serves. And Disney could do better as an employer—it has not appeared on *Fortune*'s list of the 100 Best U.S. Companies to Work For, and its employee ratings on feedback site Glassdoor.com have been solid but not spectacular.

A Harbinger of Things to Come

Scott Burns was a harbinger of things to come. So was the longtime Home Depot customer who responded to Burns's essay on MSN and had come to "dread" visits to the store. The emotional connection Burns had with Home Depot—the affection he had for it and the grief he felt

---

The Party Gone Wrong

To understand the gathering strength of worthiness, let's look at economic history in the form of a parable. Call it the parable of the party gone wrong.

> A couple threw a party, inviting many friends. Among them was a wealthy one who brought gifts and wine to the hosts. But he behaved badly. He got drunk, grabbing more than his fair share of food, insulting—and sometimes assaulting—other guests and trashing the home.
>
> Even so, the couple tolerated him and even egged him on. Tipsy themselves and eager to stay in his favor, they let him and the party get out of control.
>
> The next day, though, the couple woke up with bad hangovers. And it dawned on them that the wealthy guest's gifts weren't very meaningful, that he had all but ruined their home and had frayed their other friendships. They decided to demand better of themselves and of him if he wanted an invitation in the future.

As you might guess, the wealthy guest in the story corresponds to companies and the couple to society at large. It's an oversimplification. But the tale captures the central features of business conduct and economic culture over the past few centuries, and the past few decades in

in leaving it when it became unworthy—signals the way all of us are starting to care more about the companies we let into our lives. We may not go so far as the MSN commenter, who would "relax" in the evenings with Home Depot. But more and more, people want to be at home with the firms in which they work, invest, and shop.

This desire comes in part from companies' own efforts to bond with us and gain "mindshare." Marketing and brand campaigns have long tried to position firms as a "good neighbor," a "family," and a "friend."

For years, we didn't look too closely at those feel-good claims as we invited companies into our lives. But now companies are getting more attention from us than they ever expected. These days, having been

---

particular. Modern corporations have brought society material riches, but their benefits have come at a significant cost. At times companies have balanced the needs of different stakeholders, including employees and communities. But during the past 30 years in particular they have become obsessed with enriching shareholders. The endless thirst for profits has intoxicated them, numbing them to the harm they do to people and the planet.

We in society have been complicit with our companies. Outfitted with 401(k) plans and focused on becoming rich, we've rewarded short-term corporate results and turned a blind eye to environmental harm and human exploitation.

But we're sobering up. The Great Recession has prompted a painful reckoning. As a pause in the materialistic party that has lasted since the beginning of the industrial age, the downturn has helped us see that the bash hasn't been all that satisfying and can't continue if we want our species to survive. We're setting the bar higher for ourselves and the companies in our lives. It's not like we can't have good times with companies. But we won't invite over the ones that take things to extremes in ways that ruin our earthly home or hurt our fellow human beings. Greed is on the way out. Goodness is in.

burned by bad business behavior and chastened by the Great Recession, we want to know details like how subcontracted workers are treated, how much the CEO makes, and how big the carbon footprint is.

We are growing more intimate with companies but in a wise way. If businesses want to be with us, they've got to be worthy.

Home Depot, for its part, pushed to be a pal to do-it-yourselfers with slogans like, "You can do it. We can help." But that tagline began to ring hollow under CEO Robert Nardelli. And customers like the MSN commenter held the company accountable. "Like it or not, the advertising states, 'we are here to help,'" the commenter wrote. "It creates an expectation of service that just doesn't exist. Customers come in expecting what is advertised."[44]

In the wake of this post and the broader public scolding it got at MSN, Home Depot tried to clean up its act.

It started with Frank Blake's frank apology on the site. And thanks partly to Blake's focus on employee engagement and improved treatment of customers, Home Depot has made progress rebuilding its rickety reputation. Customer service scores have risen.[45] And its stock outperformed rival Lowe's as well as the S&P 500 Index during the two-year period ending December 21, 2010.[46]

How well Home Depot does in the future remains to be seen. But people are feeling more at home with the company thanks to its recent good behavior.

For Frank Blake and CEOs everywhere, such worthiness is increasingly vital. Companies that prove to be bad company will find themselves left alone, without any invitations. And a company without company is soon no company at all.

CHAPTER ONE SUMMARY

A convergence of forces is giving rise to a new economic era—which we call the Worthiness Era.

The Worthiness Era

- A combination of economic, social, and political forces is pressuring companies to become "good company" to their employees, customers, and investors.
  1. Some of these forces have been gathering strength for centuries and others have taken shape just in the past few years.
  2. Taken together, the forces amount to technology-fueled people power.
- To thrive in the emerging era, companies must prove to be good employers, sellers, and stewards.
- Worthiness goes beyond corporate social responsibility. It conveys a sense of intrinsic virtue, of purposefulness, and of doing the right thing without being asked.

Good Company Index

- Based on the three pillars of good employer, good seller, and good steward, we created a Good Company Index that assigns a grade from A to F for each of the publicly traded Fortune 100.
- Data shows that goodness already has its rewards. Firms with higher scores on the Good Company Index performed better in the stock market than their counterparts.

The Future of Worthiness

- Even the Great Recession could not derail the momentum behind the Worthiness Era.
- Companies that disregard the new rules of business success do so at their own peril.

CHAPTER 2

The Economic Imperative

The Disneyland employees most pivotal to the famed theme park's customer satisfaction aren't the ones roaming around in Mickey Mouse and Goofy costumes.

They're the folks carrying brooms.

Scholars John Boudreau and Peter Ramstad have shown that the sweepers who continually tidy up the park and often answer guest questions are vital to Disney. The caliber of these workers and their ability to solve problems are crucial to the holistic "magic" Disney aims to create for visitors.

"Disney sweepers have the opportunity to make adjustments to the customer-service process on-the-fly, reacting to variations in customer demands, unforeseen circumstances and changes in the customer experience," Boudreau and Ramstad have written. "These are things that make pivotal differences in the 'Happiest Place on Earth.' . . . At Disney, sweepers are actually frontline customer representatives with brooms in their hands."[1]

The importance of sweepers to Disney speaks to the way in which consumers' desire for integrated experiences is propelling companies to greater worthiness. For Disney to delight customers on premium-priced vacation packages, the company can't just focus on excellent rides, good food, and friendly costumed characters. It has to make sure even the employees carrying out clean-up duties are sharp thinkers and sociable to boot. It has to recruit the right people to be sweepers, train them, engage them, and retain them—it must be a good employer.

Consumer hunger for more than just goods and services is one of several economic factors ushering in the Worthiness Era. Others are technological change, global trade, and the public's growing focus on economic security. This chapter discusses each of these forces.

Consumer Desire

Providing a wonderful, relaxing time has been a key to Disney's success over the years. It has fulfilled children's fantasies of meeting beloved characters and taking thrilling rides while realizing parents' visions of making their kids' dreams come true. The company was ahead of the curve in recognizing that consumers want memorable experiences or "transformations," where companies help individuals realize their aspirations.[2]

This desire on the part of consumers is not new—advertisers at the turn of the 20th century were trying to tie mundane products to grander concepts.[3] But the power of brands and experiences has been recognized and tapped most extensively in just the past decade or two.

Authors B. Joseph Pine II and James H. Gilmore warned companies to think bigger than mere goods and services in the late 1990s. "Those firms that shift beyond manufacturing goods and delivering services to staging experiences and guiding transformations will ward off the commoditization that threatens businesses everywhere," they wrote. "Those that do not will find themselves subject to the vagaries of a very competitive and ruthless marketplace."[4]

Pine and Gilmore's prediction has held up well. Their notion of the "Experience Economy" helps explain not only the continued popularity of Disneyland visits, but the premium Starbucks can charge for coffee and the quick take-off of Virgin America airlines. People will pay $3 or $4 for a latte at Starbucks instead of $1 for a coffee at 7-11 because that latte is served up in a broader package that speaks of friendliness, coziness, and sophistication.

Virgin America airlines has lured travelers away from existing airlines largely because of its ultra-hipness, including a commitment to fuel efficiency,[5] cabin mood lighting, sleek black-and-white seats, and irreverent flight attendants. The airline, launched in 2007 and partly owned by Richard Branson's Virgin Group, reported a net profit by the third quarter of 2010, when it also saw revenue jump 28 percent year over year to $202 million.[6]

Yes, customers continue to patronize low-price specialists. But even discount giant Walmart has taken a page from the customer experience playbook. Walmart in 2007 de-emphasized its "Always Low Prices" motto in favor of a tagline that tries to connect bargain shopping to a more profound goal: "Save money. Live better."[7]

To deliver experiences rather than simply goods and services, companies have to maintain a consistent feel to their "brand." An unkempt bathroom at Disneyland, a rude Starbucks barrista, or a Virgin flight attendant speaking from a script breaks the spell for consumers, making them think twice about their next purchase.

Brand coherence means every customer-facing employee must provide the same high level and kind of service. And for those customer-facing employees to be able to provide great experiences, it's important that support staffers also perform at a high level.

Thus firms must recruit people with certain traits (friendliness in the case of Starbucks coffee slingers, free-spiritedness in the case of Virgin flight attendants), train them in the same processes and priorities, and inspire them to "live" the organization's values. Decent if not generous compensation and a healthy corporate culture are part of the equation. So is an ability to manage people and tasks with an eye to hard data.

Akin to the way leading companies study, segment, and engage their customers, companies seeking to provide great experiences need to analyze employee performance and impact, encourage employee feedback, and empower workers to take initiative. A key to great customer experiences, in other words, is excellent people management.

Some in the business world preach putting the customer first. Anything other than a laser-like focus on the people paying the bills is a distraction that can destroy a company in short order, this argument goes. To be sure, companies can't lose sight of customer desires and shifting market trends. But they also must not concentrate on customer needs in a way that blinds them to the importance of their own people.

"Customer experience depends on employee experience," writes consultant Bruce Temkin.[8] In his book *The Six Laws of Customer Experience*, Temkin elaborates:

> If you want to improve customer experience, then it might seem obvious that you should focus completely on customers. For most firms, though, that's not the correct approach. Where should you focus? On employees. While you can make some customers happy through brute force, you cannot sustain great customer experience unless your employees are bought-in to what you're doing and are aligned with the effort. If employees have low morale, then getting them to "wow" customers will be nearly impossible.[9]

Most Disney sweepers probably do not directly "wow" visitors so much as maintain the theme park's happiness vibe. But one sweeper made a strong impact on photographer John Harrington. Harrington, on assignment at Disney's California Adventure park in 2009, mentioned the sweeper in a blog item, saying the man stood out for his pride and purposefulness.

"A stubborn stain he spritzed with his spray bottle, and his holster held other tools necessary to do the job as if he were Michelangelo," Harrington wrote. "He even cared about his appearance as he was doing it, and he also worked during lulls in the crowd so his mopping didn't interfere with the parks' guests. I watched for a while, impressed by his overall approach as well as the details he cared about."[10]

Sweepers like this one help explain why Disney's parks and resorts were able to stay profitable during the difficult years of 2008 and 2009.[11]

Walt Disney himself would be smiling about those results and the rank-and-file folks behind them. Disney's relationship with employees was not always smooth,[12] but he understood their importance. "You can design and create, and build the most wonderful place in the world," Temkin quotes him as saying. "But it takes people to make the dream a reality."[13]

Yes it does. And to make reality dreamy for customers in search of richer experiences, businesses must act as worthy employers.

Economic Security Focus

One of Ed's closest friends recently fled the instability of the private sector. And his story captures the way workers' desire for economic security is prompting companies to be worthier.

Ed's friend graduated from an Ivy League school and earned a doctorate in Chinese linguistics from a prestigious university. The friend, whom we'll call Peter, has proven to be a thoughtful, effective advisor on the cultural challenges of Westerners doing business in China.

But after a recent stint of life-rattling job volatility, Peter gave up on private-sector employers for a steadier position in the academic world.

In the wake of losing his job at a management-consulting firm at the end of 2008, Peter spent a year seeking work. During his unemployment and underemployment as an independent consultant, tensions rose between Peter and his wife as they faced the possibility of home foreclosure. He finally found a job at an outsourcing services start-up that seemed promising. But that post soon proved shaky as well. Within a year, Peter's pay had been slashed roughly in half, and he was warned he might be laid off soon. Amid renewed concerns about how to keep a roof over himself, his wife, and their two young daughters, Peter applied for and landed a job as head of a study-abroad program in China.

The program, a partnership between two major universities in China and the United States, will be well served. But its gain is the corporate world's loss. And decisions like Peter's are playing out by the thousands and millions, as other economically shell-shocked Americans seek safer employment bets. They may not be able to find work in the relatively stable refuges of academic institutions or government agencies. But they are looking for organizations that offer something firmer than the employment quicksand so common at companies over the past few decades.

Workers want security these days. A survey of U.S. employees by consulting firm Towers Watson in late 2009 found that respondents rated "security and stability" as their top priority, ahead of both "significantly higher pay" and "opportunity to rapidly develop skills/abilities."[14] A study done earlier in 2009 found that 33 percent of U.S. employees overall cited job security as a reason for joining an organization, putting it in a tie for second place.[15] Job security was an even higher priority for top performers—those in the upper ten percent when it comes to job performance—in the United States. It was cited as a reason for joining an organization by 37 percent of them, making it the second-ranking reason after "nature of work" for top performers.[16]

Why should the Americans most able to land new jobs be the most keen on staying in one place? Perhaps because their job prowess extends to a broader insight about the labor market: it has grown increasingly perilous for Americans. In fact, job loss is particularly devastating for seasoned, well-trained professionals—for people like Peter. While older, more educated, and white-collar workers are less likely to become unemployed, they are more likely to be unemployed for long periods if they do lose their jobs.[17]

Americans' hunger for job security is part of a larger desire for economic security that has been growing in America and other parts of the world.

For decades, financial risk has been shifting from companies and government to individuals in the United States. Growing use of layoffs by companies and the erosion of benefits such as health insurance and pensions have created an economic roller coaster ride. In the early 1970s, the inflation-adjusted incomes of most families in the middle of the economic spectrum went up or down no more than about $6,500 a year. By 2004, those fluctuations had more than doubled to as much as $13,500.[18] Compounding the problem, America's safety net for workers losing their jobs has been relatively weak among industrialized democracies.[19]

The Great Recession—with its layoffs and plunging stock values—only heightened economic insecurity in the United States and elsewhere in the world. According to a 2009 study, a record-low 13 percent of Americans said they are very confident of having enough money to live comfortably in retirement. The report found retirement confidence among workers plunged by 50 percent from 2007 to 2009.[20]

How much people in other parts of the world want economic security from their workplace and from their economy overall varies according to factors including a country's economic growth, business practices, and public safety net. But in general there appears to be growing dissatisfaction with the uncertainties resulting from decades of largely unfettered global capitalism.

A BBC World Service poll from late 2009 found that dissatisfaction with free-market capitalism is widespread, with an average of only 11 percent across 27 countries saying that it works well and that greater regulation is not a good idea.[21]

Overall, the public is pushing back at the decades-long glorification of risk and of "creative destruction." After all, capitalism as we know it often destroys the plans people create—to stay in their home, to send their kids to a particular school, to retire comfortably. What's more, the desire for more stability is grounded in psychological research, which shows that a degree of certainty is a key to happiness.[22]

Still, business leaders might ask themselves: doesn't job security make employees complacent? Don't firms need to keep workers' feet to the fire—through fear of being fired or laid off—in order to spark hard work and fresh ideas? And do companies really need to care about people's desire for more stability when the U.S. unemployment rate hit 10 percent in 2009, stayed above 9 percent throughout 2010, and is expected to remain high for the foreseeable future?

Yes, a slack job market puts employers in the driver's seat. But to disregard what employees want is to risk losing them when the economy and job market heats up again. Top performers are among those itching to leave. Compared with 2008, top performers in 2009 were 14 percent less likely to want to remain with their company versus taking a job elsewhere.[23]

Job instability also can take a toll on engagement—which refers to workers' commitment to and willingness to go the extra mile for their company.[24] In a study of employees from across the globe, the Corporate Executive Board research firm found that "engagement is deflated by change and even more so by anticipation of change."[25] The research firm found that the percentage of workers worldwide who were "highly disengaged" rose from 8 percent in the first half of 2007 to nearly 22 percent in the third quarter of 2010.[26]

In today's climate of anxiety, then, the companies seeking to attract, retain, and engage top workers will have to provide some measure of security. They will have to prove their worthiness as an employer in ways such as generous severance packages, a commitment to treat layoffs as a last resort rather than a first step, and substantial training investments that help people upgrade skills and remain employable.

Transparency about company strategy and performance also can combat employee uncertainty. As can greater decision-making power by workers on the job.

As of early 2011, Peter looked forward to beginning his new job as head of the study-abroad program. Universities—and governments—cannot guarantee employment, but they have tended to offer steadier work than private-sector firms. And for that, Peter felt relief.

"I'm so over the insecurity," he said. His words speak for many people. And they serve as a warning to companies.

Global Trade

Take a look at the back of an iPod or iPhone and you'll see a pair of statements that get at the way global trade is pushing companies to be worthy.

"Designed by Apple in California"

"Assembled in China"

Apple remains headquartered in Cupertino, California, in the heart of the technology hub known as Silicon Valley. But Apple now focuses its California operations on things other than actually making electronic products. Its employees there design devices, write software, develop marketing campaigns, and negotiate relationships with content and telecommunications companies. They also manage a worldwide network of suppliers. These jobs are high-level, knowledge-work positions that all but require excellent people management.

When it comes to the actual manufacture of iPods, Apple taps a far-flung network of suppliers that culminates in the devices coming together in Chinese factories run by outsourcing partners.[27] Recurrent labor problems in recent years at a major supplier—Foxconn Technology Group—would seem to suggest Apple has turned a blind eye to sweatshop conditions behind its sleek products. But the company is keenly aware of such problems. In fact, since 2007, it has published annual reports disclosing labor shortcomings in its global supply chain in great detail, as well as documenting the company's actions to improve matters. And it is unlikely Apple will be able to reverse course.

In effect, Apple's global operations increasingly require worthiness in both the developed and developing world.

It is far from alone. An ever-more global economy is raising the bar for companies as employers.

Key sources of competitive advantage in past eras—natural resources and capital equipment—have become commodities in today's global economy. More and more, the only sustainable advantage is through people. Organizations must rely on employees or contractors to generate innovations—in product categories, in service lines, in product designs, and in marketing methods—and then execute on the resulting strategies. Succeeding in what's sometimes called a "knowledge economy" then, requires firms to excel at identifying, attracting, retaining, developing, and orchestrating talent.

The global economy's worthiness effect plays out differently in developed markets and less developed markets.

Developing Economies

A more interlocked international economy is obliging businesses to become good employers in emerging economies. Rapid growth in China and India over the past 10 years, driven largely by exports, has led to fierce competition for skilled workers and for leaders capable of managing in a global business climate. In a 2008 paper, researchers at consulting firm McKinsey & Company wrote: "The growing need for talented managers in China represents by far the biggest management challenge facing multinationals and locally owned businesses alike."[28] Forty-four percent of the executives at Chinese companies surveyed by the *McKinsey Quarterly* reported that insufficient talent was the biggest barrier to their global ambitions.[29]

Ed saw this talent gap firsthand during a reporting trip to China in 2007. Companies like Hyatt, Hewlett-Packard, and Motorola were working hard to recruit, train, and retain managers. A Hyatt executive told Ed that rising stars in the middle of a four-year development plan are sometimes poached by firms that will double their pay. Multinationals like Hyatt, in other words, are under pressure to prove their worthiness as employers.[30]

For the lowest-wage workers, however, the prognosis is less clear. Some fear that ever-more global commerce, combined with extensive use of outsourced suppliers, fuels a race to the bottom, with companies treating employees as disposable so long as a poorer region or country is desperate for work. As little-known, poorly regulated shops undercut each other to get a piece of the garment or computer manufacturing business, this argument runs, multinationals have no real incentive to make sure workers are treated well as they cut costs and maximize profits.

To be sure, globalization has led to worker abuses.[31] But beginning with the campaigns against apparel makers like Nike in the 1990s,[32] activists and the broader public increasingly have held companies accountable for the treatment of workers making their products—no matter who is listed as their employer of record.

Apple is a case in point. In 2006, Apple faced allegations of harsh working conditions in the making of the iPod at a Foxconn factory in China. In response to this criticism, Apple conducted its own probe. It found violations of its code of conduct, including overly long hours, and said the supplier was addressing them.[33]

"We are dedicated to ensuring that working conditions are safe and employees are treated with respect and dignity wherever Apple products are made," the company said at the time.[34] Indeed, the number of facilities audited by Apple rose from 39 in 2007 to 127 in 2010.

The suicides of at least 10 workers in 2010 at Foxconn, which makes iPhones and iPads,[35] indicates that Apple has not yet succeeded in eliminating poor treatment of workers by its suppliers. What is striking, however, is the candor with which Apple is addressing its failure. In its annual Supplier Responsibility reports, it has disclosed a range of serious problems in considerable detail.[36]

The 2011 report, for example, acknowledged 36 "core violations" of Apple's standards, including 10 facilities that had hired underage workers. Apple also said it commissioned an independent team of experts to review the Foxconn suicides, and that its supplier was planning to adopt the team's recommendations, including better training of care center counselors.[37] In one respect, Apple is responsible for every single labor abuse its own reports reveal. Looked at another way, Apple is taking steps to make a bad situation for many workers a bit better in a world of cutthroat global competition.

What's more, it is hard to imagine that Apple can retreat from the issue. The Foxconn suicides, for example, did not escape the notice of prospective buyers, as evidenced by a discussion forum about iPods at Amazon.com.[38] And while its annual reports on supplier responsibility did not attract much attention for the first few years, 2011 was different. With suicides at Foxconn still fresh in the public's memory, Apple's publication of the report in February 2011 generated widespread media coverage.[39] The scrutiny of both the media and ever-more-ethical consumers means that Apple, along with other multinationals relying on overseas suppliers, has little choice but to continue to force progress toward more humane labor standards for workers around the globe.

Developed Economies

The global economy also is encouraging worthiness as an employer in developed markets.

Many economists view international trade as forcing operations in the developed world to move up the "value chain" by generating new technologies, products, or services that can't easily be created in emerging economies. Indeed, high-skill jobs continue to be located in countries such as the United States.

Look no further than Apple, whose California designers—along with Apple employees in marketing and business development—have taken the world by storm with the iPod, iPhone, and iPad. In the three months ending September 25, 2010, Apple sold 14.1 million iPhones, more than 9 million iPods, and 4.2 million iPads—fueling record company revenue of $20.3 billion.[40] The knowledge-work positions behind those numbers require smart, stirring management for success. Failure to find and channel talent in an optimal way results in also-ran products like Microsoft's Zune or Sony's MP3 Walkman. Indeed, Apple is famous for cofounder Steve Jobs's inspiring, if demanding, leadership and for a culture of creativity.

On the other hand, not all operations in the United States hinge on high-skill knowledge workers. In fact, as economist Alan Blinder has pointed out, an increasing number of U.S. jobs will be focused on "personal services" that require face-to-face interaction.[41] These are jobs like massage therapist, teacher, and retail sales clerk, whose services cannot be delivered easily over telecommunications networks from Costa Rica or the Philippines or China. To excel in these personal service fields requires a company to select employees well, train them effectively, and motivate them to wow customers.

Apple neatly embodies virtually all the facets of the global economy— including the need to be a good employer on a worldwide basis. Besides managing its product designers and international supply chain, Apple employs sales specialists and technical support professionals at more than 200 retail stores. These workers provide face-to-face, personal service.

Apple takes pains to recruit the right people for its stores and to rev them up. The company's career Web site casts working at Apple as much more than a job. "Part career, part revolution," the site states. "Be part of something big." Apple's benefits include an employee stock–purchase plan, product discounts, and tuition assistance.

"Your work is going to fill a large part of your life," Jobs said at a Stanford University commencement speech a few years ago. "And the only way to be truly satisfied is to do what you believe is great work. And the only way to do great work is to love what you do."[42]

As its own supplier reports show, Apple has a ways to go to make sure that all the people creating its products are treated decently, let alone love what they do. But the pressure to tackle labor problems in its supply chain will grow. In California, China, and every other corner of the world, the companies that meet basic labor standards, foster workers' fervor, and prove worthy of their devotion will be the ones that thrive in an ever-more global economy.

Technological Change

On February 12, 2008, a marketing manager at Yahoo lost his job.

That shouldn't have been a big deal given the troubles of the Internet firm and the regularity of layoffs in the U.S. economy during the past three decades.

But this particular pink slip caught the public's eye. The employee, Ryan Kuder, "twittered" his layoff. That is, Kuder used his microblogging account at Internet site Twitter to give a blow-by-blow account of getting the ax. Among his "tweets":

> Y! layoffs today, I'm "impacted." I'm heading into work to pack my desk, get my severance paperwork and hand in my badge . . . more to come.

> Ironic that I just got my PC repaired yesterday. Won't be needing that anymore.

> Walking around saying goodbye to some great people and good friends.

> This is a serious downer. Trying to drown it in free lattes. Which I will miss.

> Lots of whispered conversations. Like people are afraid to ask who's gone.

> I'm going dark in a few minutes. The HR guy is on his way over to confiscate my laptop.

> Celebrating unemployment with a giant margarita at Chevy's.[43]

A variety of media seized on Kuder's personal-made-public report, with one commentator calling it "a new form of literature."[44] Perhaps. But equally important was the way Kuder's account, posted on the Internet, signaled the growing power of social media technologies to lay bare what happens inside corporations.

Among those who recognize the shift is business consultant Libby Sartain, who was head of human resources at Yahoo when Kuder lost his job.

"People tweet, people blog, people text," Sartain says. "You are going to have a completely transparent workplace at all times. You can't really spin it."[45]

The transparency Kuder created through Twitter is part of a broader way technological change is pushing companies to clean up their acts.

The emergence of Web 2.0 technologies in the past decade or so has enabled people to reward goodness and punish its absence. These technologies both foster a culture of disclosure and participation (which we'll talk about more in Chapter 3) and make it powerful. Social networking sites like Facebook, Twitter, and YouTube; interactive features on traditional media sites; and feedback sites like Glassdoor.com, Vault, TripAdvisor, and Yelp give people a platform for making negative and positive comments about organizations. Such comments or reviews typically stay on the Internet forever, visible to anyone searching on a Web browser.

Many sites also have mechanisms for synthesizing feedback to give people a more comprehensive picture of an organization. Glassdoor.com, for example, provides average ratings for companies based on employee reviews. Yelp does something similar for ratings on restaurants and other local services. So does technology product review site CNET.com, which supplements expert commentary with user ratings.

Investors, too, are speaking up and out about companies through technology tools. The message boards at Yahoo Finance, for example, are full of people debating the merits of different stocks. These discussions aren't only about the likelihood of gains and losses but also the social responsibility of publicly traded companies.[46]

Not only do many sites summarize the "wisdom of the crowds" with rating averages, but features such as "rate this rating" allow the very best comments to rise to the surface.

Such interactive tools are being employed by businesses themselves on their own sites. Amazon's release of its Kindle 2 digital reading device is a case in point. As of late 2009, Amazon's user review section showed that the device had an average rating of four out of five stars. But the third user review presented on the Kindle 2 page was from a customer who gave the product a mere one star. "BEWARE of the SIGNIFICANT DIFFERENCES between Kindle 1 and Kindle 2!" wrote Gadget Queen, who went on to provide a 15-point detailed critique of the device.[47]

Although it was a negative review and far from the average rating, some 17,450 of 18,600 people found the review helpful. The first two user reviews—detailed but largely positive—also had thousands of "helpful" ratings attached to them. In essence, Web 2.0 feedback and meta-feedback technologies make it likely that problems at organizations will be made public; and the more legitimate the problem, the more likely it is that it will be made public in a prominent way.

Opinions aren't the only things employees, consumers, and investors are publishing these days with the help of technology. They're also posting photos, audio files, and video images that they can capture at any moment. Smart phones and other handheld devices are commonplace and capable of recording images, video and audio. It is increasingly easy for people throughout the world to upload this content to the Internet.

For years, organizations have had to worry about the possible theft of valuable data and contend with the prospect that embarrassing e-mails and other documents will be exposed by means such as litigation and government probes. Now, in this more interactive era, there are even more ways sensitive corporate information can be disclosed: in an employee's YouTube video, through a tweet by a worker at a supplier, via a Facebook discussion page.

Some observers dispute that the rise of Web 2.0 technologies pushes companies to behave better. They point to cases where workers have been fired for blogging about their firms and to policies banning the use of social media at work. More fundamentally, critics note that the democratization of media on the Internet is leading to the demise of newspapers and traditional media, which have been among the most important watchdogs of corporate activities.

But newspapers and magazines haven't disappeared completely. And the increase in the amount and variety of information on the Internet—including government records and company documents—makes investigative reporting on companies by "citizen" journalists ever easier.

What's more, social media tools like Twitter accelerate the distribution of noteworthy news about firms. Stories can go viral. A damaging report about a company's pollution record that may have remained a regional story a decade ago now can spread across the globe rapidly as a forwarded link.

Despite the high-profile cases of employees fired for offensive blogs or tweets, workers continue to push the boundaries of what they can disclose.[48] And the ability to post information anonymously through blogs or feedback sites gives employees at even the most draconian firms an option to speak their mind.

In effect, the rise of Web 2.0 and the ubiquity of digital recording devices are disrobing companies. Increasingly, company gaffes and missteps will be outed. They can only be countered with overwhelming evidence of goodness.

And they can be countered. The era of the naked company means that companies' best sides shine through as well. As of early 2011, the top-ranked "most helpful" Kindle review at Amazon's site gave the product four out of five stars.[49]

Ryan Kuder's twittered tale showed Yahoo to be a workplace on edge and a bit disorganized about its PC repair decisions. But what company wouldn't be tense amid layoffs and imperfect in its coordination? The bigger message was that Yahoo had been a fun place, with nice perks and great people.

In Sartain's view, Kuder's account of his layoff was on balance positive for the firm.

"He didn't say, 'Yahoo sucks,'" she says.[50]

CHAPTER TWO SUMMARY

Four fundamental economic forces are increasing the premium on being a "good company."

Consumer Desire

- Consumers are increasingly seeking to purchase an experience, not just a product or service.
- This means that employees at all levels in an organization must be able and willing to enhance the quality of consumers' experience.
- This, in turn, means that employers must increasingly be "worthy" of the best efforts of employees at every level in the organization.

Growing Focus on Economic Security

- The Great Recession has fundamentally, and perhaps permanently, altered employees' preferences.
- Employees now place a much higher premium on economic security.
- High levels of insecurity undermine employees' performance.
- So, although it is currently a buyers' market for talent, smart employers will find ways to reduce unnecessary job and wage insecurity among their employees.

Global Trade

- In today's global economy, the only sustainable advantage is through people—identifying, attracting, retaining, developing, and orchestrating talent.
- In the developing world, strong demand for skilled talent and managers puts a premium on being a worthy employer, and companies face increasing pressure to treat low-wage workers well.
- In developed economies, sophisticated, inspired management is needed to bring out the best of both high-skilled knowledge workers and employees in personal-services roles that can't be offshored.

Technological Change

- The emergence of Web 2.0 technologies in the past decade or so has enabled people to reward goodness and punish its absence.

- The inner workings of organizations are being exposed as never before by a variety of interactive tools, including social networking sites like Facebook and feedback sites like Glassdoor.com, Trip Advisor.com, and Yelp.

- Many sites also have mechanisms for synthesizing feedback to give people a more comprehensive picture of an organization.

- Increasingly, company gaffes and missteps will be outed. They can only be countered with overwhelming evidence of goodness.

CHAPTER 3

The Social Imperative

On November 10, 2004, the fiancée of an employee at video game maker Electronic Arts (EA) posted a blog entry. It was an anonymous, emotional essay published at a free blogging site. And it transformed the video game industry.

In her nearly 2,000-word essay titled "EA: The Human Story," the author, who referred to herself as "ea_spouse," spoke in personal terms about the toll long work weeks were taking on her fiancé and herself.[1] At first, she explained, her fiancé's project team was expected to work eight hours a day, six days a week. Then twelve hours a day, six days a week. Then eventually extended hours for seven days a week. "The love of my life comes home late at night complaining of a headache that will not go away and a chronically upset stomach, and my happy supportive smile is running out," she wrote. She also argued that routine weeks of 85 hours on the job without overtime pay by game developers were illegal, ill conceived, and the product of corporate greed.

In another era, her essay might have been the sort of complaint shared merely with family and friends. Or perhaps, if she was particularly determined, she might have sent it to mainstream media outlets or a labor attorney with the hope that a sympathetic journalist or lawyer would take up her case.

Instead, she published her tale on LiveJournal.com, one of a number of Internet sites allowing anyone to start a Web log for free. And despite her anonymity, despite her lack of legal backing or traditional media distribution powers, ea_spouse set off a firestorm. Within weeks, the blog item had generated more than 2,000 comments.[2] It ricocheted across the Web and prompted mainstream media coverage. To her own surprise, ea_spouse's essay triggered industry-wide soul searching about work hours. It also helped bring about major management reforms at Electronic Arts.

"Truly, the power of the Internet is astounding," ea_spouse wrote on her blog in mid-December 2004, "and all other things aside, we live in a positive age when so much information can be shared so easily and quickly."[3]

She might have added, "And with such major implications for firms." Her essay and its impact highlight the way people increasingly are expressing their opinions and experiences in public and how this culture of disclosure and participation is pushing companies to become more worthy.

The rise in public expression and interactivity is one of several social forces prompting companies to ramp up their worthiness. Other factors are a growing sense of global solidarity, continued environmental concerns, and the arrival of the Millennial generation. This chapter examines each of these.

Disclosure Culture

In the past decade or so, people have begun disclosing aspects of their experience as never before. They are documenting their daily lives, emotions, observations, and opinions through public venues such as blogs, Twitter, YouTube, and Facebook pages. The number of active Facebook users, for example, jumped from 12 million in late 2006 to more than 500 million in early 2011. Half of those users log on to the site on any given day.[4]

Much of the self-expression spills over into people's experiences as workers, consumers, and investors. Facebook has page after page devoted to businesses, some of which are created by employees and consumers.

This growing publication of the personal is fueled and made forceful by emerging social media technologies. Blogging sites like LiveJournal

.com and social networking sites like Facebook make it easy for people to start online journals and discussion groups, contributing either named or anonymous entries. And the interactive, viral nature of these Web 2.0 tools—where people can comment on postings and pass links to the content to their network of friends and contacts—helps explain why the anonymous lament about working conditions at Electronic Arts elicited so many comments.[5]

Related to the upsurge in public autobiography is a rise in online involvement more generally. Through the Internet, many people are becoming more participatory as consumers, citizens, investors, and employees. They are joining conversations about the strengths and weaknesses of products and services, stocks, and employers.

Time magazine captured the emergence of "user-generated content" and the democratization of media by naming its 2006 person of the year "You."

> It's a story about community and collaboration on a scale never seen before. It's about the cosmic compendium of knowledge Wikipedia and the million-channel people's network YouTube and the online metropolis MySpace. It's about the many wresting power from the few and helping one another for nothing and how that will not only change the world, but also change the way the world changes.[6]

In this world, individuals have the power to call attention to business successes and shortcomings as never before. And they are. As mentioned in Chapter 2, they are using the site Glassdoor.com to assess employers. They are praising and panning stocks at Yahoo Finance. They are tapping Yelp to post reviews of restaurants, pet services, and dentists.

Yelp depends on people submitting unpaid assessments of local businesses. With a motto of "Real People. Real Reviews," the site has generated more than 15 million reviews since it was founded in 2004. And Yelp is popular. More than 41 million people visited it during a single month in 2010.[7]

Yelp's success speaks to a trend running parallel with the culture of interactivity: a hunger for authenticity. This can be seen partly in the rise of "reality" TV programming. Despite some contrived situations, the shows depict everyday people in struggles to lose weight, parent better, or handle tough jobs. And in the wake of scandals ranging from Enron to misleading evidence about nuclear weapons in Iraq to gargantuan CEO pay, the public is wary of traditional authority figures and their platitudes. In Edelman's 2010 trust study, respondents were more likely to trust information about a company from "a person like yourself" than from a CEO.[8]

The authentic nature of the ea_spouse essay—the way it combined principled criticism of the company with the particulars of her own story—may help explain why it served as a flashpoint for the video game field. Her indignation hit a high point as she addressed EA CEO Larry Probst directly:

> Larry: you do realize what you're doing to your people, right? And you do realize that they ARE people, with physical limits, emotional lives, and families, right? Voices and talents and senses of humor and all that? That when you keep our husbands and wives and children in the office for ninety hours a week, sending them home exhausted and numb and frustrated with their lives, it's not just them you're hurting, but everyone around them, everyone who loves them?

Many of the ensuing comments spoke about excessive hours as a wider problem in the still-maturing video game field. "White-collar slavery is alive and well in the games industry," one anonymous responder wrote.[9]

In the wake of her essay, Electronic Arts admitted a problem of long hours. It started a project to "lessen the number of late-in-the-process changes, fire drills and crunches." Soon thereafter, while facing at least one lawsuit claiming unpaid overtime wages, the company also said it would make some employees eligible for overtime pay but not offer those workers bonuses or stock options.[10]

As EA discovered, companies operating in an age of disclosure and interactivity face growing pressure to be genuine, honest, and good throughout. While nobody expects organizations to be perfect, troubles increasingly are exposed by stakeholders today. Companies will have to minimize or fix problems like cynical work cultures, faulty products, and misleading leaders. Firms also need to pay attention to how employees, customers, investors, and others are talking about them online, and to engage in those informal conversations.

Skeptics of this conclusion might argue that all the expression, autobiography, and interactivity these days amounts to narcissistic noise. To be sure, much of what is written by people online is crass, inarticulate, and uninformed. But, as discussed in Chapter 2, today's technologies help to generate average ratings of companies and to highlight particularly strong praise and criticism. As a result, the personal publication trend is amplifying the power of would-be whistle-blowers. What might have required a lawsuit or outreach to a newspaper or television station 20 years ago now can take the form of an anonymous posting about problems at a company.

Also, as mentioned earlier, much of what is posted online at sites like Facebook, MySpace, and Twitter remains there for an indefinite period. The blog entries, comments, photos, and videos are visible to job candidates, employees, customers, investors, journalists, government officials, plaintiff's attorneys, and others.

Even as late as 2010, people continued to comment on the original ea_spouse essay. Among the most recent of the responses were posts that criticized Electronic Arts.[11] One, from an anonymous commenter in 2009, offered further evidence that people publishing their experiences and opinions online pressures companies to be good: "I dislike the money churning practices of EA anyway but to hear firsthand how they achieve this is unforgivable. Rest assured that when I go into the industry (and I intend to) I will steer clear of Electronic Arts!"[12]

Global Solidarity

The death of single Iranian woman in June 2009 transfixed the world.

Neda Agha-Soltan, a 26-year-old studying music and engaged to be married, was killed during a street protest of the country's disputed presidential election. Her last moments were captured on video by a bystander, posted on the Internet, and eventually broadcast throughout the world.[13] The footage riveted people within Iran and throughout the globe, putting a face on Iran's opposition movement and eliciting empathy for the everyday people contesting the hard-line government.

In effect, Neda's death increased pressure on that government. It also signaled the way in which a growing sense of social solidarity around the world is pushing organizations of all stripes to treat people well.

Many people have come to identify to some extent as "global citizens," with strong sympathies for people throughout the world. The notion of a single human family living together in a small world has been around for centuries. But the concept is coming to fruition in the 21st century.

The more people know people from different regions of the world, the more they see themselves as global citizens—rising to 47 percent among those who know people from five or more regions, according to a 2009 study by research group WorldPublicOpinion.org.[14] Overall, the study of 21 nations found that 1 in 10 people identify principally as a citizen of the world, and another 20 percent identify themselves as being equally a citizen of the world and a citizen of their country.

"It is likely that in the future people will increasingly think of themselves as global citizens," says Steven Kull, director of WorldPublic Opinion.org. "Young people are more prone to see themselves this way. Also, with economic development people travel more, meet foreigners more and become more educated; all these developments are related to greater tendencies for people to see themselves as global citizens."

Natural disasters over the past decade, like the 2004 tsunami in South Asia, Hurricane Katrina in 2005, and the devastating 2010 earthquake in Haiti, reinforced the idea that people need each other. As did the Great Recession, when millions around the world lost jobs and felt economically vulnerable. At the same time, social networking technologies have made it easier than ever for people to establish connections with others—including long-lost schoolmates and people located far away.

The United States is one of the places where a more collective attitude has taken root over the past 15 years or so. Americans overall have come to adopt more of a "we're in this together" mindset in contrast to a "you're on your own" mentality. This can be seen in part in the growing concern with income inequality in America. In 2002, 65 percent of Americans agreed with the statement that "the rich just get richer while the poor get poorer." That figure grew to 71 percent in 2009.[15]

The notion that in America the haves keep getting more while have-nots get less is grounded in reality. The share of income in the United States going to the top 10 percent of families increased dramatically between 1982 and 2007.[16] In 2007, one study found, the top 10 percent of families accounted for 49.7 percent of income in the United States, a level higher than any time since 1917 and above the 1928 peak of the roaring 20s stock market bubble.[17]

Increased financial insecurity in the United States and elsewhere—discussed in the previous chapter—also helps explain the evolution toward an all-for-one, one-for-all sensibility.

The growing belief that people are fundamentally connected and need to look out for each other also goes a long ways toward explaining why treating employees well is one of the public's biggest concerns when it comes to corporate social responsibility. Studies by public-relations firm Fleishman-Hillard and advocacy group the National Consumers League found that when asked the meaning of corporate social responsibility, U.S. adults ranked a commitment to employees as the top response in 2006 and the second-highest response in 2007, after a commitment to communities.[18]

A more global, social mindset is leading to greater focus on the way organizations treat people, no matter where those people are located. The American social reform movement that protested sweatshops in Manhattan a century ago has had a successor in the "fair-trade" movement in the past few decades. Concerns about sweatshops and mistreated communities half a world away have hit a nerve among U.S. college students and the wider public. As mentioned in the last chapter, Apple and Nike are among the companies that have had to answer questions about overseas operations, and such scrutiny is not going away.

"A global social conscience is one of the biggest trends to have emerged in the last decade," says Amilcar Perez, vice president of marketing for Latin America at the Nielsen Company. "Global consumers are collectively speaking out and demanding that corporations make a positive contribution to society."[19]

There are countervailing forces to a global social conscience. Deep animosity still dominates in a number of hotspots in the world, religious fundamentalism is sowing discord, and extremist nationalist political parties have taken aim at immigrant and minority populations. The Tea Party movement in the United States has challenged the notion that government can solve social problems, and there are concerns that Americans and others feeling pinched by hard times will not see themselves as their brother's keeper. Indeed, Americans' support for a government safety net for the poor—although greater than in 1994—did recede some between 2007 and 2009,[20] and charitable giving fell between 2007 and 2008.[21]

But despite those declines and the doubts about the effectiveness of government, there's evidence the country and world continue a march toward greater social solidarity. Even amid the recession, the U.S. volunteer rate held steady in 2008 compared to 2007, with roughly a quarter of adult Americans volunteering 8 billion hours of volunteer service.[22] And the U.S. volunteer rate ticked up in 2009, when the number of volunteers rose by 1.6 million—the largest single-year increase since 2003.[23]

"During past tough economic times, there was a decrease in volunteering," Patrick Corvington, CEO of the federal Corporation for National and Community Service told *Parade* magazine in early 2010. "But today there's a 'compassion boom' of people helping others."[24]

A compassion boom can be heard echoing around the globe. A 2008 study of consumers in 10 countries found that 71 percent said they had either given the same or more time and money to good causes in the face of the economic downturn.[25] The same study also found that 68 percent of consumers would remain loyal to a brand during a recession if it supports a good cause. "Despite the downturn, across the globe people's sense of commitment to helping others—and to brands and companies that share that commitment—remains strong," said the report from public-relations firm Edelman.[26]

In Iran, Neda's cause did not immediately prevail. The government, which claimed her death was staged by its enemies, remained in power and may have substantial popular support in the country.[27] But the sense of solidarity inspired by her death has not been snuffed out. Among the tributes that preserve her memory—and by extension preserve pressure on the regime—is an Oxford University scholarship in her name.

There's also a Web site devoted to her. Its title encapsulates the way people more and more see themselves as united and determined to stand up for each other: "We are Neda."[28]

Going Green

Former Walmart CEO Lee Scott may prove to be the most important environmentalist in history.

This is hard to believe at first. After all, among the criticisms heaped on Walmart over the past decade or so is that it symbolizes materialism at its world-destroying worst. But under Scott's leadership, the retail giant launched an ambitious sustainability campaign in 2005. Walmart laid out short-term goals as well as these long-term doozies: to be supplied 100 percent by renewable energy, to create zero waste, and "to sell products that sustain our resources and environment."[29]

Five years later, Walmart had turned greener. The firm's "Sustainability 360" program has shown results such as several pilot high-efficiency stores designed to use up to 45 percent less energy, a 38-percent increase in the efficiency of its U.S. truck fleet, and a switch to sell only concentrated laundry detergent—projected by Walmart to save 430 million gallons of water between 2008 and 2011.[30]

Part of what makes Walmart's green push powerful is its scale, with a network of more than 100,000 suppliers, 2 million employees, and 8,000 retail locations. The firm is working with its suppliers to reduce packaging in its supply chain by 5 percent by 2013 using a 2008 baseline, which it says is equivalent to taking 213,000 trucks off the road annually.[31]

A variety of organizations have lauded Walmart's sustainability efforts, including the U.S. Environmental Protection Agency, the state of California, and the Carbon Disclosure Project—an effort by institutional investors to track the carbon emissions of major companies. In 2009, Walmart ranked as the highest-scoring consumer staples company on the Project's Carbon Disclosure Leadership Index.[32]

It's hard to know exactly what triggered Walmart's earth-friendly agenda. Public pressure and the prospect of cost savings certainly factored in the decision. But to hear Scott tell it, his own switch to a more environmentally concerned mindset played a big role. In a 2005 speech, Scott said the effort came after a year of talking with experts about how to make Walmart a better force in the world. Scott and Walmart also were trying to build on the momentum of having played a helpful role in the aftermath of Hurricane Katrina. And Scott had an ecological epiphany along the way:

> Frankly, I thought the environment was the least relevant. We are recycling responsibly and we are not wasteful—so a Walmart environment program sounded more like a public relations campaign than substance to me. But we kept talking, and as I learned more a light bulb came on for me . . . and that's a compact fluorescent light bulb! We should view the environment as Katrina in slow motion. Environmental loss threatens our health and the health of the natural systems we depend on.[33]

The flash that convinced Scott the environment is in peril helped make the company's green efforts much more than happy talk. And his conversion is part of a broader public commitment to the environment that is pushing companies to be better stewards.

Widespread concern about environmental issues dates to the 1960s, when Rachel Carson's book *Silent Spring* detailed the way pesticides were harming birds and charged the chemical industry with spreading falsehoods. During the past few decades, environmental problems like fouled waters, air pollution, and potentially catastrophic climate change have remained public priorities.

In recent years, in fact, Americans have grown more concerned about a range of environmental topics. The percentage who say they worry a great deal about polluted drinking water rose from 53 percent in 2004 to

59 percent in 2009.[34] Similarly, the U.S. public has become more anxious about air pollution, contamination of soil and water by toxic waste, and the loss of tropical rain forests.[35]

People worldwide also care about the environment. A 2009 study of 15 nations, most of them in the developing world, found that majorities of the people polled want their governments to take steps to fight climate change, even if that entails costs.[36] The study, commissioned by the World Bank, said public concern about climate change is high worldwide but generally higher in developing countries. It also found that people, particularly in developing countries, believe climate change is already having negative effects.

That conclusion dovetails with a 2009 Accenture report on electronics products. It found that 67 percent of consumers globally said they were willing to pay a premium for products that are environmentally friendly. But consumers in the emerging markets of China, India, Singapore, and Malaysia were particularly green: 84 percent of respondents in emerging markets said they would pay a premium for a product marked as being more environmentally friendly.[37]

The exact degree to which Americans and others worry about ecological issues has varied some over time.[38] In recent years, there's been heated debate on the question of global warming and whether human activities are changing the climate in a significant way.[39]

Still, the American public remains green overall—an attitude reinforced by BP's major oil spill in the Gulf of Mexico in early 2010. Fifty-five percent of Americans said environmental protection was a higher priority than energy production in mid-2010, according to a Gallup poll.[40]

Part of what is fueling the continued focus on ecological issues is the food movement that in recent years has questioned eating habits and assumptions. This push by activists, chefs, and consumers has focused attention on the carbon-intensive, industrial food system.[41]

Another important shift in the environmental equation is the addition of key evangelical Christians. In 2006, 86 evangelical Christian leaders including the influential mega-church pastor Rick Warren signed the "Evangelical Climate Initiative."[42] This effort and the broader "Creation Care" philosophy have widened the environmental tent to include people with traditionally pro-business values.[43]

The tent also is attracting a growing number of business leaders. Among them are the members of Business Leaders for Climate Solutions, a group of executives in the American Northwest. "Climate change is the defining challenge for our time. If we act now, solutions are affordable and create business opportunities for our region—failure to act poses catastrophic risks to our economy, quality of life, and future generations," reads the group's declaration of core principles. Between 2008 and early 2011, more than 1,000 business leaders had signed onto those principles, including executives from Microsoft, the Greater Seattle Chamber of Commerce, and Xerox.[44]

Another way businesses are promising to protect the planet is through the United Nations Global Compact, a voluntary initiative whereby businesses pledge to abide by 10 principles in the areas of human rights, labor, anti-corruption, and the environment.[45] A 2010 UN Global Compact-Accenture study reports: "In the course of our survey and conversations with CEOs, we have witnessed a fundamental shift since the last Global Compact survey in 2007. Then, sustainability was just emerging on the periphery of business issues, an increasing concern that was beginning to reshape the rules of competition. Three years later, sustainability is truly top-of-mind for CEOs around the world."[46]

Some critics continue to fault Walmart for doing more damage than good to the environment.[47] But it's hard to claim that Walmart leaders are merely greenwashing their business in an attempt to dupe the public. In 2009, Walmart's CEO Mike Duke—Lee Scott's successor—said the company would speed up its sustainability program. Some of the proof in the pudding: in 2009 Walmart began a sustainability rating system for products, and in 2010 it announced a goal to eliminate 20 million metric tons of greenhouse gas emissions from its global supply chain by the end of 2015.[48]

"These difficult economic times have led to an obvious question that a number of people have asked me: 'Can Walmart afford to continue to be so aggressive in sustainability?'" Duke said in a 2009 company report.[49] "My response has been very clear and direct: 'We can't afford not to. We need to accelerate and broaden our efforts.'"

Duke, like Lee Scott before him and like mainstream folks throughout the world, seems to care personally about a cleaner environment. And that global concern is prompting Walmart and all its brethren in the business world to be better stewards.

Millennials at the Gate

Snowboarding star Hannah Teter is among the prominent faces of Gen Y, one that speaks to the massive cohort's power to push companies toward goodness.

Teter won a gold medal in the 2006 Turin Olympics and a silver at the 2010 games in Vancouver. But she's devoted to more than great half-pipe tricks. Teter funnels snowboard winnings to a charity she founded called Hannah's Gold, which helps bring clean drinking water to a community in Kenya. She also raises funds for the organization through sales of Hannah Teter's Maple Blondie, a Ben & Jerry's ice cream flavor she cocreated with the company. She even launched a line of underwear to raise money for earthquake relief efforts in Haiti.

"Growing up, I knew I was privileged. I knew I was hooked-up," Teter told *NBC Nightly News*. "I just have always felt since I was young that I needed to help out in some sort of way—reach out to others in some sort of way to either change a life or give hope to a life."[50]

Teter reflects the social justice orientation and participatory nature of her generation. And she hints at how it is dragging companies in the direction of goodness.

Generation Y, sometimes called Millennials, refers to the group of Americans born in a range somewhere between the mid-1970s and the early 2000s. This group is a larger cohort than the preceding Generation X. By one estimate, there are 86 million members of the generation, more than the 78 million Baby Boomers.[51]

Millennials as a whole are "confident, self-expressive, liberal, upbeat and open to change," according to a 2010 report by the Pew Research Center.[52] Compared to Generation X, Baby Boomers, and the "Silent" generation of adults born from 1928 to 1945, Millennials are the most tolerant of gay couples raising children, single women having children, and people of different races marrying each other. Americans aged 18 to 29 also were the only age group that didn't grow more skeptical about global warming reports between March 2008 and March 2009, according to Gallup.[53]

Morley Winograd and Michael Hais, authors of *Millennial Makeover: MySpace, YouTube, and the Future of American Politics*, call Millennials a "civic" generation. "Though many people question the political sophistication of the millennials," the authors say, "they have been instilled with egalitarian and participatory values by their parents since birth."[54]

Millennials have grown up in the Internet age, and they often define themselves as distinct from other generations based on their use of technology.[55] In particular, they have embraced MySpace, Facebook, YouTube, Twitter, and the like.

Among the Millennials who tweet is Teter. When she started the underwear line, she announced the news to her more-than-1,000 followers on Twitter.

Teter tweeted in early 2010: "just launched my new underwear for charity! check 'em out! sweetcheekspanties.com!"[56]

Millennials worldwide are quite willing to help companies they approve of and punish ones they see as unworthy. A 2010 global study of people born between 1980 and 1995 found that at least 8 in 10 have taken action on behalf of a brand they trust—including sharing brand experiences with others, joining online communities, and posting reviews online. When Millennials lose trust and respect for a brand, 54 percent have told their family and friends not to purchase its products, 41 percent have boycotted the company, and nearly one-third have either posted something on their social network about the brand or have joined a community of people who dislike the brand.[57]

Civic-minded, tech-savvy Millennials not only promise to propel firms to be better sellers and stewards, but to be better employers too. Accustomed to doting parents and close networks of peers, Gen Y-ers also have high expectations that employers will give them frequent feedback, enable workplace collaboration, and provide a healthy work-life balance.

A 2008 study by the Families and Work Institute found that the desire of employees under the age of 29 to advance to jobs with greater responsibility declined 13 percent compared with their counterparts in 1992.[58]

Gen Y-ers also want to work at companies in step with their broad-minded values. "Millennials favor a corporate culture of inclusion and tolerance and will gravitate toward companies that actively promote racial and cultural diversity," author Ron Alsop writes in his book about Generation Y in the workplace, *The Trophy Kids Grow Up.*[59]

Critics argue that Millennials' demands amount to self-indulgence that shouldn't be coddled and complain about job-hopping by young people. It's also possible Gen Y's values will change as members of the cohort age, making their social justice bent less pressing to companies.

But there's some evidence Millennials' liberalism is more than just youthful optimism. In a comparison of political and social attitudes between Millennials in 2009 and Generation X members when they were roughly the same age in 1994, Millennials were found to have more liberal views on family, homosexuality, and civil liberties. Millennials also tended to be more pro-regulation.[60]

Companies that fail to address Millennials' workplace priorities risk losing a generation on track to become the most educated generation in American history.[61] And despite some me-first tendencies, Millennials tend to respect their elders[62]—a promising trait for firms.

Generation Y is big, idealistic, and interactive. The new kids on the block are pressuring firms to be worthy sellers, good stewards, and devoted employers.

CHAPTER THREE SUMMARY

Four fundamental social forces are increasing the premium on being a good company.

Disclosure Culture

- People have begun disclosing aspects of their experience as never before.
- Much of this self-expression spills over into people's experiences as workers, consumers, and investors.
- Emerging social media technologies are fueling the publication of the personal, and giving it greater potential impact.
- This creates growing pressure for companies to be genuine, honest, and good.

Global Solidarity

- People increasingly identify themselves as "global citizens."
- Increased financial insecurity is giving rise to an all-for-one, one-for-all sensibility.
- A more global, social mindset is leading to greater focus on the way organizations treat people.

Going Green

- Public concern about the environment is pressuring companies to become authentically green.
- Walmart—once the symbol of materialism at its world-destroying worst—is making major strides toward becoming much more green.
- Interest in protecting the environment is especially high in developing nations.
- The "environmental tent" continues to grow—with additions including prominent evangelical Christians, as well as growing numbers of business executives.

Millennials Emerge

- The massive, civic-minded, and technologically savvy Gen Y is pushing companies to become better sellers, employers, and stewards.

CHAPTER 4

The Political Imperative

omputer chip maker Intel, famous for its "Intel inside" motto, got dinged from the outside in 2009.

Outside the marketplace, that is. European regulators slapped Intel with a record-large fine of $1.45 billion for abusing its dominant position in the market for a class of computer chips.[1] After a lengthy probe of the market for chips known as x86 central processing units, the European Commission concluded that Intel engaged in illegal anticompetitive practices such as making direct payments to a major retailer on condition it stock only computers with Intel x86 chips.

"Intel has harmed millions of European consumers by deliberately acting to keep competitors out of the market for computer chips for many years," said European Commissioner for Competition Neelie Kroes. "Such a serious and sustained violation of the EU's antitrust rules cannot be tolerated."[2]

Kroes's indignant tone is telling. The antitrust penalty her organization levied on Intel is part of a pendulum swing back toward greater regulation of businesses by governments around the world. That regulatory push is among several political factors forcing companies in the direction of greater goodness. We define *political* here broadly to refer to the way people and organizations make decisions. In that light, this chapter looks at two other political trends besides the growth in government intervention. They are the increase in shareholder activism and the emergence of workplace democracy.

Regulation Rising

The European Commission's antitrust fine against Intel was eye-popping, but it was far from an isolated case. In recent years, governments in Europe and other parts of the world have stepped up their policing of markets and companies. Just a year before imposing the hefty fine on Intel, for example, the European Commission ordered software giant Microsoft to pay a $1.3 billion fine for failing to comply with a prior antitrust ruling.[3]

Commissioner Kroes in particular has been so tough on perceived anticompetitive behavior that she earned the nickname "Steely Neelie," as well as spot 53 on *Forbes*'s 2009 list of the 100 most powerful women.[4]

Kroes and her team at the European Commission—an organization akin to the executive branch of the U.S. Government—did not let up against Intel. In their probe of whether Intel improperly tried to shut rival AMD out of European markets through hidden rebates and other means, the regulators went beyond formal contracts and statements to analyzing e-mails obtained partly from unannounced on-site inspections.[5]

And the actions of the commission are only part of the story in Europe.

In the United Kingdom, sweeping legislation known as "the Equality Bill" began to take effect in 2010.[6] Among other things, the measure gives additional power to employment tribunals and protects employees who discuss their pay to uncover discrimination, even if their employment contract bars them from talking about their pay.[7] What's more, in late 2008 Britain's Equality and Human Rights Commission announced it would probe the financial services and construction industries because of inequality in pay or ethnic minority representation in the workforce.[8]

The U.S. push toward more regulation began in earnest when Barack Obama took office in early 2009. One of his first actions as president was to sign into law a measure that makes it easier for workers to sue employers for pay discrimination.[9] His administration declared that greenhouse gases are hazardous to public health and welfare, opening the door to tighter emission controls and regulations under the Clean Air Act.[10] The U.S. Congress passed major pieces of legislation to overhaul the health-care system and increase oversight of the financial services industry. And Obama's 2011 budget called for $25 million to crack down on the prob-lem of employers misclassifying employees as independent contractors.[11]

The 2010 U.S. mid-term election results will almost certainly slow this push toward more regulation. But given the underlying dissatisfac-tion of broad swaths of the U.S. electorate with the state of corporate America, it still seems likely that the long-term trend will be toward greater regulation, across a broad array of industries.

Greater interest in regulating companies extends to China, where a law that went into effect in 2008 strengthened the hand of workers. Among other provisions, the law gives temporary workers the right to earn the same pay as comparable workers at the firm to which they are assigned, and mandates that laid-off workers generally receive one month's wage for each full year worked.[12]

That measure is part of a shift in China in recent years to balance the country's breakneck economic growth with the goal of a "socialist harmonious society."[13] Also in keeping with that aim is China's pledge to try to reduce its "carbon intensity"—which refers to emissions of car-bon dioxide per unit of economic growth—by 40 to 45 percent by 2020, compared with 2005 levels.[14]

China's swing to rein in market excesses reflects a worldwide reevalu-ation of the costs of unfettered capitalism and growing doubts about the wisdom of unchecked markets in the wake of the Great Recession. That dramatic downturn resulted at least in part from under-regulation in the financial services industry. Exotic securities products and minimal requirements for capital reserves magnified the effects of a housing mar-ket collapse.

Even leading conservative scholar Richard Posner conceded the reces-sion revealed the dangers of overly free markets. Posner published a book in 2009 titled *A Failure of Capitalism: The Crisis of '08 and the Descent into Depression* and conceded laissez faire in the financial arena is flawed.

In a 2009 *Wall Street Journal* op-ed piece Posner wrote, "The banking crash might not have occurred had banking not been progressively deregulated beginning in the 1970s . . . competition in an unregulated financial market drives up risk, which, given the centrality of banking to a capitalist economy, can produce an economic calamity."[15]

In coming to this conclusion, Posner is in step with citizens around the globe. A 2009 poll of more than 22,000 people in 20 countries found that 67 percent want to see an increase in "government regulation and oversight of the national economy."[16] And as mentioned in Chapter 2, another 2009 worldwide poll found that just 11 percent said free-market capitalism works well and greater regulation would make it less efficient.[17] That poll, sponsored by the BBC World Service, found particular support for heightened regulations in several key emerging economies. Seventy-one percent of people in China, 87 percent of Brazilians, and 68 percent of Russians want to see government be more active in regulating business.

A U.S.-only poll published in 2009 found that a majority of Americans believe that corporations are not adequately evolving to more sustainable business practices and will require regulation to move in the right direction. The poll, by Harris Interactive, showed that only 16 percent of Americans believe that companies will make these changes on their own.[18]

The implication of such surveys and growing government intervention is that companies had better behave better. Firms that fail to demonstrate goodness as a steward, seller, and employer face fines and a corresponding decline in their good name. Evidence that we provide in Chapters 5 and 6 shows that those that abide by and do more than what is required by regulations will likely survive and benefit from an enhanced reputation.

Skeptics of this conclusion might point to mixed signals on the public's support of more regulation. A Gallup survey from early 2010 found that half of Americans believe the government should become less involved in regulating and controlling business, 24 percent say the government should become more involved, and 23 percent believe things are about right.[19] Pro-regulation forces also were dealt a blow with a U.S. Supreme Court decision in early 2010, which eased restrictions on political spending by corporations and other special interests.[20]

What's more, even well-intentioned regulations can prove to be wrongheaded. Businesses have a right to point out unintended negative consequences, to question rules, and challenge findings. Intel, for example, contested the European Commission's ruling and $1.45 billion fine and pledged it would appeal the decision.

"We do not believe our practices violated European law," Intel CEO Paul Otellini said at the time. "The natural result of a competitive market with only two major suppliers is that when one company wins sales, the other does not."[21]

But in the wake of the European Commission fine, other regulators have accused Intel of misbehavior as well. The New York Attorney General sued Intel claiming it violated antitrust law,[22] and the Federal Trade Commission filed a complaint against the company alleging anticompetitive tactics that have "stifled innovation and harmed consumers."[23]

And despite public concerns about government overregulation, people are equally if not more wary about the untamed power of large corporations—especially in light of bad behavior during the Great Recession and in the Gulf of Mexico. Based on a survey done in 2010, shortly after BP's Deepwater Horizon oil spill, the *Wall Street Journal* reported that "Nearly two-thirds in the survey said they wanted more regulation of oil companies. Majorities also favor more regulation of Wall Street firms, health insurers, and 'big corporations.'" In addition, the survey found that 63 percent of Americans support legislation to reduce carbon emissions and increase the use of alternative and renewable energy sources, even if it means an increase in energy costs.[24]

Kroes, for one, does not apologize for taking a hard line with companies. In a 2009 speech she reviewed five years of work at the Commission. "I think it's a strong record," Kroes said. "A record that has left the [European market] in much better shape than if we'd left it to the wolves."[25]

Thanks to Kroes and the broader rise of regulation, if companies want to thrive in the European market and other markets, they're going to have to act less like wolves and more like good neighbors.

Shareholder Activism

Home Depot learned the hard way about the growing power of shareholder activism.

The home improvement giant and its CEO Bob Nardelli made headlines by snubbing shareholders at the company's annual stockholder meeting in May 2006. Amid heated criticism of Nardelli's hefty pay—some $200 million over five years—and a decrease in shareholder returns, all of Home Depot's directors save Nardelli skipped the event.[26] He didn't answer the questions and wrapped the meeting up after a mere half hour.[27]

Later, Nardelli conceded the "new format" was a mistake.[28] But given widespread public fury about outsized CEO pay, Nardelli became a poster child for executive arrogance. And shareholders only grew more agitated with the company. In December 2006 a shareholder group, Relational Investors, said it would call for a review of Home Depot's strategy and management.[29] And the flap found its way into the *New York Times.*[30]

"There is no accountability to shareholders," Ralph Whitworth, head of Relational Investors, told the newspaper at the time. "Since Nardelli was made president in 2000, he's taken hundreds of millions in compensation, but the company's return to investors has been almost nothing. There needs to be someone making sure management is watching the store."

Within weeks, Home Depot capitulated to Whitworth and other shareholders. Nardelli was ousted from the firm, reportedly over his refusal to more closely tie his future stock awards to shareholder gains.[31]

Home Depot has plenty of company when it comes to facing pressure from active shareholders. Over the last decade or so, shareholders have been speaking up and calling for a variety of reforms at companies. Although their concerns vary, shareholder activists as a whole are pushing companies in the direction of greater goodness.

Shareholder activism takes advantage of the fact that companies are a kind of democracy. Key decisions are made by a vote of the owners, or shareholders. Unlike in an election for public office in the United States, where each citizen gets a single vote, shareholders get as many votes as shares owned. And in some arrangements, particular classes of shares have more voting power. Still, average shareholders have a chance to participate in major decisions such as electing board members. And individual shareholders have the ability to propose initiatives to be decided on by shareholders overall.

Shareholder priorities vary. Some activist investors are focused on seeing higher stock returns. These include "activist hedge funds" that look to turn around poorly managed or undervalued companies. Other activist investors include public pension funds, unions, and individuals determined to express their political or social values through their investments. These shareholders want changes such as improved governance, more oversight on executive compensation, better treatment of employees, and increased sustainability efforts.

Taken as a whole, shareholder activism is on the rise. Consider a study of activism trends from 2006 to 2008 that examined SC 13D disclosures. This type of U.S. Securities and Exchange filing applies to persons and institutions that take a 5 percent or greater stake in companies and reserve the right to influence management. The study by research firm Audit Analytics found that such activist shareholders expressed concern over share prices five times more in 2008 and 2007 than they did in 2006. The study also showed that activist disagreements with management on actions and strategy increased substantially, as did activist allegations that management provided misleading information.[32]

Much of the stepped-up shareholder involvement centers on executive pay. In 2007 a coalition of investors came together to push companies to adopt say-on-pay measures that would give shareholders an annual advisory vote on executive compensation. The coalition, which includes public pension funds, labor funds, asset managers, individual investors, foundations, and religious investors, made progress quickly.[33] In 2007, 51 say-on-pay shareholder proposals came to a vote, with 9 getting a majority of votes. In 2008, 79 of the proposals came to a vote, with 11 winning a majority. Another 76 say-on-pay initiatives were voted on in 2009, with 24 majority votes.[34]

These measures were themselves advisory. Even when the initiatives won a majority of votes, companies weren't obligated to adopt say-on-pay. But companies have been heeding the calls for more compensation oversight. By early 2010 more than 50 companies had voluntarily agreed to hold say-on-pay votes, up from just 6 in 2008.[35] Adopters include Aflac, Apple, CVS Caremark, Hewlett-Packard, and Valero Energy.

"Say on Pay holds corporate leaders accountable for unjustifiable CEO pay," says Gerald McEntee, president of the American Federation of State, County and Municipal Employees union, which helped organize the say-on-pay campaign. "The recklessness of too many CEOs has got to end. Shareowners are demanding sensible pay for performance programs that discourage excessive risk taking."[36]

Indeed, "Say on Pay" became law in 2010, requiring companies to hold advisory shareholder votes on executive compensation.[37] And shareholder activism isn't happening just in the United States. In Korea, for example, a nongovernment organization known as People's Solidarity for Participatory Democracy has used the position of minority shareholder to fight for reforms such as leadership change and the disclosure of executive directors' salaries.[38] And say-on-pay legislation has recently been passed in Germany.[39]

In Europe, two activist hedge funds, Centaurus and Pardus, pushed through changes at technology services company Atos Origin, including a new board chair.[40] In a 2008 report, financial services firm RiskMetrics Group saw the Atos case as evidence of a turning point for shareholder activism in Europe.

> Although in the past activists have been demonized and likened to "locusts" by some on the European continent, recent activist victories indicate that "mainstream" shareholders under the right circumstances will be willing to see beyond the rhetoric and hold incumbent directors and executives accountable for underperformance much like their investor counterparts in the US have done over the past five years.[41]

Shareholder activism has its problems. Initiatives by unions or other advocates theoretically can go too far, forcing a firm to pay excess attention to a particular set of stakeholders. And as the "locusts" reference in the quote above suggests, investors driven by greed can swarm in and destroy a decent company. It's a short hop, in other words, from shareholder activist to corporate raider. In the 1980s, raiders like Carl Icahn orchestrated leveraged buyouts that led to layoffs and asset stripping to pay back debt.

Even in the Home Depot case, there was a whiff of unfair impatience to activist demands. While the company's stock price had hovered near $40 since fall of 2004, Nardelli could point to 12 percent sales growth for the year ending January 29, 2006. Net income for that year rose 17 percent.[42]

Still, part of what irked Home Depot shareholders were signs of long-term trouble. Nardelli hit his numbers to some extent by cutting costs at the expense of service and good treatment of workers. During his six-year tenure, Home Depot's customer service rating fell to 67 from 75, according to the University of Michigan's American Customer Satisfaction Index. During the same period, rival Lowe's rose from 75 to 78.[43] And Nardelli bred resentment among his rank-and-file by replacing many full-time employees with part-time workers.[44]

"You can't s—t on your employees and deliver" results, one Home Depot shareholder told *BusinessWeek* at the time. In late 2005, the shareholder, an Atlanta attorney, had requested a nonbinding shareholder vote on whether Nardelli should be canned.[45]

Ultimately, Home Depot's shareholder activism amounted to pressure on the firm to be both profitable and principled—to be a good company. And despite the possibility of doing harm, shareholder activism overall is putting similar salutary pressures on companies throughout the economy. One study of compensation-related activism found that voting shareholders do not support proposals that try to micromanage CEO pay and instead favor proposals related to the pay-setting process.[46]

The report by researchers from Duke University, Harvard Business School, and the University of Texas at Dallas also found that shareholder activism has made a dent in the problem of egregious CEO pay. According to the study, there is a $7.3 million reduction in total CEO compensation for firms with abnormally high CEO pay that are targeted by pay-related vote-no campaigns. Vote-no campaigns are efforts to convince other shareholders to withhold their vote from one or more directors up for election.

At Home Depot, investor involvement didn't end with Nardelli's departure. The fact that he left with a whopping severance package worth $210 million further enraged investors. That unseemly amount was based on an employment agreement signed years earlier, giving the company little wiggle room when it parted ways with Nardelli.[47] But Home Depot did learn some lessons about shareholder activism.

For starters, it crafted a pay package for Nardelli's successor Frank Blake that took note of shareholders' compensation concerns. In contrast to Nardelli's 2005 base salary of $2.16 million, Blake was given base pay of $975,000 when he took over in January 2007. And while Nardelli enjoyed a guaranteed annual bonus of at least $3 million a year and the rich severance deal, Blake's contract had no guaranteed bonuses and no massive severance package.[48]

Also, as discussed in Chapter 1, the company reached out to critics on a message board at Web site MSN.

Moreover, the firm returned to respecting shareholders enough to engage with them at annual meetings. The May 2009 meeting, in fact, was fairly friendly. Blake heard compliments regarding better staff morale and the promotion of an African American to a top post.[49]

One report of the meeting quoted Gary Patton, a store employee from South Carolina who had criticized the company in the past. "This year I couldn't think of anything to complain about," Patton said.[50]

Workplace Democracy

A key to success at tech services firm HCL Technologies has nothing to do with computers. It has to do with workplace democracy.

The India-based company's "Employees First, Customers Second" program aims to upend hierarchy, engage employees, and generate innovation from throughout the firm. The effort, which dates to 2005, is the brainchild of CEO Vineet Nayar. Nayar had an employee empowerment epiphany earlier in his career, when he led a customer meeting in a different division of HCL Technologies' parent company. He noticed the customer almost completely ignoring him and focusing instead on members of the team that served the firm. The customer was happy and praised the team members at length. Nayar came away from the event convinced that having the right employees very engaged in creating value for the customer was more important than anything he could do.[51]

To engage employees, the company has involved them. One of the Employees First initiatives Nayar launched at HCL was designed to make managers accountable to employees rather than the other way around. Through the firm's 360-degree feedback program, managers not only receive reviews from subordinates, peers, and supervisors, but are encouraged to post these publicly. Nayar was first to do so back in 2005, and by 2007 more than half of the firm's 2,282 managers published the feedback they got.

Other democratizing reforms have included the extensive use of employee opinion polls, executive meetings with rank-and-file workers over company strategy, and U&I—an online forum letting employees interact directly with Nayar. Between late 2006 and July 2008, employees asked 2,492 questions. Of those, 2,346 had been answered.[52]

In 2005 employees were leaving HCL at an above-average rate and the firm struggled to compete against larger rivals. By 2009, attrition had dropped, the firm had won best-employer awards, and its revenue during the recession outpaced that of a key competitor. HCL chalked up the turnaround to Employees First and its new flatness—its effort to put employees and supervisors on an equal footing.

"Through a combination of engaged employees and accountable management, a company can create extraordinary value for itself, its customer, and the individuals involved in both companies," Nayar says.[53]

Although HCL stands out as a radical example, many companies are tapping the concept of workplace democracy. Just as shareholders are growing more active in companies, so too, in a way, are employees. Over the past 15 years or so, employees have gained power through a shift in management style away from hierarchy and toward decentralization. To be sure, rank-and-file employees have limited authority in this new workplace. They typically don't have much control over corporate strategy, nor can workers generally prevent layoffs or pay cuts. But employees at many companies now determine the way they do their jobs to a great extent and are consulted by management about matters ranging from new hires, possible productivity improvements, and levels of trust in senior leadership.

In other words, workers in the age of flat organizations are generating helpful ideas, having a say over their jobs, and holding leaders accountable. This sort of workplace democracy, then, is a force for company goodness. And it is likely to grow in significance, largely because it makes good business sense.

Flatness as a management philosophy helps companies adapt to and thrive in today's global economy. That economy has grown more integrated, fast-paced, and competitive since the 1990s thanks to changes such as the diffusion of personal computers, the emergence of the Internet, and the rise of outsourcing and offshoring.

Thomas Friedman crystallized the power of such forces to erode traditional management methods in his 2005 book, *The World Is Flat*:

> Globalization 3.0, which is built around the convergence of the
> ten flatteners, and particularly the combination of the PC, the
> microprocessor, the Internet, and fiber optics, flipped the playing
> field from largely top-down to more side to side. And this naturally
> fostered and demanded new business practices, which were less about
> command and control and more about connecting and collaborating
> horizontally.[54]

A major form of employee involvement is self-managed teams—placing workers in teams and allowing them to decide how to organize themselves and how to do their tasks. Companies increasingly are adopting this practice. According to the Center for Effective Organizations at the University of Southern California, the percentage of Fortune 1000 firms with self-managing teams rose from 28 in 1988 to 65 in 2005.[55]

In addition, companies increasingly have adopted "parallel participation practices," which are separate from a worker's regular job.[56] The most popular of these are suggestion systems, attitude feedback, and discussion groups. In 2005 more than 90 percent of Fortune 1000 companies used one or more of these methods.[57]

Workplace democracy can be a key to company success, according to scholars James O'Toole and Edward E. Lawler III. In their 2006 survey of the American workplace, O'Toole and Lawler point to evidence that companies and employees both benefit when all employees participate in decisions affecting their work and all employees participate in the financial gains resulting from their ideas and efforts.[58]

"It makes sense economically, psychologically, and practically that, the more that employees are as fully engaged as executives in the most important managerial aspects of the company, the more they will think and act like those executives," O'Toole and Lawler write.[59]

That captures the thinking of Nayar when he took over HCL Technologies in 2005. He inherited a troubled operation of some 30,000 employees. Amid heated competition and commoditization in the tech services arena, HCL suffered from above-average attrition of 30 percent in 2004.[60]

Nayar was determined to go after more complex, higher-value contracts and trusted that a more democratic workplace would help drive the change. His "HCLites" proved him right. Questions raised in the U&I forum became increasingly strategic in nature, shifting from matters like delayed performance reviews to topics including new opportunities in the technology industry.[61] Overall, employees generated a number of ideas, such as putting into place a "concept to manufacture" offering with business partners. Joining forces with manufacturing services firm Celestica, for example, HCL was able to provide a C2M service that was more comprehensive than what Nayar's team had been able to sell in the past. In addition to the product design work HCL had done previously, the new service included prototyping as well as manufacturing and after-sales support.[62]

Attrition dropped below 15 percent for the year ending June 2008, while revenue jumped 146 percent between June 2005 and June 2008 to $1.9 billion annually. And HCL continued to progress amid the Great Recession. HCL's revenue grew more than 20 percent in 2009, while rival Infosys saw its sales shrink slightly that year.

Workers thinking like executives—like stewards of the company's financial success—is part of the way employee involvement pushes companies toward goodness. Workplace democracy also helps make an employer a worthy one by addressing workers' basic human desires for control and social belonging.[63] And more decentralized decision-making can make it more likely that potential problems will be noticed and fixed before a company hurts its customers, its communities, or the environment. A more transparent, participatory company, in other words, encourages whistle-blowing and makes it hard to hide wrongdoing.

Firms that stand out for a management style with high employee involvement include Gore-Tex maker Gore Technologies, junk retrieval service 1-800-GOT-JUNK?, and household products maker Seventh Generation.

The ranks of these firms are likely to grow in the future partly because of growing amounts of attention given to workplace democracy. The annual *Fortune* list of the Best Companies to Work For shines a spotlight on worker-friendly practices, including shared decision making. In addition, advocacy group Worldblu has been publishing a list of the most democratic workplaces each year since 2007.

Radical power sharing in a company may strike some as a recipe for anarchy and disaster. Skeptics also might question whether workers truly have much authority in workplaces today. Given the decline of unions and the workplace clout they represent, doesn't the current edition of employee involvement amount to democratic window dressing at best and the exploitation of workers' ideas at worst?

But the decline of unions is owed in part to their inability to channel worker voices toward helping companies handle competition and change.[64] And while it is true that individual workers typically don't have much authority to stave off layoffs and may not own the intellectual property they create on the job, the ever-flatter nature of organizations means their contributions are increasingly meaningful.

Decentralized companies can be messy and sometimes slow to act. But firms are getting smarter about how to manage in a bottom-up manner, about when executives should be decisive and when they should be consultative.

In any event, business trends, including globalization and the participatory inclinations of younger workers, will increase the pressure on companies to hammer down their hierarchies.

WorldBlu founder and president Traci Fenton explains: "Organizational democracy is inevitable. The Internet, the demands of Generations X and Y to have a voice in the workplace, and the Gallup Organization's report that nearly two-thirds of US workers are disengaged at work are causing businesses to rethink their management models and embrace a more democratic style. The companies that choose organizational democracy will lead their industries, boost their bottom lines, and ultimately build a more democratic world."[65]

One sign that workplace democracy is on the march is the way HCL's star continues to rise. *BusinessWeek* called it one of the "World's Most Influential Companies" in 2008,[66] *Fortune* said HCL had "the world's most modern management,"[67] and Nayar has become a blogger for the prestigious management journal *Harvard Business Review*. Nayar also recently published a book about the firm's philosophy of flatness.

"One of the structural flaws of traditional management systems is that the leader holds too much power," Nayar writes in *Employees First, Customers Second*. "That prevents the organization from becoming democratized and the energy of the employees from being released."[68]

More and more, democratic workplaces are releasing that energy, and it is propelling companies in the direction of goodness.

CHAPTER FOUR SUMMARY

Three fundamental, broadly defined political forces are increasing the premium on being a good company.

Rise in Regulation

- Governments around the world have been regulating businesses with greater vigor.
- The trend reflects worldwide doubts about the dangers of unchecked capitalism, especially in the wake of the Great Recession.
- While the 2010 election makes the short-term prognosis less clear in the United States, broad-based, nonpartisan discontent with corporate behavior also points to a more highly regulated environment.
- As a result, firms that fail to demonstrate goodness as stewards, sellers, and employers face fines and a corresponding decline in their good name.

Shareholder Activism

- Taken as a whole, shareholder activism is on the rise.
- Much of the stepped-up shareholder involvement centers on executive pay.
- Shareholder activism tends to push companies in the direction of worthier behavior.

Workplace Democracy

- Workplaces are becoming more democratic and less hierarchical.
- Increased "flatness" owes in part to trends such as the rise of PCs, the Internet, and offshoring, which have made top-down management less effective.
- Workers are generating helpful ideas, having a say over their jobs, and holding leaders accountable.
- More decentralized decision making can make it more likely that potential problems will be noticed and fixed before a company hurts its customers, its communities, or the environment.

PART II

Evidence and Rankings

CHAPTER 5

Goodness Matters

A growing body of evidence shows that companies can do well by doing good. But that's only part of the story in the world taking shape. The individual trends outlined in Chapters 2, 3, and 4—when taken together—indicate that goodness is rapidly becoming necessary to doing well.

What's more, the convergence of the trends we've identified calls for a comprehensive response. Many companies during the past decade have launched disparate initiatives such as becoming an employer of choice, reducing carbon footprints, and beefing up compliance efforts. But firms that aim to succeed in sustainable ways must move to become good companies through and through.

This chapter summarizes some of the best available hard-nosed evidence that companies are doing well by doing good and risk doing poorly by doing bad. Although much of this evidence is based on large, publicly traded U.S.-based firms, the arguments presented in earlier chapters strongly point to the growing imperative for all organizations—private or public, large or small—to become thoroughly worthy.

Doing Well by Doing Good

The stock market—despite all of its wild swings and, at times, seeming irrationality—provides one of the best available lenses for understanding the payoff that good companies enjoy over an extended period of time.[1] To be sure, the performance of any given stock can be erratic, as can the performance of the entire market at any point in time. But over the long haul, the performance of "good companies" (relative to the market) has a great deal to teach us.

Fortune magazine's annual list of the best companies to work for provides one of the best available methods for looking at how being a good employer relates to subsequent performance in the stock market.[2] From 1998 to 2009 the average annual return on a portfolio of the (publicly traded) companies on this list was 10.3 percent, compared to an annual average return for the S&P 500 (the standard U.S. benchmark) of 3.0 percent.[3] Even after controlling for company characteristics, the companies on this list outperformed risk-adjusted industry benchmarks. They also exhibited significantly more positive earnings surprises—occasions when their quarterly earnings surpassed what analysts predicted they would be—than their industry benchmarks.[4]

While this evidence does not necessarily prove that being a good employer causes these results, the findings strongly suggest companies can do well by doing good as employers.

And it is not the only evidence along those lines. Dan and Laurie are registered investment advisers and since 2001 have been investing in a series of portfolios based on how well firms manage and develop their employees. The performance of these "human capital management" portfolios is listed in the table on the following page.

The longest running of these portfolios—Portfolios A and B—are based on a very simple investment strategy: firms that invest more in educating, developing, and training their employees subsequently perform better (on average) than those that spend less.[5] Once again, this finding does not prove that investing in employees causes better subsequent stock performance.[6] But the finding is striking. It suggests that executives (and investors) should pay attention to the importance of being a good employer.

Portfolios C to F are each based on broader (but more difficult to quantify) concepts of human capital management. Each of the portfolios uses a somewhat different process for identifying firms with superior capabilities for managing and developing employees. For example, one

Performance of Human Capital Portfolios, Relative to S&P 500

Portfolio	Date of inception	Total return (through 12/31/10)	Overall performance relative to S&P 500	Annualized performance relative to S&P 500
A	12/01/01	44.8%	+35.9%	+3.4%
B	01/01/03	87.1%	+44.1%	+4.7%
C	03/25/08	23.7%	+30.5%	+10.1%
D	03/25/08	−4.5%	+2.3%	+0.8%
E	10/14/08	59.0%	+33.7%	+14.0%
F	12/23/08	57.1%	+11.4%	+5.5%

NOTE: Reported portfolio performances do not include fees or expenses. S&P 500 does not include dividends. Past performance is not a guarantee of future results. Additional details are available from Bassi Investments.

portfolio is heavily weighted to firms that do an exceptionally good job of employee performance management (a specific aspect of being a good employer). Another portfolio is heavily weighted to firms that use rigorous quantitative analysis to help them invest wisely in employees' development.

Although the track record on these portfolios is short, the early signs are promising.

Similarly, other data shows that a focus on responsibility or sustainability pays off. The FTSE KLD 400 Social Index, a stock index constructed using environmental, social, and governance factors, has outperformed the S&P 500 since its inception in 1990. The FTSE KLD 400 Social Index slightly underperformed the S&P 500 during the year that ended July 31, 2010. But it had outpaced the S&P 500 on a three-year and five-year basis.[7] And SAM, the investment company behind the Dow Jones Sustainability Indexes, says its in-house research and external academic empirical work suggest that "there is a positive and statistically significant correlation between corporate sustainability and financial performance, as measured by stock returns."[8]

Sustainability also spelled success in the stock market during the recent financial crisis, according to a study by consulting firm A. T. Kearney. Although the study covered a relatively short time frame of six months, the findings were telling. A. T. Kearney discovered that in 16 of 18 industries studied, companies committed to sustainability outperformed industry averages by 15 percent from May through November 2008.[9]

The Good Company Index that we created to measure the worthiness of the Fortune 100 reinforces these findings. As we'll discuss in greater detail in Chapter 6, we decided to see how Fortune 100 companies in the same industry with different Good Company Index scores performed in the stock market. We found that companies with higher Good Company Index scores (worthier companies, in other words), did better in the stock market over the last year, the last three years, and the last five years than their industry match with a lower Good Company Index score.

In sum, then, there is much compelling evidence that good companies (and their owners) enjoy higher share-price appreciation than their less-good counterparts, and that goodness actually predicts future stock market performance.

Beyond studies of stock returns, other research indicates that companies can do well by doing good. A 2009 report by economists Scott J. Callan and Janet M. Thomas examined 441 large U.S. firms and found corporate social responsibility—referred to as corporate social performance in scholarly circles—helps rather than hinders financial success. "Empirical evidence of a positive [corporate social performance]–[corporate financial performance] relationship indicates that firms need not view social responsibility and profitability as competing goals," Callan and Thomas conclude. "In fact, firms might measurably benefit from their socially responsible decisions, if these decisions are recognized and rewarded by relevant stakeholders. This recognition might take the form of stronger consumer demand or higher worker productivity, which in turn would yield to the firm a stronger financial performance."[10]

There is another benefit from being a good company: it increases the probability of long-term survival. This is more significant than it might seem at first blush. In his summary of a study done by Shell Company on corporate longevity, Arie de Geus reports that "the average life expectancy of a multinational corporation—Fortune 500 or its equivalent—is between 40 and 50 years. . . . Human beings have learned to survive, on average, for 75 years or more, but there are very few companies that are that old and flourishing."[11]

De Geus concludes that the essential attribute of these "living organizations" is that they are a "community of humans."[12] "Like all organisms, the living company exists primarily . . . to fulfill its potential and to become as great as it can be."[13] This suggests that while companies need to be profitable to survive and thrive, existing purely for the purpose of making profits is an insufficient purpose—one that, in and of itself, is unlikely to foster corporate longevity.

In another ambitious study of long-lived corporations, Danny Miller and Isabelle LeBreton-Miller conclude that such corporations tended to be disproportionately family controlled, and that they share three core philosophies:

- Ownership Philosophy—owners are stewards (not traders)
- Business Philosophy—they are driven by a substantive mission (not quick financial results)
- Social Philosophy—they have shared values and foster lasting relationships (not one-shot transactions)

The "substantive mission" at the heart of long-lasting corporations is akin to the worthy purpose we see as key to good companies. Miller and LeBreton-Miller write:

> Substantive missions are not concocted by some strategic planner, nor are they financially driven. They flow from values residing in the bellies of family proprietors. And like all bulwarks, they are immovable. Although missions are manifested in objectives such as making a superb product, pioneering technologies, or establishing an effective brand, they are more fundamental than that. Their ultimate purpose is to make a difference in how people live, in social or scientific progress, even in the joyfulness of life.

Miller and LeBreton-Miller give the example of a well-known tire maker founded in 1888: "The Michelins had a mission to transform travel into a safer, happier experience."[14]

Similarly, in his analysis of firms that are profitable over the long term (which is, in some cases, hundreds of years), Joseph Bragdon concludes that these companies operate as, "an organic living system whose defining elements are living assets; that it exists within the larger web of life, on which it utterly depends; and that its 'reason for being' is to serve humanity in sustainable ways that don't harm the web."[15]

Consider, for example, Finland-based Stora Enso. The maker of paper, packaging, and wood products is "the world's oldest company," writes Bragdon, "It has survived for 700-plus years because from the beginning, its owners (initially a religious diocese) and managers cared about employees and the community in which it operated. Stora Enso's governance became decentralized in the mid-fourteenth century due to a royal charter and a mining statue that dispersed power among a group of master miners and established fair wages and work sequencing. Since then the company has survived and grown, thanks to an open, tolerant culture that learns and adapts from the bottom up."[16]

Research into the factors behind the survival of firms with initial public stock offerings also points to the value of worthiness. A team of scholars led by University of Southern California management professor Theresa Welbourne discovered that investments in human resources are the strongest predictors of the survival of firms five years after an IPO.[17] The HR factors Welbourne and her team investigated included the degree to which the firm valued its employees vis-à-vis other assets, seen partly in whether a company has an HR officer as a senior executive. The researchers also examined the distribution of rewards, including whether stock options or profits were shared with all employees.

People management factors proved more significant to a company's long-term health than a host of other indicators, such as net profit per share at the time of the IPO, industry type, and the risk of legal proceedings against the firm.[18]

Interestingly, Welbourne and her team also found that human-resource investments had a negative effect on the initial IPO "going out" stock price. This suggests that investors have tended to view HR as a distraction and employees as primarily a cost rather than an asset.

On the contrary, prioritizing people management is critical for sustainable success, Welbourne says.

"The reason HR factors had a positive effect on longer-term performance was due to their effects on what we call 'structural cohesion,'" Welbourne writes. "Structural cohesion is an employee-generated synergy—essentially a close-knit, high-energy culture—that propels the company forward."[19]

From a variety of perspectives, then, the data is clear: companies survive and can do well by doing good.

Benefits to Goodness Through and Through

The evidence summarized above confirms there is a long-term payoff to taking the high road to profitability. To be sure, the low road—characterized by questionable ethics, unscrupulous behavior, plundering the environment, and unvarnished greed—also can be extremely lucrative. The record profits that Goldman Sachs earned in the wake of betting against its own customers is a case in point.[20] But there are also signs that the tide is turning and that companies are going to find the low road to profitability more challenging in the future.

A more ethical approach to economic choices has been building steam over the past decade, and the Great Recession did not sidetrack the trend. Although people might have been tempted to focus narrowly on selfish needs like rock-bottom prices and rapid stock returns, by and large they opted for a higher road. Nearly six in ten global consumers polled in 2009 said a company or brand earned their business during the recession because it has been doing its part to support good causes.[21] And, as mentioned in Chapter 1, nearly three out of four Americans surveyed in 2010 said they are more likely to give their business to a company that has fair prices and supports a good cause than to a company that provides deep discounts but does not contribute to good causes.[22]

Mitch Markson, Edelman's chief creative officer, argues that companies with a commitment to positive social change will get a boost from consumers, while indifferent or harmful firms will be punished. "People today are more passionately involved and supportive than ever, yet more demanding and unforgiving, as well," Markson says.[23]

Edelman's annual surveys on the importance of a good company purpose back up the point. In 2010, 62 percent of consumers globally said they would help a brand promote its products if there was a good cause behind it, up from 59 percent in 2009 and 53 percent in 2008.[24] The 2010 report also found that 37 percent of Americans would punish a company that doesn't actively support a good cause by sharing negative opinions and experiences, while 47 percent would not invest in such a company.[25] Edelman's data is part of a wide range of evidence showing the growing benefits of goodness—and the dangers of choosing otherwise.

Consumers, for instance, are holding companies to a high green standard. A 2009 study by communications services firm WPP and consulting firm Esty Environmental Partners found that at least 77 percent of consumers in all seven countries studied say it's somewhat or very important for companies to be green. The most important step a company can take to demonstrate its "greenness" is to reduce the amount of toxic or other dangerous substances in its products and business processes, according to the report. But consumers expect much more.

"While reducing toxics heads the list of consumer priorities the data also shows that the public holds companies accountable for good environmental behavior across the board," said Dan Esty, chairman of Esty Environmental Partners. "Consumers expect companies to recycle, use energy efficiently, reduce packaging, and pursue green innovation. So to gain loyalty, a company's environmental strategy must be comprehensive."[26]

People aren't just talking about green. They are backing up their ecological words with their wallets. In the WPP-Esty Environmental Partners study, consumers in both developed and emerging economies indicated they plan to spend more money on green products in the coming year.[27] And in keeping with the Accenture report on technology products referenced in Chapter 3, consumers in developing countries were particularly keen on going green. Seventy-three percent of Chinese consumers said they will spend more on environmentally friendly products, along with 78 percent of Indians and 73 percent of Brazilians.[28]

Environmental stewardship also is an increasingly vital factor to shoppers in the developed world. In the United Kingdom, for example, average household spending on products and services that combat global warming has risen in the past decade. Spending on such items as green transport, energy efficiency, and renewable energy increased from less than $37 annually in 1999 to nearly $495 in 2008.[29]

And in the United States, organic foods—which tend to be earth-friendly because organic farming methods avoid the release of synthetic pesticides into the environment—have become mainstream. One-fourth of U.S. adult shoppers frequently purchase certified organic food or beverage products, and one-third are usually willing to pay more for organic foods, according to a 2009 report by market researcher Packaged Facts.[30]

That report discussed a broader category of "ethical" consumer products, referring to items that are green, natural, organic, humane, or the result of fair trade. Packaged Facts said the U.S. market for ethical products had grown annually in the high single- to low double-digits over the previous five years. And it predicted the growth rate would persist despite the recession, with the market approaching $62 billion in 2014 up from a projected $38 billion in 2009.

"Our survey indicates that more shoppers understand the environmental, social, and economic implications of their choices," said Don Montuori, publisher of Packaged Facts. "The result is a sizeable number of consumers who will purchase typically more expensive ethical products even in economically challenging times."[31]

Other evidence that consumers will reward good companies and punish bad ones comes from a 2009 paper by researchers Remi Trudel and June Cotte.[32] Trudel and Cotte conducted a series of experiments about hypothetical coffee and cotton products, asking people about the prices they would pay for items from companies with a range of ethical practices. Customers will pay a premium for ethically produced goods and demand a lower price for products from companies that are not seen as ethical, the researchers found.

"Stay away from goods that are known by consumers to be unethically produced or pay the price (that is, know that your consumers will *not* pay the price)," Trudel and Cotte warn.[33]

In recent years, the phrase *ethical products* has become one of the main ways researchers, marketers, and the public at large talk about sustainability and social responsibility. The term and the trend speak to the way people increasingly connect all the facets of company goodness into a coherent whole. More and more, sustainability, corporate citizenship, and social responsibility amount to a holistic concept encompassing worthiness as an employer, a seller, and a steward of people and the planet.

Signs that consumers are calling for a comprehensive approach to good corporate citizenship surfaced in a 2007 report by public-relations firm Fleishman-Hillard and the National Consumers League advocacy group. It found that U.S. adults want more from firms than the charitable giving they've done for years.

> Consistently, consumers define the meaning of and expectations for corporate social responsibility in ways that go beyond just traditional charitable contributions and philanthropic giving. . . . Consumers expect companies to contribute to their communities by volunteering time and effort to local activities, getting involved in community events in nonfinancial ways, providing jobs, and treating their employees well. Companies can no longer assume that donations alone, however much they may be appreciated, can sustain a positive reputation for social responsibility.[34]

Consumers don't expect complete purity when it comes to sustainability. Trudel and Cotte found that the price premium for T-shirts made with 100 percent organic cotton wasn't very different from the premium given to shirts with 25 percent organic cotton. On the other hand, examples of outright badness will cost companies dearly, the researchers discovered. Information about unethical behavior—such as the use of child labor or heavy use of a pesticide—led to a price penalty that was bigger than the price premium given to companies with ethical practices. In other words, "consumers will punish the producer of unethically produced goods to a greater extent than they will reward a company that offers ethically produced products."[35]

Trudel and Cotte's work suggests that (at least as of 2009) there may be a threshold at which diminishing marginal returns set in when it comes to goodness (e.g., firms enjoy smaller incremental gains from additional investments in sustainability). Our prediction is that as time passes, consumers will push this threshold to a higher and higher level. But putting this prediction aside, what Trudel and Cotte's analysis makes clear is that firms guilty of serious offenses will reap customers' wrath.

It's not just consumers who seek to do business with companies well-rounded in their worthiness. Workers also want to be part of a company that is good through and through. As mentioned in Chapter 1, 56 percent of people globally want a job that allows them to give back to society versus 44 percent who value personal achievement more.[36] What's more, a 2009 study by staffing firm Randstad asked U.S. workers about traits of their ideal employer and found that 80 percent mentioned both "delivers on its promise to customers" and "cares about their employees as much as their customers." Those answers tied for the top spot, and the responses for both were up from 65 percent and 66 percent, respectively, the previous year.[37] In other words, workers increasingly are drawn to companies that do right by both customers and employees.

Investors too are gravitating toward overall goodness. As mentioned in Chapter 1, the value of assets linked to the Dow Jones Sustainability Indexes—which grade companies on criteria including customer relations, corporate codes of conduct, labor practices, and environmental impact—grew from about $1.5 billion at the end of 2000 to more than $8 billion at the close of 2009.[38]

According to *Time* magazine, the number of socially responsible investment mutual funds, which generally avoid buying shares of companies that profit from such things as tobacco, oil, or child labor, grew from 55 in 1995 to about 260 in 2009. *Time* estimated these funds managed approximately 11 percent of all the money invested in U.S. financial markets in 2009—an estimated $2.7 trillion.[39]

It stands to reason that consumers, workers, and investors clamoring to do business with thoroughly good companies would allow such firms to succeed. By practicing enlightened self-interest, worthy companies would seem likely to woo loyal customers, attract and inspire top-notch talent, and command greater amounts of investment capital.

And in fact, evidence supports such a conclusion. The power of integrated goodness can be seen in a 2008 study by consulting company Watson Wyatt Worldwide (now Towers Watson) and public-relations firm Brodeur Partners. That report found that companies that closely mesh their external brand with their employee experience outperform peers. It concluded that tight alignment between a company's external message and its employment "deal"—the rewards and experience a firm offers to workers—leads to increased employee engagement and retention, a superior customer experience, and a 15 percent higher market premium compared to industry peers.[40]

The result is at once striking and intuitive. As the study notes, employees play a key role in "delivering the brand promise to customers" just as company brand and reputation can be crucial in attracting and retaining talent.[41]

Another example that points to the growing imperative of doing well by doing good that may take some readers by surprise is Walmart. Walmart has been far from perfect in the past decade or so, especially in the area of people management. Its minimal fringe benefits arguably have burdened communities, as employees have had to rely on public health-care systems; its low-wage strategy may have cost the company more through high attrition than the higher wages paid by rival Costco; and it has displayed callousness toward workers.[42]

Still, Walmart has taken a number of steps to treat workers better, including improved health-care benefits.[43] As mentioned in Chapter 3, Walmart has taken a leadership role in the environmental arena. And it portrays itself as a steward of hardworking, lower-income consumers. Although it is debatable whether the company's overall effect—taking into consideration its massive use of overseas manufacturers—has harmed or hurt lower-income Americans, the company's low prices undoubtedly eased some of the difficulties of the recession for many customers.

In the wake of these efforts, Walmart has seen its reputation and bottom line improve. The company was ranked as the seventh most green brand in the United States in the 2009 study by WPP and Esty Environmental Partners.[44] And Walmart's reputation improved more than any other company between 2007 and 2008, according to research firm Harris Interactive.[45]

The bottom line is that the public is showing greater and greater unwillingness to keep company with less-than-good companies. Harris found in a 2009 study that 90 percent of Americans said they give some consideration to sustainable business practices when purchasing a company's products and services—with nearly 30 percent saying they consider sustainability "a great deal" or "a lot."[46]

Harris defined sustainable business practices comprehensively as "a company's positive impact on society and the environment through its operations, products, or services and through its interaction with key stakeholders such as employees, customers, investors, communities, and suppliers." Given this definition, Americans generally aren't pleased with what they see. All but 2 percent of those polled by Harris said it is at least somewhat important for corporations to evolve to more sustainable business practices. Fifty-seven percent said corporations are not adequately evolving to more sustainable business practices.[47] And, as mentioned in Chapter 4, a large majority told Harris that regulation of businesses is in order.[48]

Overall, Harris found that a record number of Americans—88 percent—said the reputation of corporate America was "not good" or "terrible" in 2008. The figure improved slightly to 81 percent in 2009.[49]

To be sure, companies can go too far in a quest to be good to all stakeholders. Overly generous salaries, excessive charitable donations, and extreme efforts to reduce carbon footprints can bankrupt a firm or prevent it from devoting enough resources to research and development, marketing, and other crucial functions. Balance remains important.

It's also possible that Scrooge-like companies that look out for a narrow group of shareholders or stakeholders will be able to keep making profits in the years ahead. There remains a portion of the public that for ideological or other reasons does not demand much worthiness on the part of the firms in their lives.

But in the emerging era of goodness, companies would do well to err on the side of acting as Santa rather than Scrooge.

Consider this finding from Edelman's 2010 "good purpose" study: 86 percent of global consumers believe that business needs to place at least equal weight on society's interests as on those of business.[50]

That statistic points to the growing significance of a genuine commitment to goodness. So do the findings of a 2009 poll commissioned by *Time* magazine. According to the survey, 38 percent of American adults—some 86 million people—reported taking a number of socially conscious actions in 2009, including buying green products and goods from companies they thought had responsible values.[51]

In announcing the arrival of "the ethical consumer," *Time* noted: "We are starting to put our money where our ideals are."[52]

If companies want to succeed in this ethical age, they had better live up to those ideals.

CHAPTER FIVE SUMMARY

The best available hard-nosed evidence consistently shows that companies are doing well by doing good. Although much of this evidence is based on large, publicly traded U.S. firms, the convergence of economic, social, and political factors outlined in Chapters 1 to 4 points to the growing imperative for all organizations—private or public, large or small—to become thoroughly worthy.

Doing Well by Doing Good

- Good companies tend to outperform less worthy companies in the stock market.
- Companies that are a "community of humans," have a "substantive mission," and "exist within the larger web of life" are more likely to survive over the long run than companies that do not possess these attributes.
- In sum, companies survive and can do well by doing good.

Benefits of Goodness Through and Through

- A growing body of evidence indicates that companies with a commitment to positive social change will get a boost from consumers, while indifferent or harmful firms will be punished.
- People increasingly connect all the facets of company goodness into a coherent whole—more and more, sustainability, corporate citizenship, and social responsibility amount to a holistic concept encompassing worthiness as an employer, a seller, and a steward of people and the planet.
- Consumers don't expect complete purity when it comes to sustainability, but they want more from firms than just charitable giving.
- Employees and investors also are gravitating toward overall goodness.
- The public is increasingly unwilling to keep company with less-than-good companies.

Ranking Companies

More and more, people are demanding that companies in their lives be "good company." The convergence of economic, social, and political forces that we describe in Chapters 2, 3, and 4 put us at the dawn of a new economic era in which genuine, broad-based worthiness is no longer an added bonus but a necessity. Some of the world's largest companies are in the vanguard, pointing the way and serving as examples for others to follow. Many others, however, are laggards, apparently oblivious to these forces—and to the fact that ignoring them imperils their existence, their employees' livelihoods, and their shareholders' investments.

In this chapter, we quantitatively rank the publicly traded companies in the Fortune 100 on the Good Company Index and describe how you can qualitatively assess other companies outside the Fortune 100 with which you do business as a consumer, investor, or employee.

The Good Company Index

In our framework, being a good company is based on how a company acts in three different arenas: as an employer, as a seller, and as a steward of its community, the environment, and society overall. In order to (1) identify which organizations are already behaving as good companies, (2) identify which ones have a long way to go, and (3) track progress in the years ahead, we sought to create an objective system of ranking companies' actions in these areas. We explored multiple sources of information to feed into this ranking system, seeking data that ideally had all of the following characteristics:

- Reflective of our concepts of good employer/seller/steward
- Reliable and of high quality
- Available for a large number of companies
- Timely
- Publicly available

We found something of a mixed bag—lots of information available in some areas, very little in others; systematic in some, little more than anecdotal in others. Even when available, much of the existing data is still in what might be considered the "developmental" stage—information currently exists, but we expect it will become stronger and more established in the years to come, as interest in this information increases.

In some categories, we found ourselves disappointed that no available data source met all these standards. In those situations, we selected the source(s) that came closest to meeting those requirements—or in some cases, decided to create our own database in order to collect and assess the necessary information.

Because little of the comparable information that currently exists is available systematically across different countries, we focused our initial Good Company Index rankings on companies based in the United States. We further limited our rankings to the 94 publicly traded companies in the Fortune 100. (This was also for data availability reasons; much less information is available for companies outside this group or for privately held companies.[1])

In sum, we consider this first-ever Good Company Index to be an important step in the right direction. In the years ahead, we expect to both improve and update these rankings, including expanding them to a larger range of companies. (The most up-to-date information on the Good Company Index can be found at http://www.goodcompany index.com.)

Below is a brief description of the three categories of information we use for the inaugural Good Company Index.

1. Good Employer Rating. Being a good employer is foundational to being a good company. We used two publicly available sources of information in making this assessment: the *Fortune* list of best places to work (a positive indicator) and employee ratings collected anonymously by Glassdoor.com (can be either a positive or negative indicator).

2. Good Seller Rating. Providing good value to customers and treating them fairly are basic characteristics of a good company. We used customer evaluations, rating companies by *quality*, *fair price*, and *trust* (graciously provided to us by research firm wRatings) to assess the extent to which companies are good to customers.[2] These can be either positive or negative.

3. Good Steward Rating. Capturing quantitatively how well a firm cares for its community, the environment, and society as a whole involves multiple categories of company behavior. In the end, we considered four different measures of a company's stewardship:

   A. Environment. This can be either a positive or negative indicator, based on data from the Dow Jones Sustainability United States Index and *Newsweek*'s environmental ranking of the 500 largest corporations in the United States.

   B. Contribution. This component is a positive indicator of a good steward, capturing the extent to which companies use their core capabilities to contribute to society (outside their day-to-day business operations). We created the database for this measure ourselves by systematically collecting information from companies' Web sites, as well as by inviting every Fortune 100 company (by both e-mail and phone) to provide us with information on how they use their core capabilities to make contributions to society. We applied a disciplined scoring process, assigning the maximum number of points to those firms that we deemed highly systematic in using their core capabilities in service to their community or society overall.

c. Restraint. One element of being a good steward is demonstrating restraint. That is, a company ought to seek to be a good "corporate citizen" and fit comfortably into a community or society overall, rather than seek only to maximize its own well-being. Systematic information on restraint (or lack thereof) was hard to come by. But we identified good data in two areas: indicators of a company maximizing profits at the direct expense of the community and focusing disproportionately on the personal benefits derived by company executives. We used the following two measures as negative indicators of restraint:

- tax avoidance through offshore registration in tax havens (based on information from a study done by the U.S. Government Accountability Office)

- excessive executive compensation (based on data from a study commissioned by the *New York Times* as well as rankings available through the AFL-CIO)

d. Penalties and Fines. We believe that government-imposed penalties or fines are a clear negative indicator of a company's behavior as steward of the community and the environment. Therefore, any company that had been assessed total penalties or fines by U.S. regulatory bodies totaling more than $1 million over the most recently available five-year period was penalized under our system (with a larger penalty for those with total fines over $100 million). No comprehensive database of such fines exists, so we compiled the data for this rating component ourselves, based on a systematic search of corporate penalties and fines.

Maximum possible points range from –2 to +2 for both the Good Employer and Good Seller measures. Reflecting the greater breadth of factors covered by the Good Steward measures, the maximum possible point range for this category is broader, ranging from –3 to +4.

Combining the three categories yields a range of possible points from –7 to +8. We then use each company's numerical score to assign a grade ranging from F for those at the bottom (those with scores of –4 or lower) up to A for companies that we believe have achieved Good Company status (those with 5 or more points). Detailed documentation and a complete listing of our rankings on each of these dimensions can be found in the Appendix.

Good Employer Ratings

Being a good employer is basic to being a good company for at least three reasons. In the first place, employees are fundamental stakeholders and deserve to be treated and managed well. What's more, over the long run it's hard for companies to deliver great value to customers if employees are surly, disenfranchised, and/or in short supply (think Home Depot in early 2007). And if firms mistreat or mismanage workers and fail customers, the company's capacity to deliver value to its investors and other stakeholders will suffer.

Despite the importance of being a good employer, this basic aspect of corporate worthiness is currently the most challenging dimension on which to gather information systematically. *Fortune*'s 100 Best Companies to Work For list provides a starting point. We assign a positive point to each of the publicly traded Fortune 100 companies that appears on this list.

At the same time, we recognize that it is an incomplete list of good employers. By definition, only 100 large organizations can make the cut, although there are almost certainly more than 100 good, big employers in the United States. And to earn a spot on the list, companies first have to choose to go to the trouble and expense of applying for inclusion.

Data from Glassdoor.com enables us to broaden our measure of good employers.[3] As its name implies, Glassdoor.com allows its visitors to see inside of companies. As of early 2011, it had ratings of over 108,000 companies and their CEOs, based on anonymous employee ratings of the companies.[4] (It also has salary information and the inside scoop on what job interviews are like at companies.) Why would anyone take the time to provide ratings of their employers? One of the major incentives is that you have to *give* to *get*: in order to get the greatest level of inside detail through Glassdoor.com, you have to provide information (fill out a survey) on your employer (or recent past employer). We analyzed the publicly available data on Glassdoor.com, focusing only on companies that had been rated by at least 25 employees (as of April 2010).[5] One of the major advantages of Glassdoor.com is that it provides a means of identifying both highly rated and poorly rated companies, based purely on employees' perspectives.

We assigned two positive points to those organizations that are in the top octile, or one-eighth, of employee ratings of the Fortune 100 companies that had at least 25 employee ratings on Glassdoor.com and two negative points to those organizations that are in the bottom octile of the ratings. We assigned one positive point to those organizations in the second octile of the Fortune 100 distribution, and one negative point to those organizations that are in the seventh (next to bottom) octile.[6] Finally, we gave neither positive nor negative points to those organizations that fell in the middle (the third, fourth, fifth, and sixth octiles), or between the twenty-fifth and seventy-fifth percentile on Glassdoor.com within the Fortune 100. We have combined the evidence from these two separate sources (Glassdoor.com and *Fortune*'s 100 Best Companies to Work For) to assign good employer scores. (See table on the following pages.)[7]

One of the notable names that employees rate in the bottom one-eighth of employers is Hewlett-Packard, a company that has a long and proud tradition of being an enlightened and forward-thinking employer. The famed "HP Way" includes "trust and respect for individuals" as a core tenet.[8] But under the leadership of recent CEOs, Carly Fiorina and Mark Hurd, big changes have been made. The company has laid off tens of thousands of workers in the past decade.[9] Although HP under Hurd saw its stock perform well, some observers questioned whether he was doing much more than cutting costs.[10] A former HP engineer told the *New York Times* that Hurd was "wrecking our image, personally demeaning us, and chopping our future."[11] Hurd was ousted from HP in mid-2010 in a scandal involving allegedly fudged expense reports and his relationship with an HP marketing contractor.[12]

One interpretation of Hewlett-Packard's low employee rating is that

Good Employer Ratings for the Fortune 100

Lowest	Low	Middle
AT&T	Coca-Cola	Abbott Laboratories
Citigroup	CVS Caremark	Aetna
Hewlett-Packard	Dell	Allstate
Motorola	General Motors	Bank of America
Rite Aid	Macy's	Cardinal Health
Sears Holdings	Safeway	Comcast
Supervalu	Sprint Nextel	Deere
UnitedHealth Group	Verizon	Dow Chemical
	Walmart	DuPont
		Emerson Electric
		Exxon Mobil
		Ford Motor
		General Dynamics
		Home Depot
		Honeywell International
		Humana
		IBM

its employees had long been coddled, and that by putting an end to that, Hurd had put the firm on a path to sustainable long-term profitability. Or it may be that by hacking away at employee perks and privileges, Hurd weakened Hewlett-Packard's ability to sustain itself in the future. Only time will tell. But what can be said with certainty is that employees' ratings of Hewlett-Packard put it near the bottom of the distribution on Glassdoor.com, and the company's long tradition of relying on its employees as a major source of sustainable advantage has eroded.

Here's something else that can be said with certainty. The employee-provided ratings available on Glassdoor.com are highly correlated with firms' stock performance. When we compared Fortune 100 firms within the same industry and controlled for other factors (through multiple regression analysis), the most consistent factor associated with higher

Middle (continued)	High	Highest
J.P. Morgan Chase	Best Buy	American Express
Johnson & Johnson	Boeing	Apple
Johnson Controls	ConocoPhillips	Caterpillar
Kroger	Costco Wholesale	Chevron
Lowe's	General Electric	Cisco Systems
McKesson	Lockheed Martin	FedEx
MetLife	PepsiCo	Goldman Sachs Group
Morgan Stanley	Travelers	Intel
Northrop Grumman	Walt Disney	Kraft Foods
Pfizer		Microsoft
Prudential Financial		Procter & Gamble
Target		
3M		
Time Warner		
United Parcel Service		
Walgreens		
WellPoint		
Wells Fargo		

NOTES: Due to an insufficient number of employee ratings on Glassdoor.com (we used only ratings from 25 or more employees), employer ratings were not available for 22 publicly traded companies in the Fortune 100; those companies therefore do not appear in the above table (and were assigned scores of 0 for overall ranking purposes).

We combined scores from *Fortune*'s 100 Best Companies to Work For and Glassdoor .com and, for purposes of this table, assigned the highest employer rating to firms with the maximum possible employer score (2), high to firms with an employer score of 1, "middle" to firms with a score of 0, low to firms with a score of −1, and lowest to firms with a score of −2.

stock performance over three years and five years is Glassdoor.com ratings. Put another way, the higher the Glassdoor.com rating, the higher the stock performance was over three years and five years, controlling for all other factors.

Good Seller Ratings

To measure how well Fortune 100 firms treat their customers, we used 2008 and 2009 data that was provided to us by research firm wRatings. wRatings collects a treasure trove of data on customers' ratings of 17 separate aspects of their experiences and perceptions of thousands of firms.[13] Hedge fund managers subscribe to wRatings because it provides them with a leading indicator of where a firm's stock price is headed; a negative change in customers' ratings is generally followed in three to six months with a decline in a firm's stock price; a positive change is likewise followed by an increase. Similarly, CEOs use wRatings to track their competition, so they know in advance when a rival is about to get a leg up on them. We worked with wRatings CEO Gary Williams to boil their vast database down to three essential aspects that we believed would summarize a company's standing as a good seller: *quality, fair price*, and customers' *trust* in the company.

Based on this three-dimensional measure of customers' ratings, relative to all of the approximately 4,000 firms in wRatings's database, we then assigned two positive (or negative) points to those Fortune 100 firms that are in the top (or bottom) octile of wRatings' overall ranking on these three dimensions. We also assigned one positive (or negative) point to those organizations in the second (or seventh) octile of wRatings's overall distribution.[14] Organizations that fell in that middle half (between 25 percent and 75 percent within wRatings's larger database) are assigned neither positive nor negative points and are included in the middle column of our Good Seller Ratings table on pages 100 and 101, which summarizes the customer ratings from this analysis.[15]

The mediocrity of customers' experience with most Fortune 100 firms is one conclusion that jumps out of the table. Only two of these firms—Emerson Electric and Ingram Micro—are in the top one-eighth of the overall wRatings distribution. At the other end of the spectrum, Fortune 100 firms are proportionally represented at the bottom of customers' experience.

Also notable is the poor regard with which customers hold the big oil and gas firms. No doubt, this is tied up with these firms' activities that result in large penalties and poor stewardship of the environment, a discussion of which follows.

Good Steward Ratings

We take a broad view of stewardship, which includes not only firms' environmental records, but also the extent to which they show a serious commitment to being of service to the world and are able to demonstrate a degree of restraint (or conversely, an absence of greed) and avoid major penalties and fines. As noted above, the measures that we use for each of these aspects of stewardship are as follows:

- Environment. We assign a positive point for inclusion in the Dow Jones Sustainability United States Index and *Newsweek*'s environmental ranking of America's 500 largest corporations. We assign a positive point to companies in the top 25 percent in *Newsweek*'s environmental ranking of America's 500 largest corporations and a negative point to those in the bottom 25 percent.

- Contribution. We assign a positive point to organizations that use their core capabilities to contribute to society and another positive point to those organizations that do so in a systematic way.

- Restraint. We assign a negative point to organizations whose CEOs have compensation we deem excessive (based on a study commissioned by the *New York Times* as well as rankings available through the AFL-CIO)[16] and a negative point to organizations that avoid paying taxes through offshore registration in tax havens (based on a 2008 study by the U.S. Government Accountability Office).[17]

- Penalties and Fines. We assigned a negative point to firms that were assessed total penalties or fines from $1 million through $100 million (between 2005 and 2009). Two negative points were assigned to companies with total fines and penalties of more than $100 million over the same time period. Our research included a systematic review of fines by U.S. regulatory bodies as well as a scan of headlines for major fines and penalties meted out by European Union regulators.

The findings from our stewardship analysis are summarized in the table on pages 102 and 103.

We were surprised by a number of the findings with respect to stewardship. First, we were pleased by the extent to which Fortune 100 firms

Good Seller Ratings for the Fortune 100

Lowest	Low	Middle
Chevron	Aetna	Abbott Laboratories
Comcast	Cisco Systems	Alcoa
ConocoPhillips	Sprint Nextel	Allstate
Enterprise GP Holdings	Verizon	American Express
Exxon Mobil		AmerisourceBergen
Hess		Apple
Marathon Oil		Archer Daniels Midland
Murphy Oil		AT&T
Occidental Petroleum		Bank of America
Plains AA Pipeline		Best Buy
Sunoco		Boeing
Tesoro		Cardinal Health
Valero Energy		Caterpillar
		Citigroup
		Coca-Cola
		Costco Wholesale
		CVS Caremark
		Deere
		Dow Chemical
		DuPont
		FedEx
		Ford Motor
		General Dynamics
		General Electric
		Goldman Sachs
		Hewlett-Packard
		Home Depot
		Honeywell International
		Humana
		International Paper
		J.P. Morgan Chase
		Johnson Controls

Middle *(continued)*	High	Highest
Kraft Foods	Dell	Emerson Electric
Kroger	IBM	Ingram Micro
Lockheed Martin	Intel	
Lowe's	Johnson & Johnson	
Macy's	Philip Morris Int'l	
McKesson	Walt Disney	
Medco Health Solutions		
MetLife		
Microsoft		
Morgan Stanley		
Motorola		
Northrop Grumman		
PepsiCo		
Pfizer		
Procter & Gamble		
Prudential Financial		
Rite Aid		
Safeway		
Sears Holdings		
Supervalu		
Sysco		
Target		
3M		
Time Warner		
Travelers		
Tyson Foods		
UnitedHealth Group		
United Parcel Service		
United Technologies		
Walgreens		
Walmart		
WellPoint		
Wells Fargo		

NOTES: wRatings does not track four of the publicly traded companies in the Fortune 100 (Berkshire Hathaway, CHS, General Motors, News Corp.); those companies therefore do not appear in the above table and were assigned the score of 0 for overall ranking purposes.

For purposes of this table, we assigned the highest seller rating to firms with the maximum possible seller score (2), high to firms with a seller score of 1, middle to firms with a score of 0, low to firms with a score of –1, and lowest to firms with a score of –2.

Good Steward Ratings for the Fortune 100

Lowest	Low	Middle
Philip Morris International	Archer Daniels Midland	Aetna
Prudential Financial	Berkshire Hathaway	American Express
Sunoco	ConocoPhillips	AmerisourceBergen
	Costco Wholesale	Apple
	CVS Caremark	AT&T
	Dow Chemical	Bank of America
	Exxon Mobil	Boeing
	General Dynamics	Cardinal Health
	Ingram Micro	Caterpillar
	International Paper	CHS
	Marathon Oil	Chevron
	Medco Health Solutions	Citigroup
	Murphy Oil	Coca-Cola
	News Corp.	Comcast
	Occidental Petroleum	DuPont
	Rite Aid	Emerson Electric
	Tyson Foods	Enterprise GP Holdings
	Valero Energy	General Motors
		Goldman Sachs Group
		Hess
		Home Depot
		Honeywell International
		Humana
		Intel
		J.P. Morgan Chase
		Johnson & Johnson
		Johnson Controls
		Lockheed Martin
		McKesson
		MetLife
		Microsoft

are systematically using their core competencies to do good in the world. For example, Kraft Foods recently pledged $180 million over three years to get more food—and better nutrition and information—to children and families.[18] And IBM provides its speech recognition technology to help both children and adults improve their literacy skills.[19] We assigned

Middle *(continued)*	High	Highest
Northrop Grumman	Abbott Laboratories	United Parcel Service
Pfizer	Alcoa	Walt Disney
Plains All American Pipeline	Allstate	
Sears Holdings	Best Buy	
Sprint Nextel	Cisco Systems	
Supervalu	Deere	
Sysco	Dell	
Walmart	FedEx	
WellPoint	Ford Motor	
	General Electric	
	Hewlett-Packard	
	IBM	
	Kraft Foods	
	Kroger	
	Lowe's	
	Macy's	
	Morgan Stanley	
	Motorola	
	PepsiCo	
	Procter & Gamble	
	Safeway	
	Target	
	Tesoro	
	3M	
	Time Warner	
	Travelers	
	UnitedHealth Group	
	United Technologies	
	Verizon	
	Walgreens	
	Wells Fargo	

NOTE: For purposes of this table, we assigned the highest stewardship rating to firms with the maximum possible stewardship score (4), high to firms with a stewardship score of +2 or +3, middle to firms with a score of +1 or 0, low to firms with a score of –1 or –2, and lowest to firms with a score of –3 or lower.

the maximum contribution points (two positive points) to a majority— 56—of the publicly traded Fortune 100.[20]

Conversely, we noted a large percentage of Fortune 100 firms—at least 59 of them—appeared to be using offshore tax havens to avoid paying taxes.[21] Some would argue that publicly traded companies actually have a fiduciary responsibility to shareholders to lawfully minimize their tax liabilities and therefore should actively seek out tax havens. But we don't buy this thinking, and we suspect that the vast majority of tax-payers would side with us. This is a behavior that was perhaps acceptable in the past but won't be tolerated in the future.

With regard to our other restraint measure—CEO compensa-tion—we came to the by-now-unsurprising conclusion that a CEO's compensation has little to do with his or her company's performance. News accounts over the past several years have pointed out example after example of executives who are highly paid yet are underperformers.[22] As is the case with other forms of greed, we expect that this too will be much less tolerated in the future than in the past.

We were dismayed at the large number of penalties and fines levied against Fortune 100 firms. Although these fines do not necessarily indi-cate that firms have broken the law (since they often agree to pay the fine without admitting to illegal activities), it also seems reasonable to conclude that where there's smoke, there's often fire.

Some of the cases that were assigned two negative stewardship points are well known, such as the European Union's $1.3 billion fine of Microsoft for its sales tactics.[23] Others also come as no surprise, such as the large numbers of fines and penalties paid by firms in the oil and gas industry. Some of the other companies' assessed penalties are more notable, including Johnson & Johnson and renowned Berkshire Hatha-way. A subsidiary of Berkshire Hathaway was found guilty of entering into a fraudulent scheme to manipulate AIG's financial statements.[24] And a Johnson & Johnson subsidiary was found guilty of illegal kick-back schemes.[25] (It should be noted that the company called this illegal-ity to the attention of regulators. However, as of early 2010, a similar action was pending against another of Johnson & Johnson's subsidiar-ies.[26]) Johnson & Johnson also has seen its reputation tarnished by major product recalls and criticism from government officials.[27]

Some might question whether a parent company should be held fully accountable for the actions of its subsidiaries. But we think that misses the point. The parent company *is* responsible for the actions of its subsidiaries, and if the burden of monitoring those subsidiaries so that they abide by the law is too great, then the company has grown too large (and perhaps too greedy). The blame falls to both the subsidiary and its parent company.

Others might argue that the reason so many large companies break the law (or alternatively, enter into consent decrees) is because it is simply impossible for them to abide by the law. This perspective would hold that the large number and magnitude of penalties and fines paid by Fortune 100 firms proves that the law is an unreasonable constraint on commerce.

We don't accept this point of view either. The corporate activities that result in these penalties and fines are often serial in nature. Many are for repeated and/or egregious violations of the law—not for an occasional minor infraction here and there. (We have accounted for this issue by focusing only on firms that had more than $1 million in fines and penalties.)

As we compiled and assessed the database of major corporate penalties and fines, we came to four conclusions:

1. Compiling this information is hard work. There is no centralized source that makes information about rule violations by companies and resulting punishments easily available. That should not be the case—it can and should be remedied—a point that we return to in Chapter 10.

2. While we are confident that we have identified the major penalties and fines levied by federal regulatory bodies in the United States, we are equally confident that there are other, smaller penalties and fines that we have missed. We did not, for example, examine the penalties assessed by state regulators. Hence, our final calculations of fines and penalties among the Fortune 100 almost certainly understate them for some companies.

3. Breaking the law is a part of how some of these firms have gotten to be, so big. By engaging in dangerous cost cutting, fraudulent financial practices, and/or anticompetitive practices, these firms have gotten a leg up on their competition and taken advantage of society.

While they might not be too big for their own good, some have
clearly become too big for our own good.

4. Nonetheless, many of the largest firms have managed to grow large
through more worthy means: by scrupulous attention to and compliance with the law. As the world becomes increasingly transparent,
and law-breaking or other questionable behavior becomes more
readily detectable, we predict these are the firms that will prosper.

Overall Good Company Grades

The final step in creating the Good Company Index consisted of con-
solidating the employer ratings, seller ratings, and steward ratings, and
converting the numerical scores to grades. This led us to the combined
Good Company Index, summarized in the table labeled Overall Good
Company Index Grades for the Fortune 100 on pages 108 and 109.[28]

There is good news and bad news in this table. The bad news is that
only two Fortune 100 firms (Disney and FedEx) received a grade in the A
range (thereby meeting our definition of a Good Company) while a dis-
tressingly high 16 of the Fortune 100 received either a D or F. The good
news is that 35 of the Fortune 100—a little over one-third—received a
B− or better.

Some of the findings may come as a surprise—such as Walmart's
grade of C (for those who love to hate it). While there is much to dislike
about Walmart—its treatment of its employees, the significant penalties
and fines that have been levied against it, and the extremely high compensation of its CEO—there is also much to admire. As discussed in earlier chapters, Walmart is making progress. It is a leading green company,
and it uses its considerable resources to contribute to making the world
a better place. In early 2010, for example, Walmart announced a massive $2 billion campaign to help alleviate hunger in the United States.[29]
And unlike the majority of its Fortune 100 brethren, it has avoided using
tax havens. We believe Walmart has been pushed by the convergence of
economic, social, and political forces discussed earlier and has become a

more worthy organization. It still has a long way to go but seems to be headed in the right direction.

Similarly, Home Depot—which received a C+—has come a long way since its flaws were very publicly disclosed and discussed by thousands of its disgruntled customers in 2007 at *MSN Money*'s Web site. It earns average scores on both employee and customer ratings, and it consistently uses its core capabilities to make contributions to communities. For example, Home Depot provides disaster preparedness clinics at its stores.[30] The only strike against it in our scoring system is a $1.3 million penalty in 2008 for alleged violations of the Clean Water Act at its construction sites. Like Walmart, it's coming along. It's within striking distance of catching up to Lowe's, which received a grade of B−.

With the exception of Chevron, which received a C+, the oil and gas firms received Ds or Fs. The unprecedented environmental disaster caused by BP in 2010 will almost certainly hasten the changes that society will demand of these firms. But even without fundamentally changing how they operate, they would be well served by taking some relatively simple actions. For example, they could stop using offshore tax havens, reduce their CEOs' compensation, and begin to make more meaningful contributions to the communities in which they operate.

Goldman Sachs is a special case. In our grading system, Goldman Sachs received a B, a grade that some might find overly generous in the wake of the company's behavior during the housing meltdown and financial crisis. But for years, Goldman earned top marks for corporate social responsibility. It has been lauded as a good employer and a sustainability leader. And it has been generous with its philanthropy—most notably a massive $500 million donation to charity it made in early 2010. So once we took into account the company's whopping $550 million penalty paid to settle charges that it defrauded investors in a mortgage securities deal, a B is where Goldman fell on the grading continuum.

But we see Goldman's grade of B, rather than an A, as a good example of how the bar is rising for businesses. It's now clear that the kind of "responsibility" Goldman Sachs and others have practiced is no

Overall Good Company Index Grades for the Fortune 100

Company	Employer	Seller	Steward	Good Company Score	Good Company Grade
Walt Disney	1	1	4	6	A
FedEx	2	0	3	5	A−
Cisco Systems	2	−1	3	4	B+
IBM	0	1	3	4	B+
Intel	2	1	1	4	B+
Kraft Foods	2	0	2	4	B+
Procter & Gamble	2	0	2	4	B+
Travelers	1	0	3	4	B+
United Parcel Service	0	0	4	4	B+
American Express	2	0	1	3	B
Best Buy	1	0	2	3	B
Caterpillar	2	0	1	3	B
Dell	−1	1	3	3	B
General Electric	1	0	2	3	B
Goldman Sachs Group	2	0	1	3	B
Microsoft	2	0	1	3	B
PepsiCo	1	0	2	3	B
3M	0	0	2	2	B−
Abbott Laboratories	0	0	2	2	B−
Alcoa	NA*	0	2	2	B−
Allstate	0	0	2	2	B−
Apple	2	0	0	2	B−
Deere	0	0	2	2	B−
Emerson Electric	0	2	0	2	B−
Ford Motor	0	0	2	2	B−
Johnson & Johnson	0	1	1	2	B−
Kroger	0	0	2	2	B−
Lockheed Martin	1	0	1	2	B−
Lowe's	0	0	2	2	B−
Morgan Stanley	0	0	2	2	B−
Target	0	0	2	2	B−
Time Warner	0	0	2	2	B−
United Technologies	NA	0	2	2	B−
Walgreens	0	0	2	2	B−
Wells Fargo	0	0	2	2	B−
Boeing	1	0	0	1	C+
Cardinal Health	0	0	1	1	C+
Chevron	2	−2	1	1	C+
Home Depot	0	0	1	1	C+
Johnson Controls	0	0	1	1	C+
Macy's	−1	0	2	1	C+
McKesson	0	0	1	1	C+
MetLife	0	0	1	1	C+
Motorola	−2	0	3	1	C+
Safeway	−1	0	2	1	C+
Verizon Communications	−1	−1	3	1	C+
Aetna	0	−1	1	0	C

Company	Employer	Seller	Steward	Good Company Score	Good Company Grade
AmerisourceBergen	NA	0	0	0	C
Bank of America	0	0	0	0	C
CHS	NA	NA	0	0	C
Coca-Cola	−1	0	1	0	C
Costco Wholesale	1	0	−1	0	C
DuPont	0	0	0	0	C
Hewlett-Packard	−2	0	2	0	C
Honeywell International	0	0	0	0	C
Humana	0	0	0	0	C
Ingram Micro	NA	2	−2	0	C
J.P. Morgan Chase	0	0	0	0	C
Northrop Grumman	0	0	0	0	C
Pfizer	0	0	0	0	C
Sysco	NA	0	0	0	C
Tesoro	NA	−2	2	0	C
UnitedHealth Group	−2	0	2	0	C
Walmart	−1	0	1	0	C
WellPoint	0	0	0	0	C
Archer Daniels Midland	NA	0	−1	−1	C−
Berkshire Hathaway	NA	NA	−1	−1	C−
Citigroup	−2	0	1	−1	C−
Comcast	0	−2	1	−1	C−
Dow Chemical	0	0	−1	−1	C−
General Dynamics	0	0	−1	−1	C−
General Motors	−1	NA	0	−1	C−
Hess	NA	−2	1	−1	C−
International Paper	NA	0	−1	−1	C−
News Corp.	NA	NA	−1	−1	C−
Sprint Nextel	−1	−1	1	−1	C−
Supervalu	−2	0	1	−1	C−
Tyson Foods	NA	0	−1	−1	C−
AT&T	−2	0	0	−2	D+
Enterprise GP Holdings	NA	−2	0	−2	D+
Medco Health Solutions	NA	0	−2	−2	D+
Philip Morris International	NA	1	−3	−2	D+
Plains All American Pipeline	NA	−2	0	−2	D+
Sears Holdings	−2	0	0	−2	D+
ConocoPhillips	1	−2	−2	−3	D
CVS Caremark	−1	0	−2	−3	D
Marathon Oil	NA	−2	−1	−3	D
Murphy Oil	NA	−2	−1	−3	D
Occidental Petroleum	NA	−2	−1	−3	D
Prudential Financial	0	0	−3	−3	D
Rite Aid	−2	0	−1	−3	D
Exxon Mobil	0	−2	−2	−4	F
Valero Energy	NA	−2	−2	−4	F
Sunoco	NA	−2	−3	−5	F

*NA = not available

longer good enough. Take Goldman's giant gift. It came in the wake of mounting public outrage at Goldman for betting against clients, possibly worsening the Great Recession, and setting aside billions in pay while millions of families struggled financially. In other words, the hefty donation appeared reactive—Goldman responding to social pressures as opposed to acting out of a genuine sense of community stewardship.

Indeed, the hundreds of documents unearthed during government probes proved without a doubt that Goldman has been far from thoroughly worthy. One e-mail from a senior Goldman executive captures the way the company, despite its many decent qualities, was quite willing to peddle crummy products to customers: the executive described the sale of a mortgage-related security as a "shi**y deal."[31]

This unworthiness as a seller helped persuade us to make an exception to our index calculations. The mid-2010 news of Goldman's penalty and settlement with the U.S. Securities and Exchange Commission arrived after our deadline for tallying fines and penalties paid by the Fortune 100. If we hadn't extended the cutoff point for Goldman Sachs, the company would have earned our top grade of A. Given the wrongs at Goldman in recent years, we hope readers will agree this was the right decision.

Then there are the two Fortune 100 firms that unambiguously qualify as Good Company—Disney and FedEx. FedEx has delivered the goods as a good company. The package-shipping titan earned strong marks on Glassdoor.com and has made *Fortune*'s 100 Best Companies to Work For list 12 of the past 13 years.[32] The company narrowly missed earning a customer service point in our ranking system, and it has consistently outperformed rivals United Parcel Service and the U.S. Postal Service on the American Customer Satisfaction Index.[33] What's more, FedEx has proved itself to be a sound steward. This includes regularly offering its transportation and logistics expertise during disaster-relief efforts.[34]

Even with its classification as Good Company, FedEx has a black mark against it because of its use of at least a dozen subsidiaries in offshore tax havens. And there has been controversy over the way FedEx classifies many of its drivers as independent contractors rather than employees.[35]

While it stands heads and shoulders above most of the Fortune 100, it too has improvements to make.

Disney deserves special comment. It is the only Fortune 100 firm that has above-average scores in all three of the major ratings—employees, customers, and stewardship—while simultaneously having no negative points against it. For example, we did not find significant penalties or fines levied against the firm.[36] Disney scored six of the maximum possible eight points in our Good Company ranking system. It's an impressive performance.

As we sliced and diced the data from the Good Company Index, it became apparent to us that goodness does, indeed, already have its rewards. Companies with higher scores than industry peers on the Good Company Index had stronger stock market performance than their counterparts over periods of one, three, and five years (see sidebar).

How to Assess the Companies You Do Business With

The quantitative ranking provided above is a useful starting point for assessing the largest U.S.-based companies. But you do business with many other companies not on this list, and for which there isn't enough (or any) publicly available information for you to create your own ranking. So for these companies—from the "mom and pop" corner dry cleaner to the supermarket where you buy food—we suggest using a qualitative assessment process.

The indicators summarized above are tangible traits. They can be measured in pay levels, policies, and emissions. From the scores of interviews that we did in our background research, we identified five less-tangible attributes that form the foundation for being a good employer, good to customers, and a good steward.

- *Reciprocity* is the shift from an exploitation mindset to one of cultivation, of seeking mutual benefit through win-win interactions.
- *Connectivity* refers to the fundamental need (and emergent power) of human beings to be connected, informed, and effective.

Good Companies Outperform in the Stock Market

When we compared pairs of Fortune 100 companies within the same industry, we found that those with higher scores on the Good Company Index outperformed their peers in the stock market over periods of one, three, and five years.

For example, over the previous three years, the company with the higher Good Company Index score performed, on average, more than 4 percentage points better in the stock market than the paired company from the same industry with the lower Good Company Index score. (For the one-year and five-year periods, the comparable annual outperformance is 2 percentage points in each of the periods.)

By stock market performance, we mean the percentage change in share price (up or down), after incorporating any dividends paid. The analysis included 33 pairs of same-industry companies (those for which stock market data was available for all three periods and for which there were no missing elements among the components of the Good Company Index scoring system). Twenty-one of the pairs involved differences of 1 or 2 points on the Good Company Index; the remaining 12 pairs involved differences of 3 points or more. (Since Dan and Laurie are both registered investment advisors, it's important for us to add the customary precaution that past performance is not a guarantee of future performance.)

Most of the differences in stock performance occur when the difference in Good Company scores between the two paired companies is three points or greater, which corresponds to at least an entire letter grade in our overall ranking system. Companies that outscored their peers by three points or more on the Good Company Index outperformed them, on average, by 11 percentage points annually in the stock market over the previous three years. (For the one-year and five-year periods, the comparable annual outperformance is 5 percentage points and 6 percentage points, respectively.) The relative annual performance of each of these twelve industry-matched pairs over the three-year period is displayed in the figure on the opposite page.

Relative annual stock performance, previous 3 years,
for industry-matched pairs with Good Company Index
score differences of 3 or more

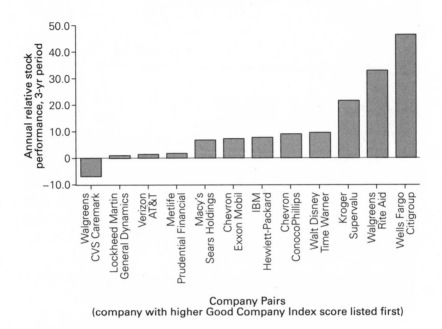

Company Pairs
(company with higher Good Company Index score listed first)

NOTE: Relative performance for each pair is calculated as stock performance of company
with higher Good Company score minus performance of company with lower Good
Company score.

For example, Chevron and ConocoPhillips are both major oil and gas
companies. Chevron earned a Good Company Index score of +1 (C+),
while ConocoPhillips scored –3 (D), a difference of 4 points, or more than
one full grade. Over three years, Chevron outperformed ConocoPhillips by 9 percentage points annually. This example, combined with the
results from the other industry pair cases, suggests that the better companies are when compared to their peers, the more they will outpace
them. Goodness comes with a tailwind.

- *Transparency* means a willingness to share information and expose the reasoning behind decisions with stakeholders.

- *Balance* means the wisdom to make judgment calls amid competing priorities.

- *Courage* refers both to taking risks and doing what is right, despite possible adverse consequences in the short run.

RECIPROCITY

Reciprocity is a core attribute of a good company. Think about the difference between Southwest and United Airlines. The organizations' commitment to reciprocity—or the lack thereof—shows up in both employee and customer relations. Southwest is near the very top of Glassdoor .com's employee ratings, whereas United is near the bottom.[37] Here's one illustrative example of why this is so. In the crisis that followed the September 11 destruction of the World Trade Center, the major airlines laid off 16 percent of their workforces. Southwest avoided layoffs altogether.[38] And although Southwest is among the most unionized of airlines, management consistently has a constructive and respectful relationship with labor.

Southwest's focus on reciprocity permeates all of its relationships. And not coincidentally, in 2010 Southwest had the top customer satisfaction ratings in the airline industry, while United had the worst.[39]

Need to cancel a reservation on a Southwest flight? No problem. Even with the lowest-price class of ticket—the "Wanna Get Away" fare—you can quickly go online, cancel the ticket, and your full payment goes into an account that you can instantly access for your next ticket on Southwest.[40] But if you need to cancel your reservation with United, you have to call them (unless you have purchased an expensive refundable ticket), wait for a customer service representative (waits of over 30 minutes are not uncommon in bad weather), and pay a cancellation fee of $150 to have your original payment applied to a new flight.[41]

United charges you this fee because they can—they've got your money and they don't have to give it back to you. Southwest chooses not to do so—even though they could—because they are committed to reciprocity.

Reciprocity plays itself out in ways large and small in the companies that you deal with day in and day out. It is the give and take between human beings that makes life better, but that is all too often lost because of "corporate policy" (as in when the customer service representative tells you that he or she cannot do what you are requesting because corporate policy does not allow it). Good companies, like Southwest Airlines, realize that they need to build reciprocity into their day-to-day operations—to base corporate policy on the principal of reciprocity.

CONNECTIVITY

Human beings have a fundamental desire for *connectivity*. And since technology enables new ways for people to be connected with one another, people's expectations have risen. Both employees and customers increasingly expect the organizations in their lives to provide them with more and better ways to connect to improve the quality of their lives.

Kaiser Permanente is leading the way in health care—an industry that is badly in need of finding new and better ways of providing its services efficiently and effectively. Kaiser uses technology to provide its customers with easy "24/7" access that they can use to schedule appointments with doctors at the customer's convenience (imagine that!), access their health-care records, see results from diagnostic tests as soon as the lab has completed them, and send questions via e-mail to their doctors.

From the customer's perspective, the system seems to be designed for their convenience, rather than that of the physicians'. It enables customers to take much more active ownership of their health care, rather than being forced to passively wait until the system chooses to deliver it.

But the system is also designed to enable employees at all levels in the organization—from the clerk who checks a customer in to a busy doctor attempting to achieve a modicum of work-life balance—to be more effective and efficient. Imagine this scenario (which actually happened to one of the authors): You are checking in to get the necessary vaccinations for an upcoming trip to a far-off, developing nation. Since this is not routine preventative care, you will be charged for it. You hand over a check for $30. "But wait," the clerk says, "I see that the only shot you need is a tetanus shot—that's routine preventative care, for which there is no charge." With a pleased smile, the clerk returns the $30 check you just wrote. There is also a pleased (and surprised) smile on your face. Or consider the doctor who sends you an e-mail at the end of her busy day that answers an urgent question you have. The doctor has saved both of you the trouble of an urgent visit the next day.

Connectivity has made everyone in these exchanges better off by reducing costly administrative errors and unproductive use of time, resulting in higher quality outcomes at lower costs.[42] The technology that has fueled this connectivity enables people to be more informed and effective, and in so doing, makes life better.

TRANSPARENCY

Transparency—the willingness to share information and to expose the reasoning behind decisions with stakeholders—builds trust and good will. In its purest form, transparency takes the form of an open-book policy. When Habanero, a Vancouver-based Web-consulting firm, adopted an open-book policy in 2002, its CEO Elliot Fishman had to take the time to train his employees to read profit-and-loss statements. Perhaps more importantly, he had to trust them not to leak information inappropriately to outsiders, including competitors.

When the firm had to find ways to cut costs during the Great Recession, his investment of time and trust paid off handsomely. Employees volunteered lots of good cost-savings ideas, both large and small. Later, it became apparent that even this was not enough, and that 15 percent of the staff had to be laid off and bonuses eliminated. "There were no hiccups because people saw it coming," Fishman said. "Being transparent leading up to our decision set us up to deal with the fallout."[43]

Transparency with customers also has its payoffs. McAlvain Group of Companies, an Idaho-based construction firm, prominently promotes its commitment to transparency on its Web site as follows: "Our open-book accounting and line-item budgeting allows our clients to identify where project costs reside by division. From design through final completion, we provide cost-saving options by analyzing schedules, means and methods, alternative construction, and constructability surveys . . ."[44]

Their CEO, Torry McAlvain, says, "In the construction business there are so many ways to make money that you don't feel good about. Our open-book policy is a way to make sure that we feel good about what we do. It promotes trust with our customers, and it drives accountability throughout our employee base. It's knit into the fabric of the organization. And it works—it's how we win business."[45]

BALANCE

Balance is more of an Eastern concept than one from the West, where businesses historically have been more focused on progress. But the ability to achieve equilibrium in different business arenas is increasingly important to companies throughout the world. They must balance the interests of different stakeholders, sometimes-conflicting values, and short-term gains against long-term goals. Among the firms that have best managed to create harmony amid discordant demands is Seventh Generation. The household product maker's very name builds balance into the business. It is a reference to a concept from the Native American Iroquois people: that decisions today ought to consider the effects on descendants seven generations into the future.

Seventh Generation puts this principle into practice by balancing consumer convenience and manufacturing ease with environmental and community stewardship. The firm isn't perfect in achieving this counterpoise. As of the publication of its "Corporate Consciousness Report" in 2009, it had not replaced a nonbiodegradable synthetic polymer in its automatic dishwashing powder and gel.[46]

On the other hand, Seventh Generation has eliminated synthetic fragrances from all its products and backed a push to grow palm oil—a major ingredient in cleaning products—more sustainably.[47] It also has dared to try to change consumer behavior. Among the company's campaigns in 2008 was a "Get Out of Hot Water" effort. It called attention to the fact that 90 percent of the energy expended when washing clothes is used for heating water, and encouraged consumers to do the laundry in cold water instead.[48]

So far, Seventh Generation is managing to be both a sound steward and a successful business. Its sales soared 51 percent in 2008, despite the

Goldman Loses Its Good Name

The scandal that surrounded Goldman Sachs in 2010 captures the danger of being a less-than-thoroughly worthy company.

Prior to Goldman's public flogging for putting its own interests ahead of clients' and for possibly contributing to the Great Recession with casino-like operations, the company had built an impressive track record of corporate responsibility and business success.

Among Goldman's honors were a top-10 ranking in *Fortune* magazine's 2009 list of the best companies to work for in America, a place on the Dow Jones index for sustainability leaders in the United States, and regular appearances on *Fortune*'s lists of the most admired companies.[57]

But these achievements shrank in importance as the firm's trading and pay practices came under scrutiny in 2009 and 2010. Amid tough economic times for many people and after receiving an emergency loan from the U.S. Government, Goldman Sachs sparked public fury by setting aside billions in pay for its bankers in 2009.[58] In April 2010, the company was slapped with a civil lawsuit by the U.S. Securities and Exchange Commission (SEC) for allegedly defrauding investors in connection with a mortgage-related transaction.[59] And documents that surfaced thanks to a Congressional hearing all but convicted Goldman in the court of public opinion.

According to the internal documents and a *New York Times* story, Goldman decided to "short"—or bet against—the mortgage market by early 2007.[60] In a December 2006 e-mail, Goldman executive Fabrice Tourre wrote, "We have a big short on . . ."[61] But, the *Times* reported, Goldman did not reveal its short position even as it sold mortgage-related securities to clients.[62] And, according to the SEC suit, it hid from clients the fact that a particular mortgage-related security was constructed with the significant involvement of a hedge fund that bet against the security.[63]

On April 27, 2010, Goldman CEO Lloyd Blankfein testified to Congress,

Great Recession. Sales fell slightly in 2009 but climbed in early 2010, and Seventh Generation expected 20 percent growth for the year.[49]

You might think of Seventh Generation employees and executives as yogis. Yogis can stand on one leg for an eternity with a placid expression,

---

"We didn't have a massive short against the housing market and we certainly did not bet against our clients."[64] But taken as a whole, the evidence indicated otherwise. It showed Goldman to be a company looking out for itself—magnifying risk in the financial system and willing to sell out clients to boost its own profits.

Such unworthiness did not go unpunished. Goldman settled the SEC case in mid-2010, agreeing to pay a record $550-million penalty and admitting that its marketing materials for the mortgage product contained incomplete information.[65]

Earlier in the year, Goldman announced a $500 million contribution to charity.[66] That amount dwarfs the typical philanthropic donation companies make annually. But the gift came across as a *response* to anger at Goldman. And the generosity didn't earn the firm much praise—a sign that corporate "responsibility" is no longer good enough. In the emerging Worthiness Era, gross examples of greed will not be tolerated, even by companies that in other respects are decent. A report from Harris Interactive in early 2010 found Goldman Sachs to have the fifth-lowest reputation of the 60 most-visible companies in the United States.[67]

Goldman has tried to recover its good name. In January 2011, it released a report outlining a series of internal reforms in areas including client service, transparency, and training.[68]

Still, Goldman's earnings for 2010 fell by nearly half.[69] A hiccup for the firm or a sign of long-term trouble?

"We have been a client-centered firm for 140 years and if our clients believe that we don't deserve their trust, we cannot survive," Blankfein told Congress.[70] Whether Goldman has been client-centered for all of its 140 years is debatable. But Blankfein was on the mark about client trust and survival. Goldman—good in so many ways—may ultimately wither because of its bad behavior.

but they are concentrating—working hard—to achieve that balance. In fact, Seventh Generation's growth during the recession took a toll on employees such that "our work/home balance is clearly out of whack," company cofounder Jeffrey Hollender wrote in the company's 2008 "Corporate Consciousness Report."[50]

Even this admission of workplace imbalance—rare among companies—is a positive sign. Seventh Generation takes balance seriously. That's good for it and all its stakeholders.

COURAGE

Good companies aren't for the faint of heart. They take *courage*, especially in this transition period when companies can continue to get a leg up on worthier rivals with low-road tactics. For a portrait of corporate courage, consider Ultimate Software and its CEO Scott Scherr.[51]

Scherr hasn't laid off a single employee since he founded the Westin, Florida-based HR and payroll software company in 1990. Ultimate has stuck by its employees in both good times and bad, including a stretch from 2000 to 2004 when the company lost more than $45 million.[52] Scherr also avoided giving pink slips to any of his nearly 1,000 employees during the Great Recession, even though Ultimate posted losses in 2008 and 2009 totaling about $4 million.[53]

"We never threw anybody under the bus," Scherr says. "The test is always the tough times."

Some might call Scherr foolish rather than brave. Why not streamline the company during downturns, cutting out dead wood and avoiding the risk of a bloated ship sinking? But Scherr and Ultimate obsess on hiring only A players. And while a small fraction of the workforce is fired for performance problems every year, Scherr views the layoff aversion as a way to preserve talent. To him, those people are the heart of Ultimate's success.

"The business is there to take care of the employees, and the employees are there to take care of the business," he says.

Ultimate also refused to change its practice of giving all employees stock-based compensation, despite the change in accounting rules a few years ago that makes companies' net income look worse when doling out stock options.[54]

Despite the recent losses, other signs show the company's gutsy reciprocity is paying off. Ultimate's revenue climbed from $179 million in 2008 to $197 million in 2009. Customer retention that year was 97 percent.[55] And without any mandate from management, Ultimate's employees trimmed back travel and expense costs during the recession to a "material" extent, Scherr says.

Ultimate ranked as the best medium-size company to work for in America in both 2008 and 2009.[56] When accepting the 2009 honor, Scherr laid out his philosophy: "The true measure of a company is how they treat their lowest-paid employee."

That's a good yardstick for worthiness—and performing well on it requires the kind of courage Scherr and crew have shown.

The more business you can do with organizations that cultivate these five characteristics, the better off we all will be.

CHAPTER SIX SUMMARY

We quantitatively rank the publicly traded companies in the Fortune 100 on a Good Company Index and describe how you can qualitatively assess other companies outside the Fortune 100 with which you do business as a consumer, investor, or employee.

The Good Company Index

The Index incorporates three subcomponents—ratings on company behavior as an employer, seller, and steward.

- To rate employers, we use information from *Fortune*'s list of the 100 Best Places to Work For and employee ratings collected anonymously by Glassdoor.com.
- To rate sellers, we use customer evaluations of *quality, fair price*, and their *trust* in the company (provided by research firm wRatings).
- To rate stewards, we consider four measures of a company's stewardship:
    1. Environment—based on the Dow Jones Sustainability United States Index and *Newsweek*'s environmental ranking of the 500 largest corporations in the United States
    2. Contribution—our assessment of the extent to which companies use their core capabilities to contribute to their community or to society overall, based on our own data collection
    3. Restraint—there are two areas related to companies' restraint for which data is available: tax avoidance through offshore registration in tax havens (based on a 2008 study done by the U.S. Government Accountability Office) and excessive executive compensation (based on a study commissioned by the *New York Times* as well as rankings available through the AFL-CIO)
    4. Regulatory penalties and fines—compiled by the authors through a systematic search for each company

Overall Good Company Grades

- Only two companies—Disney and FedEx—earned an A, thereby meeting our definition of a Good Company.

- Three companies—Valero Energy, Exxon Mobil, and Sunoco—received a grade of F.

- A comparison of Fortune 100 firms within the same industry reveals that firms that had higher scores on the Good Company Index had stronger stock market performance than their counterparts over one-, three-, and five-year periods.

How to Assess the Companies You Do Business With

We identified five less tangible attributes that form the foundation for being a good company that you can use to assess the companies with which you do business:

1. *Reciprocity* is the shift from an exploitation mindset to one of cultivation, of seeking mutual benefit.

2. *Connectivity* refers to the fundamental need (and emergent power) of human beings to be connected, informed, and effective.

3. *Transparency* means a willingness to share information and expose the reasoning behind decisions with stakeholders.

4. *Balance* means the wisdom to make judgment calls amid competing priorities.

5. *Courage* refers both to taking risks and doing what is right, despite possible adverse consequences in the short run.

PART III   Good Employer,
Good Seller,
Good Steward

CHAPTER 7

The Good Employer

Paul Levy walked the halls of Beth Israel Deaconess Medical Center. But he may as well have been walking a tightrope.

The Great Recession had hit, and Levy, CEO of the Boston hospital, had to cut labor costs while somehow preserving a high level of patient care. As he considered his options, Levy watched as a janitor emptied the wastebasket, a food service worker delivered meals, and other low-wage employees pushed patients through the halls on gurneys. He listened as they spoke kind words to patients and their families, he witnessed their cheerful presence and gentle care, and he realized that these "low-skill" workers were delivering health care.

As layoffs loomed large, this was not an idle insight. Levy knew that these workers are normally the first to go. But he also knew that patients would suffer in small but real ways as a result. Levy was not content with "normal," and so he called a meeting of all employees who were able to attend in the hospital's auditorium.

He struggled to find the right words that would explain to all present what he had seen and heard: that each of them, down to the lowest-paid employee, was critical to delivering quality health care, and that perhaps there was some way that high-wage employees could find to save the jobs of their colleagues who earned less. He didn't have to struggle for long. Before he was able to finish his thought, the auditorium erupted in applause. He had spoken a truth that touched the hearts of those present. Money-saving ideas poured in, and the hospital managed to save almost all of the positions targeted for layoffs.

In effect, Levy struck a balance when it comes to employees. Employees are both a cost and an asset. Finding the equilibrium between these opposites is most difficult in the midst of an economic downturn, but the challenge never disappears. Day in and day out, in good times and in bad, leaders and managers make myriad choices about their workers—the totality of which define their worthiness as employers.

The phrase *good employer* typically evokes images of generous, nice companies. Those attributes are part of the equation. But being a good employer, as we define it, is more complex—and more difficult to achieve. In order for any business to thrive (or even survive), there are many tradeoffs and judgments that must be made with respect to employees. To make these judgments wise ones, the worthiest employers measure workers, analyze workplace practices, and make sense of metrics in ways that might be considered cold and calculating rather than compassionate. Such data-driven management, though, can benefit both employees and employers.

This is especially true when companies possess another key element of worthiness as an employer: a compelling purpose. A company mission that goes beyond benefiting a narrow circle of stakeholders and solving a limited business problem can help focus firms on decisions and practices that both treat workers well and inspire them to give their best efforts.

Such a mission helps explain why Beth Israel Deaconess has become a standout hospital, ranked in the top 3 percent of hospitals in the nation.[1] Levy wrote on the hospital's Web site: "We care for our patients and family members like they are members of our own family."[2] That family sensibility figures into both keeping care quality high for patients and treating workers well, and it helped Paul Levy succeed in his high-wire budget act.

This chapter discusses the elements of the Good Employer, revealing a recipe for workplaces that are at once caring, exacting, and stirring.[3]

The recipe we spell out here—which is equally relevant for employers in for-profit and nonprofit sectors—is largely the product of two decades of research and client consulting by Laurie and Dan. They have conducted large-scale studies on training and other HR matters as well as helped dozens of firms of all sizes around the globe manage employees better. In the course of those efforts, Laurie and Dan have arrived at a framework for people management that has proven effective at improving business results.[4]

That framework consists of three main elements: a value-creating organization committed to employees, sound data analysis, and an inspiring purpose.

A Value-Creating Organization Committed to Its Employees

A "value-creating organization" might sound like a corporate motto more appealing to CEOs or shareholders than to employees. But the truth is that great places to work also have to be places that create value for customers and other stakeholders, including owners who expect a good return on their investment. Only those organizations are capable of a long-term commitment to their employees, providing job security and opportunities for development and advancement. It can be a self-reinforcing cycle because organizations committed to employees typically bring out the best in their workers—who in turn create value.

In other words, chief among the ingredients for a value-creating organization is a long-term commitment to employees.

An organization with a long-term commitment to its employees is one where employees

- are rewarded for developing skills needed to meet the organization's business goals
- are provided with opportunities for advancement
- receive recognition for their accomplishments
- feel secure in their jobs

It is this last point—job security—that has been among the most contentious in recent decades. Globalization and changes in technology have rendered lifetime job security a quaint relic of the past. As the pendulum has swung, some employers have gone too far in the opposite direction and shed workers at the first sign of trouble (or even before it). This, too, is not sustainable. A tendency toward hair-trigger layoffs is one of the manifestations of an excessive focus on short-termism. And, not surprisingly, it has long-term, negative consequences. It is a form of unworthiness.

You may remember the old saw from the days when socialism was more prevalent: "They pretend to pay us and we pretend to work." So too it is with job security. They employ us—at least for the moment—and we pretend to do a good job. But it is unlikely in the face of chronic job insecurity that employees will either choose to or be able to perform at their best.

After all, why should employees give the gift of discretionary effort— that little extra push that is needed to ensure perfect quality, that little extra gesture that could delight a customer, that creative idea that generates cost savings—if they don't know whether or not they will be laid off tomorrow, or next week, or next month? Moreover, the chronic state of worry that this produces renders employees less effective. They start devoting effort to polishing their resumes and networking, leaving less energy for work.

Sure, fear of job loss can induce a frenzied devotion to cranking out the work, at least for a while. The problem is that it's rather like an overworked adrenal system. When the body is chronically stuck in fight-or-flight mode, it eventually becomes disabled. So while fear can motivate a workforce in the short-run, it is generally a lousy long-run strategy.

Worthy employers—employers that are committed to their employees—get this. HCL Technologies, the India-based technology company whose "Employees First, Customers Second" ethos was highlighted in Chapter 4, announced a no-layoff policy in the midst of the Great Recession.[5] What's more, in recent years HCL has increased employees' income security by reducing the percentage of compensation that is variable (based on bonuses). HCL appears to have been handsomely rewarded for its foresight, enjoying significant growth during the downturn and gaining market share against rival Infosys Technologies. That's what happens when employees reciprocate their employer's commitment and give the gift of their discretionary effort.

Other elements are necessary to complement commitment to employees in developing and maintaining a value-creating organization. These fall into three primary categories: leadership, work, and learning.

Reams and reams have been written about leadership. It all boils down to what leaders say and what they do—their communication and their behavior.

The work environment is more complex. It consists of multiple components, including hiring practices, job design, work processes, conditions, accountability, and compensation practices.

Much has also been written about an organization's ability to learn. This too can be winnowed down to two components—formal means for fostering learning and informal means for doing so. We discuss each in turn.

Leadership

COMMUNICATION

Communicating is easy. Effective communication is hard—especially if there are more than two people involved. Hence, this is a struggle for many organizations. It takes time, effort, intention, and skill on the part of leaders throughout an organization. It requires that leaders and managers effectively communicate what is expected of employees and, perhaps harder still, that they be genuinely open to two-way communication. Failure in this regard can lead to disaster.

On March 23, 2005, there was an explosion and fire at BP's Texas City refinery that killed 15 people, injured over 170 others, and resulted in enormous financial losses. It was one of the most serious U.S. workplace disasters in nearly two decades. Within the next five months, the Texas City refinery experienced two additional (but less disastrous) process safety incidents. An intensive investigation concluded that weak leadership resulted in a corporate culture that "left safety processes to the discretion of managers and did not define what was expected of them . . . and that employees did not report accidents and safety concerns because they feared repercussions or judged that the company would not do anything about them."[6] A classic communication problem, with deadly consequences.

The benefits of effective communication by leaders, while typically more subtle, are nonetheless real. When Paul Levy at Beth Israel Deaconess Hospital acted on the courage of his conviction and spoke forthrightly to his staff about the need to make sacrifices to protect low-wage employees, he was handsomely rewarded for having done so. The hospital staff came up with ideas that generated enough savings to preserve all but 70 of more than 600 jobs that had been slated for layoffs.

That's quite a payoff for one courageous communication. And truth be told, it probably was not just this single communication that generated such a tremendous outpouring of goodwill and good ideas from employees—although clearly Levy's speech that day was critical. Rather, Levy had a consistent track record of focusing relentlessly on communication with employees. That is, for all intents and purposes, what he sees as the main job of a CEO.

BEHAVIORS

Leaders' actions also speak very loudly. Essential leadership behaviors include

- working collaboratively with employees to eliminate barriers to effective work
- seeking and using input from employees in making decisions and plans
- following and demonstrating the organization's values
- exhibiting principled and ethical behavior

Leaders' behaviors have one of two manifestations—action and inaction. Toyota's extraordinary fall from glory in 2010 is a case in point. Despite their much-lauded focus on quality and safety, leaders at the top of the organization apparently ignored customer feedback on safety problems with the accelerators in Toyota's cars. After a series of deadly crashes, governments around the world forced Toyota into massive and expensive recalls of their vehicles. The damage to Toyota's brand and its finances were enormous.

An NPR reporter noted "Older workers [at Toyota] haven't really been that surprised. Many of them believe that, in fact, the problems stem from this extraordinary corporate culture. . . . The cost-cutting just was too great."[7]

Leaders' (in)actions revealed that saving on costs was more important than honoring Toyota's stated values of quality and safety. In their quest for growth through cost cutting, Toyota's leaders jeopardized the lives of customers and therefore the company's long-term prospects.

A more positive example of leadership behavior comes from FedEx CEO Fred Smith. Smith responded to the Great Recession by chopping pay at the top, starting with his own. In a December 2008 blog item titled "Minimizing Job Losses and Protecting FedEx for the Long-Term," Smith announced his salary would be cut 20 percent and other senior executives would have their salaries reduced by 7.5 to 10 percent. The rest of the salaried workforce exempt from overtime pay rules would take a 5 percent cut. The salary cuts did not affect hourly employees—workers such as couriers and package handlers.[8] The move was in keeping with values Smith has been touting since he founded the company in 1973. The company's "People-Service-Profit" philosophy stresses caring for FedEx employees as a foundation of great service, which will lead to a strong bottom line.[9]

"I am asking all our team members to keep focused on delivering an outstanding FedEx experience to our customers and to each other," Smith wrote in the 2008 blog item.[10] "That has made all the difference during past economic challenges in our history. Our ultimate success depends on it again today, and I know we'll come through."

Smith's salary action inspired employee Kimberely Howell Jones, whose pay fell by 5 percent. "Thanks for Walking the Walk," she wrote in response to the original blog. "During these tough times, it was good to know that our Leadership team led by example. The pay cut was difficult, but I knew I wasn't in it alone."[11]

Together, the company did indeed bounce back quickly from the recession. For the year ending May 31, 2010, FedEx saw revenue grow 20 percent to $9.4 billion. It also posted a profit of $419 million, compared to a loss of $876 million the year before.[12]

As is the case with leaders' communications, the benefits of exemplary behavior are typically more subtle. But you may have experienced it directly at some point in your working life. Think about the difference between the best and worst boss you've ever had. We're willing to bet that your best-ever boss was pretty good at helping you to work more effectively, sought and used your input, followed the organizations' values, and was a principled and ethical person. And we're also willing to bet that your worst-ever boss had serious deficiencies on one or more of these fronts.

Now think about the difference in what you were willing to do to help these two different bosses achieve their goals. Play that out hundreds and thousands of times over. That's a key difference between good employers and the rest of the pack. The good ones are filled with leaders at all levels who are worthy of the best efforts of their employees. If you don't currently have the good fortune of working for such an organization, wouldn't you prefer to find one?

Work Environment

HIRING PRACTICES

No organization can hope to create value if it doesn't pay careful attention to hiring the right people and getting them up to speed once they are on the job.

In the supercharged competitive market for technology workers, Symphony Services—an India-based technology company—depends heavily on employee referrals to fill its open positions. This is a smart practice because employee referrals can be both an inexpensive and highly effective way to find good job candidates that fit in well with an organization's culture.

To ensure that it remains worthy of these ongoing referrals, the company provides complete transparency to employees about where those they have referred are in the hiring process. An employee can check online at any time to see how many interviews have been conducted with the person he or she referred and when the next step of the process is scheduled. If ultimately that person is not hired, the employee can find out the reason why (with, of course, appropriate protections provided to ensure the job candidate's privacy). This creates an environment of transparency, fairness, trust, and accountability, in exchange for which Symphony Services' employees reward it handsomely. Over 50 percent of the company's job postings are filled through employee referrals.

Zappos.com, the upstart online retailer acquired by Amazon.com, is legendary for its exceptional customer service and ultra-speedy delivery of purchases to customers. It has a very clever way of ensuring that it hires the right people—those who will thrive in its slightly wacky culture and continue to deliver on Zappos's renowned customer service. Every new employee goes through four solid weeks of customer loyalty training, and about halfway through, new hires are offered $2,000 to quit. That offer generally comes from the training team, although CEO Tony Hsieh sometimes offers the money himself. Since Zappos's entry-level customer service representatives earn about $11 per hour, $2,000 represents a hefty chunk of change. The deal is good for the duration of the training class, so new hires have a couple of weeks to consider it.

The offer has the effect of requiring that employees pay $2,000 for the privilege of working at Zappos. Those that turn down the cash are the ones who really want to be part of the organization's zany, customer-centric culture. Very smart.

JOB DESIGN

Zappos's unorthodox ways don't end with its training and hiring process. As other employers are exercising increasing scrutiny over call center employees' every working moment and keystroke, Zappos is doing just the opposite. Its call center jobs are designed to give employees an unusual degree of autonomy and authority in deciding how best to do their jobs.

One day a Zappos customer service rep was handling what seemed, at least initially, to be a routine request from a female customer for assistance in returning a pair of men's boots. Detecting that the customer seemed upset, the service rep asked if anything was wrong. Yes, the woman replied. Her husband, for whom she had purchased the boots, had just been killed in a car accident—hence her need to return the boots.

The service rep kindly responded that she didn't need to worry about a thing. All she needed to do was put the boots outside her front door, and the service rep would take care of the necessary (but nonstandard) process for having the boots picked up and returned. After taking care of that, the service rep spent a bit of time scouting around on the Internet (which is expressly prohibited in many call centers), located the funeral parlor where the memorial service was being held, and arranged for a beautiful bouquet of flowers to be delivered from Zappos. One of the people attending the service posted a tweet on Twitter about the bouquet. The posting went viral, and Zappos earned an extraordinary amount of free PR for this small act of humanity by an empowered call-center employee.

Not too long thereafter, at the ripe old age of 10 years and with only 1,300 employees, Zappos was sold to Amazon.com for roughly $1.2 billion in the midst of the worst economic downturn since the Depression. The "bouquet incident" was just one small part of creating extraordinary economic value, value based on lots of smart choices about how to get the people side of the business right.

Circuit City represents the other end of the spectrum in this regard. In 2008, just seven short years after business author Jim Collins identified it as one of only eleven "great" firms in *Good to Great*, Circuit City was bankrupt. One of the now-widely acknowledged factors that contributed to its speedy demise was a 2007 decision to fire 3,400 of its most highly paid sales employees and replace them with lower-paid employees.[13] With the benefit of hindsight, it is now apparent that there was a reason why those 3,400 folks were highly paid—they had the skills, talents, and experience necessary to be successful, and their lower-paid counterparts did not. Because Circuit City did not clearly understand and define the skills necessary for its sales staff to be successful, it failed to properly design its sales jobs. This proved to be a fatal error.

PROCESSES

Another critical nuts-and-bolts factor that shapes whether an organization has a workplace capable of creating value for its customers and other stakeholders is the extent to which it has effective processes in place for getting work done. We have met many senior leaders who believe that they have no responsibility for ensuring that their organization's work processes are sound—that this is a responsibility that can be delegated to others at lower levels in the organization.

It is, indeed, true that senior executives cannot and should not be involved in the day-to-day minutia of refining and honing work processes. But any number of post-mortem organizational autopsies have revealed that abdication of responsibility on mission-critical work processes can result in a speedy death.

In 2002, Dan and Laurie conducted an analysis of the work, learning, and leadership environment at Riggs Bank. Founded in 1836, Riggs was a proud Washington, D.C. institution, with its main branch perched across the street from the White House. It had successfully branded itself as the "most important bank in the most important city in the world" and boasted that it was the personal banker of more U. S. presidents than any other bank.

In our report to Riggs, we called their leaders' attention to a dearth of defined processes—particularly with respect to hiring practices and employee training—in its international banking unit. Our warning fell on deaf ears. Within two years, Riggs found itself embroiled in a Justice Department investigation that eventually ended with the finding that Riggs's international division had violated a number of money-laundering laws. Shortly thereafter, Riggs was sold for a pittance to PNC Bank. Many jobs were lost, shareholders' value was destroyed, and a venerable 168-year-old institution ceased to exist. Process matters.

CONDITIONS

Conditions is a work environment category closely related to processes. By this we mean decisions and practices, some small and some large, that are made hundreds of times every day. For good or for ill, these decisions create the conditions in which people find themselves working.

Just as people need to floss their teeth, eat right, and exercise in order to have the best shot at a healthy future, organizations have to attend vigilantly to their own "hygiene" factors. It's not sexy stuff, and hands-off executives would prefer not to be bothered. But people can't hire someone to floss their teeth or exercise, and organizations can't outsource this stuff either. Getting the day-to-day, essential discipline right is a critical task in maintaining an organization's health and its ability to create value for customers and other stakeholders.

Among the conditions that are necessary for an organization to remain healthy and viable are

- a conscious, relentless focus on how to create great value for its customers
- a guarantee that employees have access to necessary materials and technology
- a physical environment that contributes to performance
- a place where learning is valued and new ideas are welcomed

You can get most of this right but be missing one piece of it—and a single piece can prove to be disastrous.

Self-delusion is disconcertingly easy. For example, what might be mistaken as a focus on creating value for customers could, in truth, be a focus on cost-cutting that crosses the line into dangerous. That seems to have been the case at Toyota. The veteran Toyota employees cited earlier believed that the emphasis on cost cutting negatively affected Toyota's "reputation for safety and quality, which were always its watchwords."[14]

When it comes to workplace conditions, *vigilance* is the watchword.

ACCOUNTABILITY

Accountability is the key to creating vigilance.

At some fundamental level, all of the corporate disasters mentioned in this chapter are grounded in issues related to accountability:

- The employee deaths, injuries, and financial loss that resulted from the 2005 explosion at BP's Texas City refinery resulted from an absence of accountability on safety.

- The customer deaths attributable to Toyota's faulty accelerator resulted from an absence of accountability for adhering to the company's stated values of quality and safety.

- Circuit City's decision to lay off its most highly paid sales people suggests that there was a lack of true accountability within the company for the quality of customer service (although Circuit City was ultimately held accountable by its customers).

- Riggs Bank's descent into oblivion happened because employees were not held accountable for abiding by the law.

These lapses in accountability speak volumes about what a company values most. In all four of these examples, the decisions that ultimately led to these disasters reveal what leaders in these organizations were truly seeking. In each case, maximizing corporate profits was held to be more important than the publicly stated values of the company.

There is no denying that this form of unworthiness can lead to spectacular short-term gains. But ultimately such a strategy is not sustainable. As one of our colleagues is fond of saying, "It's what you get away with in life that kills you."

And in a world of increasing transparency, the expected life span of organizations that engage in these unworthy behaviors is likely to shrink. Toyota's problems in one market quickly spilled over into its other markets. Things can unravel very fast these days.

True accountability requires attention, focus, and effort by leaders at each and every level in an organization. But it cannot occur without the authentic commitment of leaders at the very highest level of an organization, including the Board of Directors. It demands that employees at all levels—from the CEO and senior leadership team all the way down to the factory floor—be held accountable for producing quality work and exhibiting decision making and behaviors that are consistent with the organization's commitments to customers and other stakeholders.

The litmus test for this is an organization's systems for making promotions and determining compensation (including, very importantly, bonuses). If, for example, promotions and/or bonuses are based almost exclusively on meeting short-term profit targets, there will be enormous pressure for employees at all levels to meet these targets at the expense of whatever stated principles exist, or even at the expense of customers. This short-term focus is a path that moves organizations toward unworthiness.

FAIRLY COMPENSATING EMPLOYEES

In addition to creating a culture in which employees can and will perform at their best, fairly compensating them is an essential, foundational element of being a worthy employer. At some level, this is pretty simple stuff. Wages and salaries are easy to measure, and there are a variety of sources for easy benchmarking across employers, jobs, skill levels, and experience. Benefits can be trickier, but sources are also available in that domain to help employers identify appropriate levels of benefits.

At the end of the day, fairly compensating employees is hardly sufficient. While there are always some individual exceptions, survey after survey reveals that the top drivers of employees' commitment to their employer (measured either by voluntary turnover rates or an employee's intention to remain with an employer) has much more to do with other culture elements (such as the factors discussed above) than with compensation.[15]

For example, studies find that primary contributors to employee commitment include

- management concern for employees and customers[16]
- participation in decision making and autonomy, along with supervisory career support (information, advice, and encouragement)[17]
- nonmonetary recognition and competency development[18]

It's much less expensive to stimulate employees' discretionary effort through these nonmonetary practices than to attempt to purchase it through above-market compensation packages.

Learning

The ability to learn is an increasingly essential attribute for individuals and organizations around the globe. Globalization and changes in technology have both separately and together resulted in what economists blandly call a "skill-biased" economic evolution. That is to say, there is an increasing return to knowledge and skills. As a result, all economic entities around the globe—individuals, families, employers, and governments—are increasing the resources they devote to education.

There is an increasing return to learning for all who invest in it. But therein lies the catch-22. Investing requires a long-term focus; it requires an ability to balance the tradeoff between profits in the here-and-now for greater returns in the future.

Short-termism contributes to a chronic tendency on both the part of employers and individuals to underinvest in learning. Those who are able to overcome this tendency are rewarded handsomely for doing so.

Learning is an economic elixir. It makes both people and organizations more adaptable, more able to respond to change, more nimble. It serves as the bedrock for innovation; it is impossible to innovate without learning something new. And when it occurs in workplaces, it is one of those rarest of opportunities—where employers' and employees' incentives are in perfect harmony. In the vast majority of cases, it makes both better off.

There is one important exception. When learning is used to improve efficiencies that ultimately lead to employees being laid off, there is understandable reluctance on employees' part to play ball. This, in turn, leads to stagnant environments where innovation is unlikely to occur, and decline is not far behind.

In an environment where learning thrives, it occurs in two ways: formally and informally. Both are critical in increasing an organization's ability to create value.

FORMAL LEARNING

Because of its long-standing commitment to employees, the Container Store's annual employee turnover rate is in the single digits. (This compares with turnover rates in retail stores that are often in excess of 100 percent annually.)

While low turnover carries with it significant organizational benefits of its own, it has a huge side benefit as well. The Container Store makes unusually large investments in employee training—with a full-time trainer assigned to each of its retail stores. It is able to make this investment because it is confident that its employees will be sticking around long enough for the company to reap the benefits of the investment. Employee training, in turn, makes employees more knowledgeable, less frustrated, and hence, less likely to quit, all of which produce delighted customers.

The result is a virtuous cycle of low turnover, value created for the company's delighted customers, and profits that then fuel additional investments. This is just the opposite of the vicious cycle that other retailers too often create when they fail to invest in employees: generating high employee turnover rates, dissatisfied customers, and ultimately razor-thin profit margins.

Symphony Services, the India-based technology company, is another example of how a company in an improbable industry uses investments in employee training to create an extraordinary competitive advantage. The labor market for technology workers in India is extremely competitive, with an average annual employee turnover rate of about 30 percent. Many employers conclude that because of this high turnover rate, they can't afford to invest in employee training.

Symphony Services turns that logic on its head. It makes huge investments in developing its employees' skills; and then, because their employability is enhanced, they paradoxically don't need to look outside the company to hone their skills and stay competitive. The large investment that Symphony Services makes in its employees provides them with the wherewithal to leave, but there is no need for them to do so.

As a result, Symphony Services is growing by leaps and bounds and is on a buying binge—acquiring other technology companies across the globe.

INFORMAL LEARNING

The means by which employees learn informally can be just as important (some argue even more important) than formal learning. Increasingly, work and learning are becoming blurred. Need to know something right now to help you get a task accomplished or a question answered? Just do a quick Internet search, and you are likely to find exactly what you need. Need to know who in your company knows the answer to your question? Just look on the company intranet to find the expert in that area who can quickly get you the knowledge you need. Need to be able to troubleshoot a problem? An electronic support system is likely to be able to help you figure it out. Just-in-time, bite-size learning increasingly happens all day long in many organizations. And it looks very much like work.

With over 40,000 employees disbursed around the globe, and 75 percent of its revenues this year coming from products that didn't exist at the beginning of the year, technology company EMC is a good example of how informal learning can propel a business forward. With such short product-life cycles, standard operating process and bureaucratic decision making are precursors to death. And so EMC relentlessly promotes social networking as a way of getting work done faster, speeding innovation cycles, and reducing travel and meeting costs.

Got a problem that needs to be solved at EMC? No need to call a meeting—throw it out to EMC's social network and they'll solve it for you in a fraction of the time and cost that would be required through traditional ways of working and learning. Polly Pearson, EMC's former VP of Employee Branding, is a zealot about the economic value that EMC's social network creates.[19] But it isn't all about revenues and profits. With pride in her voice she shares the story of a young Asian EMC engineer who was diagnosed with an aggressive form of cancer that required an immediate bone marrow transplant. His doctors told him that because of his ethnicity, he had a zero percentage chance of finding a donor match. Not content with this answer, Polly threw the problem out to EMC's social network. EMC employees, in turn shared the problem with their social networks—customers, competitors, and friends. In short order, two perfect matches were found.

There is no value that can be placed on that. It makes people proud to be at EMC. It makes them more willing to contribute to EMC's mission and makes EMC more worthy of the gift of their discretionary efforts. It fuels another virtuous cycle.

Creating Business Intelligence for Being a Good Employer

So back to the beginning. Balance—masterfully managing the tension inherent in employees simultaneously being a major cost and a major asset to their employers—is the trademark of a worthy employer.

Traditional systems of measurement, which are so key to running a business, often make it more difficult to be a worthy employer. Although CEOs proclaim "Employees are our most important asset," employees are nevertheless measured as costs. In addition, in publicly traded firms, investments in employee development are counted as overhead costs in annual reports and financial statements. Hence, one way to boost profits in the short run is to cut these costs.

But doing so increases the likelihood that future productive capability will be harmed, since those cut "costs" are actually investments necessary for future production and growth. In essence, traditional measurement fuels short-termism. For publicly traded companies (particularly those in the United States, where the influence of financial markets on management practices has been so pervasive), this has resulted in a chronic tendency to underinvest in the people side of the business.

At some level, of course, it makes sense for employees to be accounted for as costs. After all, they are not *owned* by their employer—and that is a good thing. But the lopsidedness of traditional measures does get in the way of balance. And hence, it gets in the way of being a worthy employer.

There is a nascent movement underway to correct this imbalance by collecting, compiling, and analyzing data in new ways to create true insight—actionable business intelligence—that helps employers better measure (and therefore manage) employees as both costs and assets.

The basic idea is pretty simple: it relies on taking disparate pieces of data and combining them in such a way as to create understanding that is not evident to even the most tuned in and intuitive of managers (or, for that matter, to anyone staring at mountains of unfiltered data).

Google, not surprisingly, is one of the pioneers in this regard. For example, in 2006 Google conducted an extensive survey of all of its long-time employees, with questions touching on personality, behavior, and other characteristics, such as pet ownership. The company then linked the data to various performance outcomes, including results of employee reviews and a measure of contributions to the company as a whole. The resulting analysis yielded insights on employee traits that were tied to better performance in a variety of job areas. Google then started looking for those job-specific characteristics as it hired new employees.[20]

Similarly, Google recently began to analyze data from employee reviews, promotion, and pay histories to identify which of its employees are most likely to quit (getting "inside people's heads even before they know they might leave," according to an HR executive at the company)[21] and then to work proactively to address their concerns before they actually take steps to leave. By using existing data both to identify potential new hires who are most likely to contribute to organizational success and to retain valuable existing employees who might be inclined to leave, Google is using "human capital analytics" to improve its capacity to create value.

Thus, the tools now exist that allow more organizations to apply analytics to create actionable business intelligence on the people side of the business. Done correctly, this has two benefits: It enables organizations to more efficiently create value for their customers and others. Simultaneously, it enhances their capacity for long-term commitment to their employees by providing quantitative information that can counterbalance the cost-focused nature of the standard accounting system. It makes it easier for organizations to develop the virtuous cycles described earlier in this chapter.

In order for this nascent movement toward more insightful business intelligence to have the greatest possible effect on the people side of an organization, however, it's first necessary for organizations to move beyond the broadly accepted focus on employee engagement that exists within most HR departments. Attention paid to employee engagement is currently the primary mechanism that reflects an organization's recognition that employees are assets as well as costs. Unfortunately, it has little, if anything, to do with how work gets done and value gets created in an organization. It is entirely possible, for example, that employees may be fully engaged—in the flow—in an organization with rampant inefficiencies, poor hiring decisions, and no significant organizational learning.

Organizations should not fall into the trap of equating employee engagement with business results. While engagement is necessary to produce results, it is not sufficient; and the two should not be confused with one another.

Moving beyond employee engagement toward measures that truly reflect employees' central roles in their organizations' creation of value will require that organizations begin to get serious about human capital analytics. Google is showing the way.

Inspiring Purpose

Goodness as an employer requires more, though, than sound metrics and more than the other ingredients we discussed above, such as a commitment to employees. It also requires an inspiring purpose. By purpose, we mean two things. In the first place, we refer to the "for whom" question—the people the company is designed to benefit. Then there is the "for what" question—what is the company trying to achieve?

For a long time, the "for whom" question has been answered by companies in a narrow way. A "maximize shareholder value" philosophy has governed many companies over the past several decades, indicating a dominant focus on company owners (and typically top executives, who received large quantities of stock or stock options) and little concern on the part of firms for their workers or the communities they touched.

Increasingly, though, companies are expanding what we might call

the *people purpose* to include employees as stakeholders. Whether explic-
itly written into company bylaws—and demonstrated through workers
owning stock—or implicitly adopted as an ethos, a stakeholder mindset
helps ensure that companies will treat workers with dignity and respect.
Remember HCL Technologies: its Employees First initiative is both a
business strategy as well as a declaration that employee welfare is central
to the company.

As HCL's strong results in recent years indicate, a broad people purpose also can spur employees to put forth their best efforts. After all, the
workers know they have a serious stake in the organization's success.

A compelling "for what" purpose also can bring out the best in employees. A cause that fires up the imagination, stirs the spirit, or otherwise taps our better nature is likely to make us work hard and feel alive
on the job.

It may be a grand vision such as IBM's goal of a "smarter planet."[22]
"To fill the earth with the light and warmth of hospitality" is the mission
of Hilton Worldwide. FedEx has updated its shipping services mission
to include greenness as a goal—it now aims to "connect the world in
responsible and resourceful ways."[23] The ambition also can be more mod-
est.[24] Former Coca-Cola CEO Roberto Goizueta used to focus on the
way the company's soft drinks helped small merchants make a living.[25]

The point is that it is a moving mission. This is an old, intuitive idea,
one rooted in traditions such as community barn raising and cathedral building. The importance of purposeful work also has reemerged
recently. A "noble cause" is critical to the highest-performing teams and
organizations, according to authors Dave Logan, John King, and Halee
Fischer-Wright. In their 2008 book *Tribal Leadership*, they estimate that
less than 2 percent of workplace cultures have arrived at the ultimate,
fifth stage, including the team that produced the first Macintosh computer. Such teams or "tribes" have transcended concerns about individual
achievement or even winning against other groups.[26]

"Their language revolves around infinite potential and how the group
is going to make history—not to beat a competitor, but because doing so
will make a global impact," the authors write.[27]

In his 2009 book *Drive*, author Daniel Pink draws on a range of scholarly research to question the conventional wisdom that rewards and punishments are all you need to motivate workers.[28]

Companies "should move past their outdated reliance on carrots and sticks," Pink says. "That was fine for simple, routine 20th-century tasks. But for creative, conceptual 21st-century work, companies are much better off ensuring that people have ample amounts of autonomy and that their individual efforts are hitched to a larger purpose."[29]

Many companies today fail to spell out such a larger purpose. Instead they often set out business goals with a laser-like focus. Sure, it's wise for businesses to specialize in a particular niche with products or services. But firms seeking an inspiring aim cannot limit their vision to something as cramped as, say, "providing the best room-reservation software for the high-end hotel market." It's hard to imagine workers getting fired up about such a narrow purpose.

For most companies, though, there's a way to tie what they do to a broader goal that moves people. Remember Coca-Cola helping small merchants earn a living. Or if you're making room-reservation software, you could link your company's product with that larger vision that Hilton espouses. Perhaps something like: "We make it possible to spread the warmth of hospitality."

It's the old adage about the two bricklayers. One says he's making a wall, while the other says he's helping to construct a soaring cathedral. Which do you think is pouring more of his soul into the work?

That said, a lofty-sounding corporate purpose will fall flat or lose its uplifting power if it is not genuine. If a company claims to be about environmental stewardship but cuts corners on pollution controls or routinely puts short-term profits ahead of the planet's health, it will not fuel employee passion or optimal performance.

A stirring, inclusive vision not only helps inspire employees on a daily basis but also can buoy an organization during tough times. Consider Beth Israel Deaconess Medical Center and a 2010 scandal it weathered involving CEO Paul Levy. Levy was fined $50,000 by the hospital for "poor judgment" regarding a personal relationship with a former female employee.[30] Officials with the Massachusetts Attorney General's office probed the matter, finding that the woman was the only nonphysician director who received a bonus in all four years they reviewed. They also found that the positions she held at Beth Israel were newly created for her and not filled after she left. The investigation, though, found no evidence the hospital misused charitable funds to pay the employee's salary, travel expenses, or severance.[31]

Levy apologized in 2010 for his "errors of judgment in this matter."[32] He resigned from Beth Israel the next year, saying he needed "new challenges."[33]

It's hard to say whether Levy steered clear of more serious lapses because of the hospital's ethos of treating "patients with the utmost respect and compassion, like our own family members and friends." But that mission seemed to help the organization remain on an even keel even as the scandal unfolded throughout 2010. Board president Stephen Kay told the *Boston Globe* in September that the hospital was having "a great year," adding "we have more patients than we've ever had before."[34]

The company also appeared to remain a good employer overall. In late 2010, Beth Israel spent $3 million in appreciation bonuses—$500 for full-time workers and up to $250 for part-time employees.[35]

Cynics might see this as Levy trying to buy back the sympathies of his employees. But even before those payments were announced, and despite the scandal, some Beth Israel employees were giving the hospital high marks on Glassdoor.com. In August, a clinical research assistant rated the organization a 4 out of 5. Despite noting that "some internal competition and politics makes (the) workplace awkward at times," the employee called Beth Israel a "great place to work," citing learning opportunities and a "friendly, supportive staff."[36]

The hospital, in other words, continued to strike a balance between treating employees as costs and assets. All companies seeking to be good employers must do this. By caring for workers, being careful about how they're managed, and providing them with a compelling overall purpose, companies will find they can be good to their employees *and* to the rest of their stakeholders.

CHAPTER SEVEN SUMMARY

The phrase *good employer* evokes images of generous, nice companies. While such attributes are part of the equation, being a good employer is more complex—and more difficult to achieve. There are many moving parts, tradeoffs, and judgments that companies must make with respect to employees.

The framework we provide is largely the product of two decades of research and client consulting by Laurie and Dan. It consists of three main elements: a value-creating organization committed to employees, sound data analysis, and an inspiring purpose.

A Value-Creating Organization Committed to Employees

- Great places to work also have to be places that create value for customers and owners. Only those organizations are capable of a long-term commitment to employees, which creates a virtuous cycle that brings out the best in employees—who in turn create value.
- Beyond commitment, the necessary elements fall into three primary categories: leadership, work, and learning.
  1. Leadership boils down to what leaders say and what they do—their communication and their behavior.
  2. The work environment consists of multiple components, including hiring practices, job design, work processes, conditions, accountability, and compensation practices.
  3. Learning includes both formal and informal means for fostering employee skill development and knowledge sharing.

Creating Business Intelligence for Being a Worthy Employer

- The trademark of a worthy employer is the ability to masterfully manage the tension between employees as costs and employees as assets.
- The accounting system currently treats employees as costs. This creates constant balance sheet incentives to reduce expenditures in this area, without regard for employees' value creation.

- Collecting, compiling, and analyzing data can create actionable business intelligence that helps employers better measure and manage employees, as both costs and assets.

Inspiring Purpose

- Goodness as an employer also requires an inspiring purpose by which we mean two things.

  1. The "for whom" question. Whom is the company designed to benefit? Companies ought to expand their purpose to include employees, not just shareholders, as stakeholders.

  2. The "for what" question. What is the company trying to achieve? A cause that fires up the imagination, stirs the spirit, or otherwise taps our better nature creates an environment where people work hard and feel alive on the job.

Good employers, then, are at once caring, exacting, and stirring.

CHAPTER 8

The Good Seller

From its origins as a shipper of valuables in the 1850s to its charge card with the famous tag line, "Don't leave home without it," American Express has had a long legacy of strong service. But the company left the 20th century without it. AmEx hovered in the 50th percentile for service quality during the years 1999 to 2004, according to research firm wRatings.

Like many companies, American Express was focused on cost containment. The priority was reducing time on the phone with customers. American Express's nod to service came primarily in the form of a checklist for such behaviors as saying the customer's name three times during a call and avoiding 10 seconds of awkward dead time on the phone.[1]

This not only led to a stiff experience for customers but also robbed employees of the autonomy that helps make for meaningful work. Annual turnover in its service centers, although not as high as the 100 percent annual turnover sometimes experienced in the call-center field, was nonetheless in the double digits.

"Over time, the service had eroded," concedes Jim Bush, executive vice president of world service at American Express.

To their credit, executives at American Express saw the service slide as a serious problem. Bush took over the company's service organization for the United States in 2005, where he began a push to upgrade customer satisfaction partly by upgrading the employee experience.

Instead of ending calls as quickly as possible, AmEx call center agents now seek to deepen relationships with customers by providing relevant information and asking about their use of the card. This might sound like the irritating "upselling" consumers frequently face. But under the new American Express program, dubbed Relationship Care, agents typically aren't selling anything new. Rather, they try to help customers understand all the features of their card so they will use it more.

The company now tracks actual customer feedback instead of measuring adherence to scripts. Call center agents not only have more discretion, but can more easily earn bonuses based on customer satisfaction scores.

The service surge is paying off. American Express's wRatings scores on service quality dipped in the first several years of the initiative but spiked to the 97th percentile in 2009.

American Express embodies key features of good sellers. Good sellers offer safe products, communicate honestly, and seek reciprocal relationships. The win-win scenario of American Express customers taking greater advantage of card features—thereby spending money that translates into transaction fee revenue for the company—falls into this latter category. Good sellers also show restraint, avoiding practices like aggressive upselling.

American Express isn't perfect. In fact, a lawsuit filed against American Express by the U.S. Department of Justice in 2010 paints the firm as profoundly unworthy with respect to customers. The suit claims that AmEx's rules for merchants restrict price competition.[2] American Express counters that the suit itself threatens competition.

It's difficult to judge the case at its outset. But the suit highlights hurdles related to being a good seller, including the difficulty of pursuing a higher-touch, higher-cost path with customers. And on the face of the suit, it seems AmEx may not be tackling the issue with as much candor as it should.

Still, the company is doing better by customers than its peers, according to J.D. Power and Associates. The research firm ranked AmEx tops in credit card customer satisfaction from 2007 to 2010.[3]

American Express also shows that goodness through and through fuels goodness as a seller. It recognizes that worthiness as an employer is at the heart of outstanding service. And worthiness as a steward reinforces the company's worthiness as a seller. For example, its commitment to community service doubles as a recruiting tool for service-minded employees.

What's more, American Express demonstrates that an expansive purpose helps firms focus more fully on the well-being of customers. Underpinning American Express's worthiness as a seller is its vision "to become the world's most-respected service brand." It's a mission at once ambitious and empathetic. After all, serving others ultimately requires a degree of care for them.

This chapter spells out the characteristics of good sellers, showing how they must combine commercial savvy with service in the best sense.

Safety

As a rash of incidents in recent years has shown, many companies have not taken product safety to heart. Reasons vary. Firms may be overly focused on cost cutting, as may have been the case with Toyota. The company was slapped with a $16 million fine in 2010 for failing to promptly disclose problems with accelerator pedals.[4] They may be obsessed with profits or so fearful about bad publicity that they cover up problems rather than address them head-on. They may be under the threat of cheaper knockoffs. That's long been a challenge in many manufacturing fields, including toys.

Toy giant Mattel, like many other firms, has turned to China's giant shop floor to lower its costs. Not only have Mattel and others tapped Chinese workers, but they have further cut expenses by farming out the manufacturing tasks to independent operators. In many cases, suppliers are pitted against each other to deliver products at the lowest price.

A reliance on outsourced suppliers in China contributed to recalls of millions of toys that plagued Mattel in 2007.[5] That year, the company announced a number of recalls of lead-tainted toys and ultimately paid a penalty of $2.3 million in a settlement with the U.S. Consumer Product Safety Commission.[6]

The Mattel case and a host of other recalls in recent years on products ranging from pet food to drywall shows that the system of using contract Chinese suppliers is riddled with risks. Despite nominal efforts by Chinese officials to toughen regulations in the country, observers don't expect government efforts to bring quick results. More than ever, companies have to make extra efforts to make sure their products have a clean bill of health.

Better oversight of supply networks in Asia and elsewhere is part of the solution. Mattel, for example, took a number of steps along these lines after its recall black eye in 2007. It beefed up lead testing requirements and increased inspections of vendors and subcontractors.[7]

But efforts to monitor suppliers may not be enough, especially in light of evidence Chinese contractors find ways to flout such supervision.[8] Companies also ought to consider bringing in-house more of their manufacturing tasks, so they have greater control over the safety of the final products.

Mattel has acknowledged the wisdom of this approach. In 2007, company executives told the *New York Times* that they were trying to shift more toy production into factories they own and operate and away from Chinese contractors and subcontractors.

"We do realize the need for increased vigilance, increased surveillance," Jim Walter, senior vice president of worldwide quality assurance at Mattel, told the newspaper.[9]

The company's efforts to better safeguard customers appear to be working. Between January 2008 and early 2011, Mattel did not recall any products related to lead contamination.[10]

Reciprocity

At a basic level, reciprocity is about creating mutual benefit. Customers give money to a company in exchange for a product. When both parties feel good about the transaction, reciprocity is in effect. The roots of reciprocal relations are consistency and creativity. Consumers on the one hand want the companies in their lives to provide reliable, trustworthy goods and services—the same high-quality haircut or durable work boot over and over. But they also want to be surprised. Delighted by an innovative product that meets a known need or establishes a wholly new category of experience—think hybrid cars, Silly Bandz, and the full-body interactivity of the Wii and Xbox Kinect video game systems.

Reciprocity also means fulfilling promises. In other words, the company will deliver the products and services it says it will.

Home Depot fell down on this fundamental feature of mutually beneficial relations under former CEO Bob Nardelli. As a slew of online comments and formal surveys indicated, the company's level of service deteriorated to the point that it was violating its marketing slogan: "You can do it. We can help."

In effect, as Scott Burns pointed out in his *MSN Money* essay, Home Depot was building its bottom line on the backs of customers. Minimal staffing levels cut labor expenses for the company but cost customers in the form of wasted time.

Reciprocal treatment of customers moves companies away from the buyer-beware mentality that has long ruled commercial transactions. This concept, known also by the Latin phrase caveat emptor, lends itself to a zero-sum outcome—where one side of the transaction loses while the other gains. Amid ever-greater intolerance of corporate greed and a growing desire for social responsibility, consumers expect the dominant philosophy to be seller take care.

Some companies are forging reciprocal relationships with customers. Among the standouts are Amazon.com and its unit Zappos.com. And they show there are multiple paths to sound customer stewardship.

For its part, Amazon.com has focused on low prices, selection, and convenience. In selling books, CDs, and many other products, Amazon provides customers with service that is high-tech, low-touch, and highly reliable. The giant online retailer also has taken steps to improve the service level of partner merchants, including user ratings that keep merchants on their toes and a program to ship items on behalf of partners. Thanks to such efforts, Amazon was the top company in *BusinessWeek*'s 2009 report of the customer service "champs."[11]

Zappos ranked seventh on that list. Amazon acquired Zappos in

2009 and pledged to preserve its independent brand and culture. That culture differs dramatically from Amazon's when it comes to customer service. Zappos is all about the human touch—including extended phone calls with customer service representatives and handwritten notes from them. Zappos aims to wow customers, partly with a free shipping policy on both purchases and returns.

Both Amazon and Zappos offer customers a reciprocal relationship. Busy consumers gain from Amazon's notable efficiency while the company's highly automated system saves on labor costs. Zappos's unscripted phone service and generous returns policy all but guarantee shoppers will be happy. And while Zappos's operation costs may be higher because of lengthy customer service conversations and shipping expenses, it gains from greater loyalty. In 2009, for example, Zappos ranked second only to insurance company USAA in the percentage of customers who would "definitely recommend" the brand, at 69 percent.[12]

In *Bloomberg Businessweek*'s 2010 customer service leaders report, Amazon slipped from the top spot. But it still ranked as the 11th best service provider.[13]

Honest Communication

It almost goes without saying that a good steward of customers will communicate honestly with them. Candor is crucial in moments of crisis, when a company has faltered on product quality or safety. But it's also an ongoing duty. To care for customers well, companies must reveal what their products are made of, how they're made, how they operate, and how they should be used safely and for optimal performance.

Disclosures by sellers often are mandated by law. This is especially true for food and drug products. But increasingly, good customer stewardship calls for going beyond required labels and traditional instruction manuals. It means more interactivity in the form of feedback mechanisms that allow companies to spot and fix problems quickly. It also means taking transparency to a new level, allowing customers a view into a company's operations, finances, and future strategies.

Conscious, ethical consumers want to know how their buying decisions affect workers and the environment. They want to see evidence that the businesses they patronize do not profit-gouge, pay CEOs obscene amounts, or skimp on philanthropy. A more-participatory public also is coming to expect a say over product development decisions.

What does this new naked corporation look like? It may mean letting customers rate products without censure on company Web sites, as retailers like Best Buy and Amazon do. It can include liberal rules on employee blogging and Twittering, as Zappos has.[14] It might mean clearer reporting about financial results, as Microsoft has done with its interactive Investor Central site.[15] It could involve business strategies and dilemmas being laid bare.

A few years ago, for instance, Southwest Airlines CEO Gary Kelly used a company blog to raise the possibility of the airline adopting assigned seating. Over 600 people commented on the idea, convincing the company to stick with its first-come, first-serve approach.[16]

Radical openness to customers is counterintuitive. Business success for decades was based on finding a secret formula that no one else could duplicate and exploiting that proprietary knowledge. Exposing everything means rivals can get the goods besides customers. But in the era of Web 2.0 citizen muckraking, secrecy is less of an option. Loyalty is largely a function of trust, which turns ever more on transparency.

And the culture of interactivity means that customers assist companies that reveal themselves warts-and-all. The more-than 11,600 online reviews of Amazon's Kindle (as of early 2011) help the company find flaws and create desired features.[17] Southwest's blog serves as a low-cost focus group. Media organizations like the *New York Times* are inviting readers to submit their own images and comments about news events, which can allow the organizations to provide better coverage.[18]

"The new breed of naked executives... discover that once people are interested in you, they're interested in helping you out—by offering ideas, critiques, and extra brain cycles," author Clive Thompson wrote in a 2007 *Wired* magazine essay. "Customers become working partners."[19]

Consider how Goldman Sachs might have fared differently if it had exposed its negative stance on the housing market during the early stages of the mortgage meltdown. Yes, it might have sacrificed some short-term profits, but transparency would have done immense good for Goldman's standing among customers and the public, especially in contrast to other financial services firms that failed to comport themselves well in the downturn. Goldman could have emerged from the financial crisis with a much cleaner name, rather than with its reputation in the gutter.

Restraint

That fact that Goldman Sachs was rated as one of the least-respected companies in early 2010 shows the importance of restraint in customer care. In effect, Goldman could not bring itself to limit its gains from negative mortgage bets for the sake of clients. Apparently it was not alone in this practice.[20] And the challenge of reining in greed for the good of customers applies to companies throughout the economy.

The food and beverage industry faces the question of moderation more than most. Excessive amounts of fast food and sugary drinks are among the causes of the growing obesity epidemic in the United States, which has intensified scrutiny of the roles played by companies like McDonald's, Coca-Cola, and PepsiCo.

Fast-food firms also have established a major presence in school cafeterias with meal options of questionable nutritional value. And as exposés like the documentary *Supersize Me* have shown, companies in the food industry have sought to convince consumers to patronize them constantly.

Ed once spent much of the day with a public relations official from a major beverage company. The spokesman explained that his firm's vision was to have customers turn to one of its drinks every time they felt thirsty. The spokesman himself personally followed the prescription, downing multiple caffeinated drinks each workday.

We wouldn't want to ban sugary drinks or other food types that have a limited place in a healthy diet. And companies like McDonald's and Coca-Cola have launched healthy-lifestyle campaigns designed to encourage exercise. But for the most part, the food industry's approach to consumers tends to be *all consuming* and dangerous to the public's health.

Invasive food industry marketing speaks to another key point about restraint with respect to customers. Good sellers respect customers' privacy. This has become a more significant matter given the way electronic data collection can allow companies to monitor consumers' behavior extensively. And companies increasingly are spying on Internet users for marketing purposes.[21] In 2010 the *Wall Street Journal* found that the 50 top Web sites in the United States on average installed 64 pieces of tracking technology onto the computers of visitors, usually with no warning.[22]

Companies should not seek comprehensive knowledge of customers under the guise of providing more intelligent, targeted product suggestions. Despite all its accolades, Google has flirted with crossing this line.[23] So has Zappos. A *New York Times* story detailed the way a consumer who viewed a pair of shoes at Zappos.com found herself hounded by Zappos ads for this same pair of shoes. "For days or weeks, every site I went to seemed to be showing me ads for those shoes," Julie Matlin told the newspaper. "It is a pretty clever marketing tool. But it's a little creepy, especially if you don't know what's going on."[24]

A Zappos marketing official told the *Times* that "the overwhelming response has been positive" to this sort of "retargeting" activity.[25] But others have warned against such surveillance and the privacy risks it represents. Good companies will respect customers enough not to be nosy—to mind their own business.

Being a Good Seller Doesn't Come Cheap

It sounds simple enough to be a good seller. Offer customers safe products, be honest with them, avoid ripping them off, and show some restraint. But it is not easy to get all this right, especially when companies have to compete in cutthroat, global markets and earn a decent return for shareholders.

American Express illustrates this difficulty. It competes largely on service instead of price. This means service not only to customers but also to merchants that accept the card, who benefit in part from marketing programs provided by AmEx. One source of funding for high service levels—and American Express profits—is the fees the company charges to merchants when people use an AmEx card for purchases.

But the fees and the rules for merchants accepting the card raise questions of whether AmEx is fully worthy of customers' and merchants' business.

American Express isn't the only credit card network with transaction fees and rules for merchants. The Justice Department suit against AmEx also named MasterCard and Visa as defendants, saying all three had policies "that prevent merchants from offering consumers discounts, rewards and information about card costs, ultimately resulting in consumers paying more for their purchases." But the Justice Department said American Express has the highest merchant fees of any credit card network. And both MasterCard and Visa agreed to a proposed settlement.[26]

Among other things, the settlement allows merchants to "express a preference for the use of a particular credit card network," "promote a particular credit card network," and "communicate to consumers the cost incurred by the merchant when a consumer uses a particular credit card network, type of card within that network, or other form of payment."

In a *Washington Post* op-ed, American Express CEO Ken Chenault argued the settlement terms would allow merchants to engage in "pressuring their customers to use a different card when they pay."[27] He also said there's no guarantee merchants will pass on any fee savings to consumers and warned the settlement terms would increase the already significant market share of MasterCard and Visa.

"If the government is allowed to do away with the protections we build into our merchant contracts, the net result would be more business for the two dominant networks," Chenault wrote. "Visa and MasterCard already control 70 percent of the market. When dominant parties gain even more market share, no one will be able to negotiate freely or fairly with them. The inevitable result would be higher costs for merchants and less value for consumers."

He may be right. But on the surface, it looks as if the American Express rules for merchants effectively gag them. It seems the company ought to make its case for the use of its card—and for the fees behind higher quality services—to consumers. To convince them rather than keep them in the dark.

The issues raised by the lawsuit may prove to be a serious stain on AmEx's record as a good seller. Still, the company has shown itself to be among the best in customer service overall. Reciprocity is at the heart of worthiness as a seller, and the Relationship Care program is a particularly good example of that principle in action.

Consider some results of the program. When agents reinforce card features through Relationship Care, customer service scores rise by an average of more than 10 percent, the company says. Indeed, in a 2009 report J.D. Power & Associates found that 82 percent of American Express cardholders were aware of the benefits and services associated with their card, compared with an industry average of 70 percent.[28]

And by devoting more attention to its customers, American Express is boosting its top and bottom lines. Relationship Care conversations contribute to an increase in card-member spending of 8 to 10 percent on average, the company says. For the second quarter of 2010, AmEx's net income tripled to $1 billion from $337 million in the second quarter of 2009.

"While the economic environment remains uneven, our net income and billed business are back at, or near, their pre-recession levels," Chenault said in mid-2010.[29]

Thorough Worthiness Reinforces Goodness as a Seller

In effect, American Express shows that the business that takes care of its customer will find those same customers taking care of the business—even lifting it out of a recession in short order. American Express also illustrates the way goodness as an employer and as a steward can reinforce goodness as a seller—creating a virtuous cycle that's good for customers and all stakeholders.

GOOD EMPLOYERS MAKE GOOD SELLERS

As we discussed in Chapter 2, great customer experiences depend heavily on companies creating a great experience for their employees. Jim Bush acknowledged this relationship from the outset of his quest to ramp up customer satisfaction at American Express. The company polled existing customer care agents to find what would boost the quality of their service. Among their answers were improved incentives, more career mobility, more flexible hours, and streamlined processes.

In response, American Express increased job flexibility and created new job categories so agents could progress through four levels rather than remaining stuck in one. The company also changed its compensation plan, allowing agents to more easily earn bonuses based on customer service scores.

In addition, the company changed the job title from customer care representative to customer care *professional*. Agents got business cards for the first time.

These were more than symbolic gestures. Agents no longer merely recite company scripts, but use their discretion to figure out how American Express products can help customers solve problems. That's made the job harder in a way. Agents like Teresa Tate, who works out of an American Express service center in Phoenix, now have to think on their feet. But Tate wouldn't have it any other way. "We are getting more and more power to make the decisions at our level," she says.

Tate, who used to run a restaurant, takes calls from AmEx cardholders who operate small businesses. She is now freer to share her wisdom and her concern for these customers. "I genuinely feel like I'm in this company's finance department," she says of her callers. "Having been in small business myself, you need that support."

This sort of passion and compassion for customers translates into high levels of service, into reciprocal relationships.

American Express's worthiness as an employer predates the Relationship Care program. The company has made *Fortune*'s list of the 100 Best Companies to Work For 11 of the past 12 years.[30] Going even farther back, American Express offered employees one of the first private sector pension plans in 1875.

These days, AmEx combines kindness with cleverness in its people management. It offers a 401(k) plan that's in the top 15 percent when it comes to company generosity.[31] And AmEx has worked harder in recent years to help struggling employees succeed at the firm, rather than usher them out the door.[32] At the same time, AmEx employs workforce metrics to fortify worthiness as a seller. Agents' performance and pay are determined to a large extent by how well they fare on customer feedback surveys. The results are exposed directly to agents, who can view their recent customer satisfaction results, their aggregate results, and how they stack up against peers.

Relying too heavily on financial incentives can backfire. And workplace measurements can be misguided. Look no further than the way American Express used to track the robotic repetition of customer names. But AmEx designed its compensation system based partly on employee feedback. And the strong results of the Relationship Care program suggest the pay approach isn't distracting employees or hurting service. What's more, the continual customer feedback measurements act as a self-correcting mechanism for agents—and therefore help keep service quality high.

By blending employee autonomy and a supportive culture with smart metrics—the sort of workplace philosophy we spell out in Chapter 7— American Express shows that worthiness as an employer works to make companies worthy sellers.

GOOD STEWARDS MAKE GOOD SELLERS

At American Express, goodness as a steward also feeds into customer satisfaction. The company, for example, is rated as the fifth-greenest financial service company of 27 industry peers, according to *Newsweek*'s 2010 green ranking of America's largest 500 companies.[33] This strong showing came after AmEx finished second in the industry in 2009. American Express's "environmental efforts outshine those of other credit card companies," in part by offering cardholders guidance on environmentally favorable travel, *Newsweek* said.[34]

Given the rise of the ethical consumer we've discussed earlier in the book, such environmental stewardship by American Express amounts to a kind of reciprocity—we will help you live out your eco-values as you provide us with business.

Community stewardship also supports goodness as a seller. American Express has a long history of community service, including a program to match employees' charitable donations. These days, the company uses its frequent presence at fund-raising activities as an informal recruiting vehicle, says Tom Parker, an American Express vice president of human resources based in Phoenix.[35] People volunteering at a five-kilometer run to benefit cancer research likely have a service-oriented personality, Parker explains. He says recruiting employees at such charity events fits in with a broader push to hire people with a service ethos.

"We continue to focus on recruiting employees who understand what it means to build and deepen a relationship with a customer," Parker says, "versus someone who just has experience working in a high volume phone center environment."[36]

You can see how worthiness all the way around becomes a virtuous cycle. Serving customers well increases business, which gives American Express more resources to give back to the community as a steward. Which in turn makes it more of a magnet for people who love to serve. At the same time, superior customer service makes agents proud, which strengthens the company's reputation as a good employer. American Express, in fact, has used stories from its Relationship Care program in its recruitment advertising.[37]

The service message also is getting around by word of mouth.

During a recent training session for new employees at the company's Phoenix service center, trainee Jennifer Paez revealed that her mother owned a beauty salon and used an American Express card for her business. Paez said her mother always seemed to have a good experience when talking with American Express agents. "Every time she gets off the phone she feels better," Paez said. "I want to be one of those people who makes that happen."[38]

With pumped-up agents like Paez, service quality at American Express is likely to keep on rising.

A Good Seller on Purpose

Worthiness that permeates a firm and promotes goodness as a seller also ties back to a worthy company purpose. To a purpose that extends well beyond a short-term focus on shareholders and executives. The American Express vision "to become the world's most respected service brand" can sound a bit dry, especially compared with more uplifting company missions, such as Hilton's vision "to fill the earth with the light and warmth of hospitality." But American Express interprets its vision broadly, saying the overall service goal animates the company's commitment to community service. A quote from children's rights advocate Marian Wright Edelman on the AmEx Web site puts the philosophy in a nutshell: "Service is the rent we pay for living. It is the very purpose of life and not something you do in your spare time."[39]

Of course, uplifting talk is cheap. But American Express backs that rhetoric up. On the Good Company Index, the company earned our highest score for community contribution. We found it systematically assisted society, in part through efforts to boost leadership skills in nonprofits.[40]

Building the world's best "service brand" to American Express is about more than just business success. And precisely because of that, the company is succeeding in the service business.

Good Sellers Take Center Stage

Despite very real concerns about consumer privacy and other continuing shortcomings of companies with respect to customers, good selling behavior is on the rise. Evidence of the shift can be seen in the results of the American Customer Satisfaction Index, a measure developed at the University of Michigan. The index has climbed, more or less steadily, from less than 71 in 1997 to nearly 76 in 2010.[41]

This is how it should be in a capitalist economy, at least one that prevents the creation of monopolies and polices against predatory practices. Companies cannot remain in business without proving worthy of customers' business. The bar is set high these days. And it's heading higher.

For American Express, it is more a matter of revisiting where the bar was. Good service was essential to its success as a charge card company, as a traveler's check provider, and even to its initial business as a shipper of goods across a still-wild nation. Chenault explained as much in a corporate citizenship report:

> When American Express was formed in 1850, transporting personal goods and valuables was an uncertain proposition at best. Yet we guaranteed that a package would be delivered intact. If not, we reimbursed the sender in full. We stood behind our promises even if we could not control every circumstance. And because we did, we earned a reputation for delivering world-class service. Throughout our history, American Express has been defined by the extraordinary care we take to serve our customers, wherever and whenever they need us.[42]

Well, maybe not for its entire history. And maybe not when it comes to entirely candid communication with customers. But when its service slipped several years ago—when the company grew less caring about customers—American Express remembered itself. Bush sees the Relationship Care effort as a return to the firm's roots. "We brought it back to its heritage," he says.

American Express may have left its service legacy behind earlier this century. But the company went back home and got it.

CHAPTER EIGHT SUMMARY

Good sellers offer safe products, communicate honestly, seek reciprocal relationships, and practice restraint.

Safety

- Recent incidents reveal that many companies still have not taken product safety to heart. Reasons vary. Companies may be overly focused on cost cutting, obsessed with profits, so fearful about bad publicity that they cover up problems, or under the threat of cheaper knockoffs.

- A host of recalls shows that the system of outsourcing to Chinese suppliers is riddled with risks.

- Efforts to monitor suppliers may not be enough. Bringing more manufacturing tasks back in-house may be necessary to gain greater control over the safety of final products.

Reciprocity

- Reciprocity—creating mutual benefit—is a cornerstone of the Worthiness Era.

- Reciprocal relations depend on consistency, creativity, and fulfilling promises—delivering the products and services a company says it will.

- Buyer beware is yielding to seller take care.

- There are multiple ways to forge reciprocal relationships with customers.

Honest Communication

- To care for customers well, companies must reveal what their products are made of, how they're made, how they operate, and how they should be used safely and for optimal performance.

- Increasingly, good customer care calls for going beyond required labels and traditional instruction manuals to embrace greater interactivity.

- Ever-more "ethical" consumers want to know how their buying decisions affect workers and the environment, and the public increasingly expects a say over product development.
- In the age of the naked corporation, less-than-forthright communications will almost certainly breed distrust and disloyalty, while transparency can create competitive advantage.

Restraint

- One of the defining attributes of the Worthiness Era is that corporate greed is being restored to its rightful place—a vice that will no longer be tolerated, rather than a virtue to be admired.
- Marketing approaches that cross the line from informative to invasive are increasingly being viewed with disdain by consumers.

Thorough Worthiness Reinforces Goodness as a Seller

- Being a good seller is easier for companies that are also good employers and stewards, creating a virtuous cycle of thorough worthiness that generates financial rewards.

CHAPTER 9

The Good Steward

Seventh Generation is among the most environmentally responsible companies in the world today. But leaders of the household and personal care products company will be the first to tell you they aren't perfect.

They did just that in their 2008 Corporate Consciousness Report. "We are still working to replace the remaining synthetic ingredients in our products and to eliminate the contaminant 1,4-dioxane from our cleaning products," cofounder Jeffrey Hollender wrote.[1]

A likely carcinogen, 1,4-dioxane can form in cleaning products when modifying natural oils with the petrochemical ethylene oxide and sulfur trioxide.[2] Both Seventh Generation's fabric softener and its dish soap liquid tested positive for 1,4-dioxane, the company said in the report.

Despite this admitted black eye, Seventh Generation's track record has been a bright shade of green. Among numerous environmental awards, it was ranked as the best company on the planet by Better World Shopping Guide, a buying resource for ethically minded consumers.[3] And Seventh Generation's actions back up this honor. For example, the company in 2008 upgraded its product-testing regime, which led it to discover phthalates in its automatic dishwasher gel with a synthetic green apple scent. Although the particular phthalate found—DEP—is not a suspected carcinogen or endocrine disrupter, other phthalates have been found to be probable or possible health hazards.[4] The company discontinued use of the green apple scent, replacing it with a natural grapefruit fragrance.[5]

The firm, founded in the late 1980s, also has taken steps to reduce its carbon footprint. It estimated that a plan to decentralize manufacturing and distribution operations would cut delivery miles to retailers by 48 percent.[6]

It's all in line with Seventh Generation's deep commitment to environmental and social responsibility. The company's very name refers to the Iroquois concept that decisions today should account for their effect on the next seven generations.

Seventh Generation embodies many key features of a good steward. To start with, it communicates honestly with the public and other stakeholders about its effects on people and the planet. And its warts-and-all candor about challenges in making effective cleaning products that are environmentally sound—in contrast to many glossy, annual reports that only tout a company's greenest side—captures the kind of transparency that is increasingly necessary.

Seventh Generation also takes care of communities and the environment. This includes philanthropic giving, work to limit the environmental damage of its operations and products, and efforts to educate the public on eco-friendly habits, such as washing clothes in cold water.

Beyond all this, Seventh Generation demonstrates another vital trait of good stewards—a degree of restraint. In particular, the company embraces the precautionary principle, which presumes a chemical may cause harm unless tested and shown otherwise. After all, DEP has not been shown to carry health risks like its chemical relatives. Still, the company is erring on the side of caution.

Those sorts of choices typically mean higher costs, at least in the short run. Additional testing and product development efforts shrink the bottom line. As such, demonstrating restraint can be difficult for the typical firm, with its quest for boundless growth and near-term profits for shareholders.

But taking the high road on potential chemical risks is not a hard choice at Seventh Generation. After all, the firm is acting as a steward for the current generation and six more down the line. And this isn't just a motto dreamed up by a clever marketing team, with only halfhearted support from executives. A mission to leave the world a better place has been central to the company for more than two decades.

"From the very beginning, we've pushed to have a real impact on our competitors, suppliers, communities, and government," the Seventh Generation Web site states.[7] "Products may be the vehicle, but far-reaching, genuine change is the mission."

Recast with a more encompassing purpose, worthiness with respect to communities and the environment comes more naturally to companies. This chapter spells out the features of good stewards.

Communities

Good stewards take care of the communities they touch. They abide by laws and regulations, care for employees, and pitch in to solve local and global problems. Ideally, companies harness their core capabilities to optimize their impact on communities. But in doing so, businesses should use discretion in the way they tout or tie strings to their philanthropic efforts. Good community stewards also show restraint when it comes to executive compensation, use of tax havens, and the presence of their brands.

WORKERS

We wrote about being a good employer in great detail in Chapter 7. But upstanding employee relations deserve some mention in the context of community stewardship as well. That's partly because people care that local employers do right by their workers. A few years ago, public-relations firm Fleishman-Hillard and the National Consumers League advocacy group asked Americans about their definition of corporate social responsibility. A commitment to employees was the top answer in 2006 and the second-ranking response in 2007, behind commitment to communities.[8]

And even within the category "commitment to communities," care as an employer matters, according to the 2007 study of over 2,000 U.S. adults. Asked about expectations of local companies' participation in or contribution to their communities, 11 percent of respondents focused on responsibilities as an employer—such as treating employees well and providing a livable wage. Employee-related concerns ranked second to the expectation that companies make nonfinancial contributions like volunteering time, mentioned by 29 percent of respondents. What's more, 76 percent of survey respondents said salary or wage increases should be placed above charitable contributions.[9]

Those findings aren't surprising in light of the importance of jobs to a community's overall happiness. In Chapter 2 we highlighted the public's growing focus on economic security. No one expects companies to guarantee employment to workers in any community. But over the past three decades, American firms have tended to ax jobs first and ask questions later. For example, 75 percent of U.S. companies made either broad or targeted workforce reductions between the beginning of the financial crisis and early 2010, according to a study from consulting firm Towers Watson. The U.S. figure compared with 67 percent in Europe, 66 percent in Latin America, 62 percent in Canada, and 45 percent in Asia-Pacific.[10] Some layoffs in recent years were made in particularly callous fashion, either right before the December 2008 holidays[11] or in a way that shifted blame for business troubles to workers themselves.[12]

Some companies, though, have shown greater care for local workers and therefore proven to be better stewards of their communities. During the recent downturn, some sought to cushion the blow of layoffs with generous severance benefits. Retailer Zappos.com, for example, laid off 124 employees in 2008 but gave the affected workers a farewell package that included six months of paid COBRA health coverage. And given the importance of good, stable jobs to communities—and a raft of research questioning the long-term payoff of layoffs[13]—some companies worked hard to avoid layoffs altogether in the recession.

Solving Problems—with Core Capabilities

Apart from taking care of workers, good stewards of communities work to improve society. For decades now, companies have given back in the form of donations to charitable groups that feed the hungry, care for the sick, and address other social ills. Some of these corporate gifts are remarkably generous.

Still, corporate giving alone is not what establishes companies as good community stewards. In the 2007 Fleishman-Hillard/National Consumers League study, when respondents were asked about their expectations for companies doing business in their own communities, three times as many favored nonfinancial contributions, such as community involvement and volunteerism, over financial contributions.[14] And, as mentioned in Chapter 1, a survey of global consumers in 2010 found that 64 percent believe it is no longer enough for corporations to give money; they must integrate good causes into their everyday business.[15]

Companies have gotten the message. It's common these days for businesses to organize volunteer brigades to clean beaches, fix up schools, and build homes for low-income people. But these sorts of generic acts of generosity, while good in themselves, aren't the best a company can do. When companies contribute in ways that tap their core strengths, they maximize their ability to solve the world's problems. Such acts also can signal genuine company commitment to a mission of serving many stakeholders—as firms take the time to apply their particular capabilities to tough dilemmas.

Increasingly, companies are doing just that.

One example of a company tapping its particular strengths is the way Procter & Gamble works to fight the problem of girls in the developing world missing several days of school each month while menstruating. The consumer products giant launched a program called "Protecting Futures," which works with partner organizations to provide puberty education, sanitary protection products, and sanitary facilities to help vulnerable girls stay in school. The program also supports research on the issue. Since 2006, Protecting Futures has worked with eight partners in 17 countries, reaching more than 80,000 girls in the developing world.[16]

This effort shows reciprocity in action. On the one hand, society gets top-notch help: Procter & Gamble has great capabilities in encouraging the use of female sanitary products in different cultural contexts. On the other hand, P&G benefits from the philanthropy. The Protecting Futures project gives it a chance to showcase its products as well as learn more about new markets and product categories.

A virtuous, sustainable circle is possible. Companies that act as good stewards by using their specialized talents are rewarded in the marketplace. That business success allows them to continue providing such stewardship, which in turn leads to more business success.

Authors Michael Porter and Mark Kramer call for a close link between corporate strategy and philanthropic initiatives. They say corporate social responsibility "can be much more than a cost, a constraint, or a charitable deed—it can be a source of opportunity, innovation, and competitive advantage."[17]

Restraint

It is important, though, to point out a risk in tying corporate social responsibility efforts to company business strategies. It's a risk related to restraint.

Companies can go too far when it comes to philanthropy connected to core competencies and corporate strategies. They can, in effect, seek to capitalize on catastrophe or misfortune to burnish their image or bolster their market share. It's possible to imagine that P&G is cynically using the issue of missed school days by girls in the developing world to create a new, potentially lucrative market.

Whether targeted corporate social responsibility efforts amount to thinly veiled attempts to boost the bottom line is a matter of both largesse and restraint. Do companies give a significant amount of their resources? And do they limit their attempts to enrich or glorify themselves?

This brings us to a second arena where moderation on the part of companies is merited: marketing. There comes a point when corporate presence is oppressive. When companies, in effect, overstay their welcome.

In her book *No Logo*, author Naomi Klein argues that companies are relentless in their efforts to force their images on people: "[T]his corporate obsession with brand identity is waging a war on public and individual space: on public institutions such as schools, on youthful identities, on the concept of nationality and on the possibilities for unmarketed space."[18]

Klein points out a key truth—that historically, and especially over the past several decades, companies have tended to lack moderation in their marketing. They have been, as she puts it, "brand bullies."[19]

For companies to be good stewards of communities, they must shift from bullying the public with their brands to knowing when to butt out. Yes, businesses ought to register their good deeds at least on their Web sites and annual reports so people can evaluate their corporate citizenship. But genuine stewards don't need their names on computer rooms or on big banners touting their sponsorship of cancer fund-raising races. Gifts given quietly speak loudly about true community stewardship.

Companies often are themselves quiet about two final areas where restraint is important: CEO pay and tax havens. Firms too often have rewarded executives with multimillion-dollar compensation packages that reward risky, short-term thinking and mock the notion of community stewardship.

The recession revealed some of these excesses starkly. One 2010 study found that CEOs of the 50 firms that had laid off the most workers since the onset of the economic crisis took home nearly $12 million on average in 2009, 42 percent more than the average pay for CEOs at S&P 500 firms as a whole.[20] Good stewards of communities will rein in egregious executive compensation. By doing so, they improve the chances of managing with a long-term view, free up resources that can be used to pay rank-and-file workers better, and can invest more in philanthropic activities.

In a similar way, worthy community stewards will avoid use of tax havens.

Unfortunately, tax havens are like a second home to many major U.S. firms. Using a conservative methodology, we calculate that at least 59 firms in the Fortune 100 have employed tax havens. Those tax-avoidance practices take a toll on government revenue—and therefore on the services available to communities. A 2009 report by the Congressional Research Service indicated corporate profit shifting to low-tax locales could cost U.S. taxpayers as much as $60 billion per year.[21]

Not all big companies shirk their U.S. tax duties through tax havens.

Disney, UPS, and Walmart are among the firms that avoid the practice, and thereby go beyond the letter of the law to do the right thing as community stewards. Increasingly, all companies will be expected to do the same.

Environment

Stewardship of the environment means taking care of the planet.

Good environmental stewardship starts with staying within the limits of relevant laws and regulations. It includes good-faith communication with stakeholders, such as documenting and disclosing a company's environmental impact. It means minimizing ecological harm. And good environmental stewards go further, taking steps to fix ecological problems. As with stewardship of communities, environmental stewardship also requires a measure of restraint.

ABIDING BY THE LAW

Environmental stewards rigorously abide by the law. Governments throughout the globe have established many rules designed to protect the earth's resources, and more environmental regulation is likely.

Companies, though, have been less-than-squeaky clean when it comes to complying with these laws. Even in the wake of notorious incidents like the *Exxon Valdez* oil spill that fouled hundreds of miles of Alaska's shoreline in 1989, firms continue to run afoul of environmental rules. This is especially true for companies in the energy sector, according to our research on government fines slapped on Fortune 100 companies. For example, ExxonMobil was penalized in 2008 for failing to comply with a 2005 U.S. Clean Air Act settlement agreement. The oil giant agreed to a pay a penalty of nearly $6.1 million in connection with the alleged violations.[22]

As of early 2011, it remained unclear what amount of fines would be leveled against BP and other firms responsible for the Deepwater Horizon explosion and oil spill in the Gulf of Mexico. But in December, 2010, the U.S. Government sued BP and other firms involved in the spill, seeking penalties under the Clean Water Act and asking the court to hold most of the defendants "liable without limitation" under the Oil Pollution Act. Authorities continued to probe the incident, considered one of the worst accidental oil spills in history at approximately 4.9 million barrels.[23] But news reports in the wake of the disaster indicated BP did not follow proper procedures as it tried to get a well ready that was behind schedule.[24] And the bipartisan commission that investigated the spill came to this damning conclusion in its January 2011 report:

> The immediate causes of the Macondo well blowout can be traced to a series of identifiable mistakes made by BP, Halliburton, and Transocean that reveal such systematic failures in risk management that they place in doubt the safety culture of the entire industry.[25]

Industry defenders say a spotless environmental record is all but impossible. They argue that pollution-prevention equipment and procedures can be costly, translating into a lower standard of living for consumers and society at large. But such excuses for treating environmental rule breaking as an acceptable cost of doing business will increasingly ring hollow. More and more, consumers, workers, and investors will reward environmental stewards, not scofflaws.

COMMUNICATION

The public also will reward the companies that communicate clearly about their ecological impact, while distancing themselves from firms that are less than transparent. Candid communication is important to environmental stewardship in part because abiding by the law often is not enough to protect the planet. Regulations can lag behind what's called for by scientific consensus or the general public.[26] The generation of greenhouse gas is one example. The science is abundantly clear that current levels of greenhouse gas emissions put the earth on a collision course with catastrophic climate change. But the 2009 talks in Copenhagen failed to result in a binding agreement for tough new limits on carbon emissions. And country-specific efforts to tackle the problem of global warming have gotten bogged down in domestic politics.[27]

As a result, citizen-consumers hoping to help solve environmental problems have to rely on marketplace pressures by patronizing green firms. To do that, the public needs companies to come clean about their ecological impacts.

Good stewards are doing so through various voluntary reporting efforts.

Among them is the Carbon Disclosure Project (CDP). Launched in 2000, the not-for-profit organization based in the United Kingdom collects and distributes information about the effects of companies on the earth's climate, as well as develops international carbon reporting standards. As of early 2011, roughly 3,000 organizations in some 60 countries measure and disclose their greenhouse gas emissions and climate-change strategies through the CDP, up from 235 in 2003.[28]

Lord Adair Turner, chairman of the United Kingdom's Financial Services Authority, has pointed to the power of the project in putting companies on a path of better environmental stewardship.

"The first step towards managing carbon emissions is to measure them because in business what gets measured gets managed," says Turner, whose organization regulates the financial services industry in the United Kingdom.[29]

The Dow Jones Sustainability Indexes, highlighted earlier in the book, also are fostering extensive reporting on environmental effects. Companies filling out the questionnaire for inclusion on one of the indexes are asked to estimate their total direct greenhouse gas emissions in terms of metric tons of CO_2 gas or its equivalent. They also are probed about their total energy consumption, total water use, and total waste generation, as well as their targets for these categories and the trends of their performance against the targets.[30] The number of companies globally that completed the Dow Jones questionnaire more than doubled between 1999 and 2009, from 304 to 656.

Still, many companies are falling short of good environmental communication by engaging in "greenwashing." That term has emerged in recent years to describe businesses that try to cloak less-than-good environmental stewardship with eco-marketing or branding. As mentioned in Chapter 1, a 2009 study by consulting firm TerraChoice Environmental Marketing found that 98 percent of consumer products were green-washed in some fashion, such as the use of irrelevant claims, undocumented statements, or false labels.[31]

Good environmental stewards not only steer clear of greenwashing but also admit challenges connected with making their operations greener.

Seventh Generation cofounder Jeffrey Hollender makes this point in *The Responsibility Revolution*, a book he cowrote recently with former *Fast Company* editor Bill Breen.

"Given that every organization is to some degree imperfect, it's vital that companies be transparent about their social and environmental shortcomings as well as their successes," Hollender and Breen write.[32]

MINIMIZING ENVIRONMENTAL HARM

Seventh Generation's quest to make products without 1,4-dioxane fits into another characteristic of a good environmental steward: limiting environmental damage.

Good stewards, that is, will not just talk the talk about going green. They will walk the walk, following the old hiking principle to have a minimal impact on nature. Initial steps include office recycling and use of energy-efficient appliances and equipment. More elaborate efforts range from weatherizing factories and other facilities to redesigning products and packaging for reduced waste and pollution to evaluating entire supply-chain and logistics networks to cut down on carbon emissions. At the far end of the scale are company strategies to make the entire lifecycle of products green, which includes planning for the eventual reuse of exhausted products.

Newsweek ranked computer maker Hewlett-Packard as the greenest of America's largest companies, saying it was the first major information technology company to report greenhouse gas emissions associated with its supply chain.[33] HP also has taken the idea of a sustainable product lifecycle farther than many firms. For example, it has placed environmental stewards on design teams to identify design changes that could reduce environmental impact throughout a product's lifecycle.[34] HP also lets consumers recycle a number of products, including its inkjet and laser printer cartridges as well as rechargeable batteries.[35] The program covers computer hardware made by both HP and other companies.[36]

HELPING THE PLANET

Good environmental stewardship is about more than minimizing the bad a company does to the earth. Given the range and severity of ecological troubles at hand—from perilous climate change to tainted drinking water to polluted oceans—good companies also will do the planet good. They will play active roles in solving major environmental problems, by means such as donations, direct involvement in conservation projects, and innovative green business initiatives.

An example of such a business initiative is the Sustainable Product Index project launched by Walmart in 2009. The effort aims to create a simple rating for consumers about the sustainability of products, giving them a window into the quality and history of the goods they buy. The retailer began with a survey of its suppliers on the topics of energy and climate, material efficiency, natural resources, and people and community.[37]

And as big as its own operations are, Walmart is thinking bigger about the index. It helped to create a consortium of universities that will work with suppliers, retailers, nongovernment organizations, and government to create a global database of information on the lifecycle of products from raw materials to disposal. Walmart provided initial funding for the Sustainability Index Consortium but invited all retailers and suppliers to contribute.

"Higher customer expectations are a permanent part of the future," Walmart CEO Mike Duke said when the index project was announced. "At Walmart, we're working to make sustainability sustainable, so that it's a priority in good times and in the tough times. An important part of that is developing the tools to help enable sustainable consumption."[38]

The Sustainable Product Index is going to be a mighty tool, predicts Harvard Business School professor Rosabeth Moss Kanter, who recently wrote a book about companies that use their power to improve society, knowing that their innovations will create profits as well as social benefits. Walmart's sustainability index effort qualifies the company as one of these "SuperCorps," she wrote in a 2009 blog item.

"Walmart has just changed the game with respect to environmental issues," Kanter wrote. "By rolling out an environmental labeling program disclosing to consumers the environmental costs of making products sold at Walmart, the $401 billion retail behemoth has transformed green standards from nice-to-have to must-have."[39]

Moderation

Environmental stewardship must be about both action and restraint. About expanding what is green and reining in greed.

Taking proper care of the environment means seeking to operate in harmony with the natural world. And that, in turn, requires an end to the endless hunger for growth that has long defined corporate success. A constant quest for more revenue and profits typically translates into environmental trouble—into things like the development of land for new offices or factories, the extraction of more natural resources and the selection of materials and methods that are cheap to companies and consumers but costly to the environment.

We are not saying stewardship of the planet requires a rejection of growth altogether on the part of companies and entire economies. But moderation increasingly is a must.

What does this mean in practical terms? It means killing products where a life-sustaining alternative can't be found at a reasonable price. And it entails substituting ecologically benign materials and processes for destructive ones, even if that means greater expenses and fewer profits. In 2009, for example, Seventh Generation eliminated 1,4-dioxane from its hand dishwashing liquid.[40]

Seventh Generation practices another key behavior related to stewardship and restraint: going to great lengths to make sure new products are not harmful. This approach was codified as the Precautionary Principle in a 1998 conference of scientists, government officials, environmental leaders, and others.

It is summed up as follows: "When an activity raises threats of harm to human health or the environment, precautionary measures should be taken even if some cause and effect relationships are not fully established scientifically."[41]

Seventh Generation put the precautionary principle into effect when it nixed its green apple–scented dish cleaner because of possible problems with the phthalate DEP.

Such a go-slow approach isn't the dominant philosophy behind much of the regulation governing the U.S. economy today. But more and more, it will be the only acceptable approach for companies. In a seller-take-care world, good environmental stewards will err on the side of caution.

Stewardship Takes Shape

Exercising restraint, working to leave less of a trace on the planet, and helping to solve social and environmental problems can involve higher costs, especially in the short run. But stewardship increasingly pays off. As noted earlier, Walmart's reputation has risen in recent years. Going green also has been good for HP. At the same time that HP's sustainability efforts reduce landfill waste, they also give the company a look at the guts of competitor machines, provide feedback on how customers use products, and improve the design process.

"Our environmental stewards help product designers see that if you make a product that is easier to take apart at its end of life, it's easier to put together in the first place," John Frey, HP manager of corporate environmental strategies told *IndustryWeek* magazine.[42]

Seventh Generation also shows the connection between good stewardship and business success. Its decentralized distribution plan promises not only to cut greenhouse gas emissions but trim transportation costs as well. And consider the company's quest to create dish soap without 1,4-dioxane. Changing the manufacturing methodology led Seventh Generation to increase the percentage of renewable materials in the soap by 27 percent, and the resulting product had 53 percent better performance in a technical study.[43]

Seventh Generation's sales jumped 51 percent in 2008 to nearly $140 million. Although the company's sales slipped 2.8 percent in 2009, sales climbed in early 2010, and Seventh Generation expected growth of 20 percent for the year.[44]

In general, stewardship is starting to shape the business world. As we discussed in Chapter 2, more and more business leaders are adopting an ethos of sustainability. Business schools are also making environmental concerns key to the curriculum in growing numbers of "green MBA" programs.[45] A related development is the emergence of social entrepreneurship, the idea that business principles can be harnessed in the service of solving a social or environmental problem. A host of organizations and foundations now support people with visions to improve society, such as McKinsey & Company alumnus Vikram Akula, who founded SKS Microfinance to give loans to poor women in India.[46]

What's more, some states are considering bills that would make it easier for corporations to formalize the values of stewardship in their governing documents.[47] Vermont, for example, passed a law in May 2010 that allows organizations to form "for-benefit corporations" that aim to create public benefits such as improving the environment, improving human health, and promoting the arts or sciences.[48] Earlier in the year, similar legislation became law in Maryland.[49]

Those legislative milestones are partly the work of a consulting firm, B Lab, which is behind a parallel effort in the private sector to redefine business success. B Lab certifies B Corporations, which are companies that pledge to incorporate the interests of employees, consumers, the community, and the environment into their governing documents.[50] As of early 2011, 371 companies had agreed to those principals. The companies represent 54 industries and annual revenue of $1.8 billion.[51]

Among the B Corporations, not surprisingly, is Seventh Generation. It has been among the leading companies calling for a new philosophy of business. It has sought to be worthy in all aspects.[52] And just as American Express found its efforts to improve customer service bolstered by good behavior as an employer and a steward, Seventh Generation's aim to be a worthy steward has been reinforced by its worthiness as an employer and seller.[53]

To be sure, Seventh Generation has hit rocky patches. In late 2010, for example, it weathered a leadership crisis. The company removed Jeffrey Hollender from its board of directors and fired him from his post as "chief inspired protagonist." The move to oust the longtime face of the firm took place about a year and a half after Hollender stepped down as CEO, naming PepsiCo veteran Chuck Maniscalco as his replacement as part of a plan to increase annual revenue to $1 billion.[54]

Maniscalco resigned in September 2010. But Seventh Generation's board persuaded him to stay on as a transitional CEO, and as of late 2010 he was considering applying for the permanent job again.[55]

Fast Company magazine said the shake-up raises the question of whether growth ever can be sustainable. "In order to expand further, Seventh Generation seems to think that it needs to dispose of the man who infused the company with the green business values that it champions. Whether Seventh Generation can retain those values after Hollender's departure remains unclear."[56]

Company officials, though, have a different view. They portray Hollender's departure as a sad incident but one more about the difficulties of a founder letting go of the firm he helped launch than any real change of course.[57] Dave Rapaport, Seventh Generation's Director of Corporate Consciousness, says the company has every intention of retaining its world-changing values.

"We certainly hope to," he says. "You shouldn't just take our word for it, you should watch us."[58]

Rapaport's comment indicates the company isn't backing away from the transparency that has been a bedrock of its sound stewardship. We will keep watching Seventh Generation. As will sustainability advocates and the company's employees, suppliers, and growing numbers of customers. If it continues to demonstrate good stewardship through thick and thin, we wouldn't be surprised if Seventh Generation endures for many more generations.

CHAPTER NINE SUMMARY

As both transparency and consumers' expectations continue to increase, so too will the concept of corporate stewardship. The emerging concepts go well past traditional concepts of corporate social responsibility.

Good stewards take care of the communities they touch, in the following ways:

- abiding by laws and regulations
- caring for employees
- using their core capabilities to help solve local and global problems
- exercising discretion in how they apply and communicate about their philanthropic efforts
- showing restraint when it comes to executive compensation, use of tax havens, and the presence of their brands

Stewardship of the environment means taking care of the planet, including the following:

- staying within the limits of relevant laws and regulations
- good-faith communication with stakeholders, such as documenting and disclosing a company's environmental impact
- minimizing ecological harm
- going further, taking steps to fix ecological problems
- incorporating a measure of restraint, such as adopting the "precautionary principle" in the development of new products

PART IV The Future

CHAPTER 10

The Worthiness Era

The forces we've sketched out in this book dovetail with other key, emerging business trends—all of which are converging to create a future in which companies increasingly must prove they are worthy of consumers' business, employees' best efforts, and investors' dollars. The growing importance of organizational agility and the rise of Asia as an economic power have worked against the arrival of the Worthiness Era. But in both cases, factors in play are now propelling company goodness to the fore.

The stakes are high that companies take goodness to heart in the coming years. Without better stewardship of communities and the environment, humanity will continue on the path toward climatic disaster. Without better employer practices, millions of people will suffer unnecessarily in dissatisfying, anxiety-producing jobs. And without increased worthiness as sellers, companies will continue to sell products and services that too often harm customers physically and financially. The degree to which the Worthiness Era takes hold also has implications for the future of capitalism and America's prosperity in the years ahead.

Partly because the stakes are so high, we see a role for governments to help shepherd in the Worthiness Era. Market forces are the main engines pushing companies in the direction of goodness. But governments also have a role to play in ensuring that worthiness rules the day through new laws on disclosures and better enforcement of regulations to deter bad behavior.

This chapter explores each of these themes to paint a fuller picture of the Worthiness Era, why it is important, and what public officials can do to help bring it about.

Worthiness Meets the Agile Organization and Emergent Asia

Among the most important trends shaping the business world are (1) the pressure organizations face to become more agile in their operations and (2) the emergence of China, India, and other Asian nations as economic powerhouses. In the past, both of these developments have corresponded with less-than-admirable behavior by businesses. But, as we shall see, worthiness is at work in both cases, making them complementary if not reinforcing factors with respect to the shift to greater company goodness.

THE AGILE ORGANIZATION

Business agility refers to an organization's decision-making speed. An agile organization is able to alter strategy, change operations, develop new products, and get them to market quickly. Agility has been a watchword for a decade or so as the pace of business has picked up amid more global competition and technological advances such as sophisticated supply-chain management tools.

So far, companies have sought to increase their agility largely by slimming down. They have outsourced aspects of their operations, such as information technology, human resources, and finance and accounting. They have aimed to concentrate on their core competencies and limit fixed costs.

Companies also have tried to bring the lean philosophy to their labor force. Besides eliminating employees through the outsourcing of business functions, companies have ramped up their use of contingent workers, including part-time employees, independent contractors, and agency temps. The number of paid employees at temporary help services firms in the United States climbed 27 percent from 2002 to 2007 to 3 million. By contrast, total nonfarm employment in the United States rose just 6 percent from December 2002 to December 2007 to 138 million.[1] In

2010, *Bloomberg Businessweek* estimated that 26 percent of Americans have nonstandard jobs, including part-time employment, independent contractors, and temps.[2]

The recession reinforced the business push to trim back. Not only did companies lay off millions of workers but also the bulk of U.S.-based firms said they expected a long-term decrease in staff size.[3]

Up to now, many corporate agility efforts have worked in opposition to worthiness. A focus on becoming leaner has lent itself to a short-term mindset and transactional, zero-sum relationships—to practices such as short-staffing stores to save costs at the expense of customer service. And the corporate obsession with shrinking has led to greater job instability for workers, which has contributed to record job dissatisfaction and sagging employee engagement in the United States.

But the agility story has a sunny side as well. It's becoming clear that true agility isn't defined simply by cutbacks—by seeking to be as unencumbered as possible. At some point, a preoccupation with paring back becomes organizational anorexia. Overly skinny firms are both weak and slow. For example, some of the companies that outsourced their HR operations several years ago, expecting they could wash their hands of personnel matters entirely, found themselves stuck in troubled contracts.[4] Companies and vendors underestimated the complexity of the tasks involved. Similarly, the practice of pitting manufacturing suppliers against each other has backfired for companies in the form of product or labor problems, as scandals at Mattel and Apple indicate.

What's more, layoffs often leave unproductive workforces in their wake, as remaining employees wrestle with survivors' guilt, worry about their own fate, and struggle to figure out how to juggle additional tasks. Management professor Wayne Cascio has documented the way pink slips frequently fail to pay off for companies. "Studies have tracked the performance of downsizing firms versus non-downsizing firms for as long as nine years after a downsizing event," Cascio wrote in a 2009 report. "The findings: *As a group, the downsizers never outperform the non-downsizers*"[5] (emphasis in the original).

The ability to move fast, companies are learning, involves both weight and strength. And strength has to do with beefing up rather than breaking down connections with workers, suppliers, and customers. To be sure, companies can grow fat and bureaucratic. Some streamlining of workers and processes may be needed. But quickness also has to do with reciprocity and trust. As consultant Stephen M.R. Covey has pointed out, lower trust taxes a firm through lower speed and higher cost.[6] And a growing field of research is highlighting the power of the *connected enterprise*—meaning companies with active, decentralized networks of communication and healthy relationships within their walls as well as with external parties such as suppliers and customers.[7]

Companies have started to move toward greater connectivity and stronger ties. HR outsourcing deals now focus more on creating partnerships with frequent interaction between company and service provider.[8] In general, businesses have moved toward selecting preferred vendors with whom they have deeper relationships. Those bonds, in turn, offer greater odds that final products will be safe and environmentally sound. And after years of trying to minimize customer service costs through skimpy staffing levels, outsourcing, or a focus on minimizing time on the phone, companies like Home Depot and American Express are investing in thicker ties with customers—which can lead not only to heightened loyalty but also better real-time feedback.

There also are signs agility can mesh with goodness as an employer. Internet retailer Zappos, for example, grew to top $1 billion in sales in less than a decade with a philosophy of company as a tight-knit community. While many companies have outsourced janitorial services, Zappos brought their janitors back in-house to stay true to this vision. By trusting employees to do the right thing, the Zappos team is able to make changes on the fly, whether that means a merchandise buyer jumping on a new shoe style or a customer service agent addressing a shopper's unique problem.

The fact that so many workers want job security these days, and that top performers in particular want it, all but forces companies to offer a degree of employment stability. Showing workers they won't be tossed overboard at the first sign of trouble and helping them to safeguard their employability through training and career development help will improve employee engagement. And workers who are engaged—and marshaled intelligently toward company aims—are likely to boost a company's speed of business by giving their best efforts.

Outsourcing is unlikely to go away as an agility strategy, but it isn't incompatible with worthiness. Closer ties between companies and their suppliers offer the promise of more enlightened treatment of workers. Some major companies, in fact, are starting to act more and more like the HR departments of their suppliers. Look at FedEx and its network of global service providers, which helps the delivery company in countries where it does not have on-the-ground presence. FedEx sends instructors around the world to train those suppliers in skills and leadership and also offers them training online.[9]

Consider Apple and its manufacturing suppliers. Scrutiny of working conditions in its supply chain has led Apple to get increasingly involved in the way those firms treat employees. It has issued detailed clarifying standards on topics such as dormitories, medical nondiscrimination, and juvenile worker protections—in one case specifying that employees under 18 cannot work at heights in excess of two meters. It launched a social-responsibility training program, through which more than 300,000 workers have received instruction on worker rights and local labor laws. And working with one supplier, Apple started offering workers computer-based training, including associate degree programs linked to three universities.[10]

Apple's suppliers up to now have had a very mixed record on labor issues. But some of the firms providing outsourcing services have proven to be among the most decent and inspiring employers in the world. Outsourcers such as HCL Technologies are keenly aware that the engagement of their workforce determines the level of quality they give to clients.[11]

Even if we move in the future to a radically decentralized economy of individual free agents and ad hoc teams, elements of worthiness will persist. The reputation of organizations will matter a great deal. Akin to the way eBay sellers must maintain a good track record if they hope to keep making deals, there will likely be mechanisms for rating the trustworthiness of companies—no matter how small. Companies that don't treat contractors fairly and generously, that don't pursue reciprocal relationships, will not attract the best talent. Nor will they inspire people to give their best.

RISE OF ASIA

India and China are becoming economic powers in the 21st century.

China's share of world economic output rose from 3.6 percent in 1990 to 11.4 percent in 2008 and is expected by the International Monetary Fund to jump to 16.9 percent by 2015. India, for its part, accounted for 2.8 percent of global economic output in 1990. That figure jumped to 4.7 percent in 2008 and is projected to climb to 6.1 percent in 2015.[12] Together, then, China and India's share of world economic output was just 6.4 percent in 1990 but is expected to soar to nearly a quarter of global production by 2015.

Much of Asia's economic activity over the past few decades has concentrated on manufacturing. And much of that factory work has been plagued by poor working conditions. Especially in countries with authoritarian governments like China and Vietnam, basic labor rights such as the freedom to form independent trade unions are lacking.[13] In addition, factories operating in Asia often have had few pollution controls amid weak environmental regulation regimes.

In many cases, multinational corporations have taken advantage of cheap labor, substandard worker protections, minimal product safety regulations, and limited environmental protections in Asia. The standard defense by such firms is that their presence in developing nations helps such countries move toward greater human rights and a higher standard of living. To be sure, a more capitalist, Western-welcoming Asia has lifted millions from dire poverty. But fundamental labor protections remain missing, and workers continue to suffer from harsh conditions, especially at third-party suppliers to Western brands. And too often, Asian operations have generated hazardous products at significant environmental cost.

In this sense, Asia's rise could be said to have been a net contributor to bad company behavior. There's the potential for much more unworthiness. Perhaps most alarming is the prospect that billions of consumers in China, India, and other parts of Asia will start generating as much greenhouse gas through cars and other products as Western consumers, catered to by companies more interested in short-term sales and profits than long-term prevention of climate catastrophe.

But the Asian equation is starting to change. The region's economic emergence is beginning to become more of a force for good. In the first place, industry codes of conduct are maturing and having more influence. Partly because activists are holding companies' feet to the fire, firms increasingly have to demonstrate that they and their supplier networks abide by labor and environmental standards.

There's also homegrown momentum for company goodness in Asia. A series of Chinese labor strikes in 2010 suggest lower-skilled Chinese employees are increasingly unwilling to accept unworthy wages or working conditions.[14] In addition, a new generation of managers and executives is coming of age in China and India with promising attitudes. Although China's rapid growth has led to a shortage of skilled managerial talent in some quarters, many young and middle-aged leaders in China are seeking to combine the best of Western and Eastern thinking.

Ed met some of these leaders in the course of a reporting trip to China a few years ago. Among them was Angel Yu, then vice president for human resources and administration at Adidas for mainland China, Hong Kong, and Taiwan. Yu represented the entrepreneurial spirit unleashed by Deng Xiaoping in the late 1970s. Early in the market reform period, Yu left a fairly stable teaching post to pursue her fortune in the free-trade zone set up in Shenzhen. A series of career advances led to her post at Adidas, where she had significant responsibility over the multinational clothing company's Asian operations. She also earned an office with commanding views from the 32nd floor of a Shanghai skyscraper.[15]

Ed asked Yu for her thoughts about how Western and Chinese principles can be combined in leaders. She boiled it down to a simple phrase: "Balance 'performance culture' and 'family-oriented culture.'"[16]

Taken seriously, that pairing would mean economic progress that expands opportunities and standards of living—the best of the West, as it were. But it would also draw upon the Eastern attention to harmony and personal relationships that ideally would mean leaving no one behind.

A better way to lead businesses also is brewing in India. Earlier in the book we highlighted HCL Technologies CEO Vineet Nayar, who emphasized employee empowerment and transparency from the top. He's not the only Indian executive working on worthier management styles. A 2010 article in the *Harvard Business Review* based on interviews with executives at 98 of the largest India-based companies concluded there is a "distinctive Indian model" of leadership centered on investing in employees.

"Far more than their Western counterparts, these leaders and their organizations take a long-term, internally focused view," the authors wrote. "They work to create a sense of social mission that is served when the business succeeds. They make aggressive investments in employee development, despite tight labor markets and widespread job-hopping. And they strive for a high level of employee engagement and openness."[17]

As leaders in China and India are moving in the direction of goodness, employees in Asia are seeking holistically worthy employers. A 2008 survey by the Nielsen Company found that more than in any other region in the world, people in the Asia/Pacific region ranked work/life balance as their biggest concern.[18]

"The bottom line for employees is that they are looking for something more than compensation," Aon Consulting said in a 2008 report about the Asian workforce. "Stimulating jobs and promotion opportunities top their lists, as well as enlightened leadership and an excellent work environment."[19]

Asian consumers, for their part, also are pushing companies toward greater worthiness. As mentioned earlier, 84 percent of consumers in China, India, Malaysia, and Singapore say they would accept a higher price for a green product, compared with 50 percent in the United States, Japan, France, and Germany.[20] The greater greenness may have something to do with the way global warming and rising seas pose a particular threat to Southeast Asia, with its heavy concentration of population near coastal areas.[21]

In addition, Asian governments are poised to be a force for company goodness. Although China and India have butted heads with developing nations about how to hammer out an accord for combating climate change, their insistence on an accord that fairly allocates the carbon space countries can take up in the future represents a long-term view.[22] Moreover, both the Indian and Chinese governments have been encouraging clean tech through tax policy and other measures.[23] China led the world in clean energy investments in 2009 for the first time, according to a study by the Pew Environment Group.[24]

And as mentioned earlier, China passed a law in 2008 strengthening worker rights. The country's leaders have stressed the need to blend economic growth with social harmony.

A focus on societal success, whether by top Chinese politicians or business people like Angel Yu and Vineet Nayar, undermines bad company behavior. As the tiger and dragon leap onto the world stage, it's unlikely they will fight the emergence of the Worthiness Era. Over time, they are more likely to serve as guardians of company goodness.

The Stakes Are High That Worthiness Wins

The stakes are high that goodness prevails among companies.

In the first place, better company stewardship of the environment is critical to avoiding climatic catastrophe. The long-term threats posed by global warming include millions more people facing coastal flooding each year; higher death rates from heat waves, floods, and droughts; and increasing risk of extinction for up to 30 percent of species.[25]

According to the Intergovernmental Panel on Climate Change, global greenhouse gas emissions due to human activities rose 70 percent between 1970 and 2004, with the largest growth coming from energy supply, transport, and industry.[26]

Companies alone cannot stave off global warming and its apocalyptic possibilities. But businesses clearly play a major role in shaping the environmental future. While governments and global policy bodies can get bogged down in climate negotiations—witness the limited results of the Copenhagen talks—companies can take swift steps. And though the actions of any one individual are small, company environmental efforts can be big—as we are seeing with Walmart's green campaign.

Still, without a shift to sincere stewardship, we can expect more greenwashing instead of green-worthy behavior. More Gulf oil spills, energy-hungry products, and carbon-intensive supply chains. With poor stewardship, in other words, businesses will push our planet over the ecological edge. Companies acting as good stewards, on the other hand, could lead us on the path of true sustainability.

Besides warding off environmental ruin, company worthiness is vital to the well-being of billions of workers. At a basic level, fundamental rights such as freedom from forced labor, safe workplaces, and the ability to bargain collectively will be honored to a much greater extent when good employers are the norm. Such rights remain a real concern for many of the world's 3 billion workers.[27] The International Labour Organization estimates that about 2.3 million people die from work-related accidents and diseases each year, including close to 360,000 fatal accidents.[28]

On one end of the spectrum, some workers merely survive their jobs, but at the other end are workers thriving because of their jobs. Paychecks and health benefits can allow workers to take care of themselves and their families. Challenging projects and career progress can lead to great personal satisfaction. Inspiring company missions and accomplishments can help make life meaningful.

Scholars James O'Toole and Edward Lawler III define *good work* as employment that satisfies three major human needs: "(1) the need for the basic economic resources and security essential to lead good lives; (2) the need to do meaningful work and the opportunity to grow and develop as a person; and (3) the need for supportive social relationships."[29]

But in their comprehensive study of the American workplace published in 2006, *The New American Workplace*, Lawler and O'Toole found too little good work in the country. "Flexible working hours, company-sponsored tuition reimbursement, benefits for part-timers, employee participation in decision making and profit sharing, the redesigning of jobs to make them challenging, and the providing of on-the-job developmental opportunities all seem to have positive effects on worker productivity and job satisfaction but are not widely used," O'Toole and Lawler wrote.[30]

Worthiness also matters when it comes to consumers. Despite the "quality is job one" mantra of the past few decades, many companies have fallen short of the good seller standard. Massive recalls of toys and other products shook consumer confidence in 2007. And safety problems weren't isolated to that year.[31]

Much of the blame for product safety issues relates to poor design. Another factor is the ever-more global supply chain, with links in countries with less regulation than in the United States.[32] Unless firms hew to high standards of quality and safety, products emerging from their global operations risk harming consumers the world over.

Health hazards facing consumers extend to the food supply. Each year, about 76 million people contract a food-borne illness in the United States, with about 325,000 requiring hospitalization and some 5,000 dying.[33] Of course, not all of those cases can be pinned on bad company behavior. But businesses share some of the blame, as evidenced by recent outbreaks of salmonella in peanut butter and E. coli in spinach.

Unscrupulous selling practices hurt consumers not only in the gut but the pocketbook as well. The U.S. housing boom, for instance, was rife with ethically dubious behavior by businesses, such as steering people into unfavorable mortgages and betting against clients through mortgage-backed securities. And collectively, the shortsighted actions of financial services firms helped trigger a recession that has left much of the world worse off.

A broad shift of companies to become good sellers will result in safer products, healthier finances, and greater peace of mind for people throughout the globe.

In fact, without greater goodness, companies may find the global populace increasingly opposed to capitalism itself. Yes, the end of the Cold War seemed to signal capitalism's victory over communism. But amid recurring mistreatment of workers, communities, consumers, and investors by corporations, the model of private-sector companies pursuing their interests in largely unfettered markets is under fire.

The Great Recession especially seemed to prompt suspicion about laissez-faire economics. As noted in Chapters 2 and 4, recent global polls have shown widespread dissatisfaction with capitalism and support for more government regulation.[34]

It's true that many people also are wary of excessive government involvement in the economy. But doubts about the wisdom of business-friendly market systems run deep these days—as deep as the disastrous oil leak in the Gulf of Mexico. Concerns about capitalism were stoked by evidence that the oil industry cut corners on disaster prevention, relying for instance on "failsafe" well devices with a failure rate of an astounding 45 percent.[35]

New York Times columnist David Brooks took note of simmering anti-market sentiments in a mid-2010 essay. Brooks said that even as BP and the Obama administration sparred over the Gulf spill, they were both on the same side of a larger, global struggle over the best political-social-economic system:

> On the one side are those who believe in democratic capitalism—
> ranging from the United States to Denmark to Japan. People in this
> camp generally believe that businesses are there to create wealth
> and raise living standards while governments are there to regulate
> when necessary and enforce a level playing field. . . . On the other
> side are those that reject democratic capitalism, believing it leads to
> chaos, bubbles, exploitations and crashes. Instead, they embrace state
> capitalism. People in this camp run Russia, China, Saudi Arabia,
> Iran, Venezuela and many other countries.[36]

Although there are worthy elements in some of those societies, by and large they tend to be repressive. Western observers tend to believe that cronyism eventually will undermine state capitalism. But Brooks notes that "state capitalism may be the only viable system in low-trust societies, in places where decentralized power devolves into gangsterism."

Company worthiness, therefore, plays a key role in this global rivalry over economic philosophies. Bad company behavior erodes trust and public willingness to embrace a version of democratic market capitalism. Good company actions, on the other hand, encourage people to reject an authoritarian approach to the economy—an approach that threatens the very existence of companies as we know them.

The success of the Worthiness Era has special significance for the United States. The rise of good companies is a key to preserving the country's major role in the world economy, the U.S. standard of living, and the American Dream itself.

As we have outlined earlier in the book, the high-paying, knowledge-based, creative jobs that have evolved in the developed world all but require companies to be good employers. For the next iPad to be designed here, the next anti-cancer drug to be discovered here, the next clean-energy breakthrough to be developed here, U.S. companies will have to be among the best at caring for, coordinating, and encouraging workers.

Otherwise those tasks will flow to other developed nations or to emerging economies like India and China. U.S. wages and incomes will continue to stagnate for the bulk of workers. And the baseline bargain at the heart of the American experiment—that working hard will pay off in the form of a comfortable life and a hopeful future for your children—will disintegrate.

Of course, it is misleading to talk of "U.S. companies" given the global nature of so many firms and their lack of national loyalties. And the fate of the U.S. economy also is in the hands of political leaders, education officials, and workers themselves.

Still, the relative worthiness of U.S.-based companies and the U.S. operations of foreign companies will go a long way toward determining whether America prospers in the years ahead.

GOVERNMENT POLICY AND THE WORTHINESS ERA

As we've noted, market forces—consumer, employee, and investor choices—are the primary reasons the Worthiness Era is at hand. But with so much at stake, we see a role for governments to help give birth to this new economic chapter.

One way governments can help usher in the Worthiness Era is by enforcing regulations more effectively. Skimpy enforcement in areas such as environmental protection, wage and hour laws, and consumer product safety amounts to rewarding scofflaws. Good companies that scrupulously play by the rules typically have higher costs than companies that cut corners on pollution safeguards, overtime pay, and the like. Only when government officials hold rule breakers accountable in a tough, fair fashion will worthier firms stand out as they should.

Earlier in the book, we detailed a pendulum swing back to more regulation on the part of governments. That momentum can't come too soon in some areas. BP's Gulf of Mexico oil spill, for example, revealed a fox-guarding-the-henhouse mindset at the U.S. agency charged with regulating the offshore oil drilling industry—the Minerals Management Service. That agency, renamed the Bureau of Ocean Energy Management, Regulation, and Enforcement in the wake of the BP disaster, apparently failed to enforce a rule that required oil companies to submit proof that a key piece of their disaster-prevention equipment would work.[37] The piece in question, the blind shear ram on the blowout preventer, failed in the BP spill.

The National Commission assigned to study the Gulf spill agreed that oversight of offshore drilling must be upgraded: "Fundamental reform will be needed in both the structure of those in charge of regulatory oversight and their internal decision-making process to ensure their political autonomy, technical expertise, and their full consideration of environmental protection concerns."[38]

Disclosure is the second major way government can help bring about the Worthiness Era. The evolution of the Internet and government Web sites has made it possible for regular citizens to gather a large amount of information about companies, especially public companies. But it still remains difficult for people to piece together a complete portrait of a company's relative worthiness. Consider the challenge of assessing a firm's adherence to laws and regulations. Dozens of U.S. federal agencies exist that may have dinged a company for violating particular rules, to say nothing of the hundreds of state and local government groups that monitor business behavior.

Our own quest to create a measure approximating how well the Fortune 100 played by the rules proved to be very time consuming because no central clearinghouse for the information exists in the United States. We ended up limiting our research to fines and penalties levied by federal agencies. And, as mentioned earlier, we were surprised by how often some companies run afoul of the authorities. For some firms, it seems, breaking the rules—even when it involves paying a fine or settlement—is simply a cost of doing business.

We intend to update our research annually on major federal penalties for the Fortune 100. But that will remain a very constricted data set, given the millions of companies operating in the United States. To help the public distinguish between law-abiding firms and those with less respect for the rules, governments ought to establish a central database of information about company infractions. In the United States, a logical place for it would be in the Federal Trade Commission, with its mission of "Protecting America's Consumers."

Better disclosure shouldn't just be about revealing companies' rap sheets. We believe there is a key piece of doing-good data at companies that governments ought to expose: the amount of money spent developing employees. Companies tend to be reluctant to share this information publicly, but this data is important for a number of reasons. For one thing, these investments tend to be a win for companies and investors. As mentioned earlier, research by Laurie and Dan has shown that heavy investment in employee development corresponds with a stock outperforming peers in the market. In this regard, there's a strong case to be made that the U.S. Securities and Exchange Commission and other stock-regulating agencies should require this key piece of information to be disclosed to investors on an annual basis.

What's more, money spent on improving employee knowledge and skills signals a company cares about the career development and employment security of employees. It also shows the firm making contributions to improve a community's capacities.

Some may argue that spending on employee development is an imperfect measure. After all, some training programs and approaches may be more effective than others.[39] But we believe that using the measure of spending on training and development per employee is a good start—it has repeatedly proved to be a predictor of subsequent stock prices.

Still others will take issue with adding yet another regulatory burden on companies. Yes, regulation can overreach and bury businesses in red tape. But if anything, governments in the United States and other parts of the world have erred in the other extreme. They have tolerated companies behaving badly on a regular basis.

Since the 1990s, a number of activists have called for a radical response to egregious business behavior: revoking corporate charters. This so-called death penalty for corporations involves state officials declaring that companies have violated the legal instrument that allows them to operate. Charters have been revoked for smaller firms in the last two decades for reasons such as failure to pay taxes.[40] And in the late 1990s, a group of organizations and individuals petitioned California's attorney general to revoke the charter of oil company Unocal.[41]

The effort did not succeed. And the strategy of revoking charters for major firms has its challenges. Among these is a business-friendly climate in Delaware, where a large number of big companies are incorporated. Still, the notion of revoking charters is back in public discussion. That's thanks partly to the success of the movie *The Corporation*, a documentary that highlighted the Unocal case and was sharply critical of companies.[42]

The main policy implications we've outlined above involve a relatively light government touch: enforcing laws on the books and shining more light on good and bad behavior. But we're not averse to government officials deciding to take a stronger stand for worthiness by revoking corporate charters. We believe consumers, investors, and employees in the years ahead will help good companies flourish, all but driving bad companies out of business. But if firms refuse to play by the rules, they don't deserve to stay in the game.

CHAPTER TEN SUMMARY

How the Worthiness Era plays out in the future will be determined in no small part by the continued push for business agility as well as developments in emerging Asian economies. The stakes are high that worthiness wins; while market forces are the main engines pushing companies in the direction of goodness, governments also have a role to play in ensuring that worthiness rules the day.

Worthiness Meets the Agile Organization and Emergent Asia

- The need for agility—in large part driven by increased global competition—has caused U.S.-based firms to focus on core competencies, limit fixed costs, rely on outsourcing, and use layoffs liberally.

- It is becoming clear, however, that true agility isn't defined simply by cutbacks—by seeking to be as unencumbered as possible. At some point, a preoccupation with paring back becomes organizational anorexia. Overly skinny firms are both weak and slow.

- The ability to move fast involves both weight and strength. Strength has to do with beefing up rather than breaking down connections with workers, suppliers, and customers. It requires reciprocity and trust.

- In emergent Asia, product safety and environmental protections are still weak, and workers continue to suffer from harsh conditions, including at third-party suppliers to Western brands.

- In this sense, Asia's rise could be said to have been a net contributor to bad company behavior.

- But the Asian equation is starting to change:
  1. Activists are holding companies' feet to the fire.
  2. Lower-skilled Chinese workers are less willing to accept unworthy wages or working conditions, and a new, more enlightened generation of managers and executives is coming of age in China and India.
  3. Asian governments are beginning to take important steps in the right direction.
  4. Asian consumers are also pushing companies toward greater worthiness.

The Stakes Are High That Worthiness Wins

- Better company stewardship of the environment is critical to avoiding climatic catastrophe.

- Company worthiness is vital to the well-being of billions of workers. Beyond health and safety initiatives that help workers survive their jobs, companies can help employees thrive in their lives.

- Worthiness also matters to consumers, and without more of it, companies may find the global populace increasingly opposed to capitalism itself.

- The relative worthiness of U.S.-based companies and the U.S. operations of foreign companies will go a long way toward determining whether America prospers in the years ahead.

Government Policy and the Worthiness Era

- Market forces—consumer, employee, and investor choices—are the primary reasons the Worthiness Era is at hand.

- With so much at stake, there is a role for governments to help give birth to this new economic chapter. The main policy implications involve a relatively light government touch:

  1. Enforcing regulations more effectively is required; only when government officials hold rule breakers accountable in a tough, fair fashion will worthier firms stand out as they should.

  2. Additional corporate disclosures mandated by the government will help the public distinguish between good and bad behavior. For example, governments ought to establish central databases about

     a. company infractions to help the public identify law-abiding firms and those with less respect for the rules

     b. the amount firms invest in learning for employees, information that is crucial to stockholders, employees, and communities

If companies refuse to play by the rules, they don't deserve to stay in the game. Government officials should take a strong stand for worthiness in cases of consistent and egregious failure to abide by the law, by revoking corporate charters.

CHAPTER 11

A Hope*fully* Idealistic Vision

We hope we've made our case that the Worthiness Era is at hand. That companies, more and more, will have to prove to be good employers, sellers, and stewards to succeed. And that companies that don't do this risk being left behind, out in the cold by a public that is increasingly ethical in its economic choices.

But we realize you may remain skeptical. You may be saying: "This sunny vision is too good to be true. Companies may be talking up sustainability, being an employer of choice, and taking care of customers, but they haven't truly changed their stripes. They're still profit-maximizing organizations obsessed with shareholders' short-term gains. This Worthiness Era business is hopelessly idealistic."

Conversely, the more conservative of you may be saying, "This vision is unrealistic. Companies may try to tap green consumer trends and fire up workers. But they can't put excess attention on employees, communities, and the environment. Profitability will suffer, and their ultimate stakeholders—shareholders—may lose everything. This Worthiness Era business is hopelessly idealistic."

It is idealistic to think of companies taking the lead on global warming, consumer safety, and being a good employer. But the Worthiness Era isn't hopelessly idealistic. It is hope*fully* idealistic.

That is, the idealism here is realistic, making this vision full of hope. The pressures and trends we have described are tangible. And pursuing worthiness these days is practical for firms. Take stewardship of the environment. Yes, greenwashing exists and will likely persist for some time.

But taken as a whole, the evidence indicates the *green* of the crop, as it were, will rise to the top. Companies, for instance, won't get their products onto Walmart's shelves unless they disclose their ecological impact as never before. More and more investor dollars are seeking sustainable companies, making the cost of capital partly a function of planetary protection.

And firms are being forced to focus on climate change as never before. The U.S. Securities and Exchange Commission issued guidance in early 2010 on how a company may have to disclose impacts of climate change and related legislation on its business.[1]

It's helpful to put the discussion of stewardship today in historical context to see how much progress has been made. American business executives as a rule didn't even talk directly with environmental advocates in the 1960s and 1970s. The "Council on Sustainable Development" created by former President Bill Clinton in the 1990s was one of the first occasions for that direct dialogue. Now companies have ongoing conversations with environmental groups and researchers.[2]

David Buzzelli, a former executive with Dow Chemical who cochaired Clinton's Council on Sustainable Development, is hopeful about the future for two other reasons. First, he sees promise in the way business schools increasingly train MBAs to include sustainability and social responsibility in their conception of business goals. Second, he notices greater consumer focus on the environmental impact of their decisions. In a capitalist economy, he says, that is the key to real change. "People are voting with their pocketbooks," Buzzelli says. "That's the most important driving force."[3]

Scott Scherr, CEO of HR software provider Ultimate Software, sees a similar sea change under way when it comes to attitudes about employees. Most companies may be far from the kind of commitment to workers Scherr has shown at Ultimate, with its 20-year legacy of no layoffs. But Scherr detects greater concern about treating talent well. More and more of the HR leaders he talks with about people-management software report directly to the CEO. "There's absolutely something going on," Scherr says.[4]

And, as mentioned in Chapter 8, a similar story is unfolding with respect to customers. Better seller behavior is on the rise, as seen by improvement in the American Customer Satisfaction Index since 1997.[5] Despite a dip in the second half of 2010, customer satisfaction levels from the fourth quarter of 2008 to the end of 2010 were generally higher than in 2007 and surpassed scores from 1997 to 2006.

The Great Recession could have crushed the momentum toward better corporate behavior. Consumers, workers, and investors could have concentrated strictly on selfish needs like low prices and high returns. But they didn't. People continued to seek out good companies. It's worth repeating findings from Edelman's 2009 study of 6,000 consumers globally. Fully 61 percent bought a brand that supports a good cause even if it wasn't the cheapest brand, and 64 percent said they would recommend a brand that supports a good cause, up from 52 percent only a year before.[6]

This new economics of purposeful profit is unlikely to dissipate with a recovery. It will be easier, rather than harder, for people to buy, take jobs, and make investments based on their principles. Indeed, in 2010, 70 percent of global consumers said that a company with fair prices that gives back is more likely to get their business than a company that offers deep discounts and doesn't give back.[7]

And other forces supporting the worthiness era are likely to strengthen. The march toward more technology-enabled transparency continues. Witness the successful demands that BP provide a live video feed of its oil spill at the bottom of the Gulf of Mexico. It is hard to imagine that a generation ago a major corporation could have been pressured into exposing a catastrophic blunder in real time, with the unflattering images broadcast nearly nonstop on television.

And the participatory culture of disclosure is unlikely to ebb anytime soon. If anything, it seems to be expanding into the massive Chinese working class. Consider the way Chinese workers at a Honda plant used cell phone text messages and the Internet to organize strikes for higher wages in mid-2010. The workers in Zhongshan uploaded video of security guards roughing up employees and urged coworkers to resist factory bosses.[8]

It turns out those workers were inspired in part from an earlier protest in another Honda factory in Foshan, China, where workers used Internet forums to organize.[9]

The Honda strikes are part of broader shift in China, where younger workers are standing together and standing up for themselves in ways older Chinese workers didn't. Listen to Lan Yimin, a 22-year-old migrant worker in the Pearl River Delta. "The young generation has a wider social circle," she told the *China Post*. "We talk more about factory conditions and we know more about our legal rights."[10]

This is the world that is emerging. One that is fundamentally a more connected one. Where people are, in effect, keeping each other company like never before.

Bad companies won't be invited into the new world taking shape. They will wither. Good companies, though, will find themselves welcome. And they will flourish.

APPENDIX

Good Company Index: Scoring and Sources

In calculating the Good Company Index Scores for the companies represented in this book, we used data from a variety of sources, which are listed at the end. (The most up-to-date information on the Good Company Index can be found at http://www.goodcompanyindex.com.)

In some categories, companies were ranked from high to low into *octiles*, or eighths, which were used to assign category scores that make up the Good Company Index ratings. For example, a company that falls in the top 12.5 percent (the equivalent of the top one-eighth of the overall distribution) would be in the first, or top, octile. A company that falls between 75 percent and 87.5 percent would be in the second octile, and so on.

Overall Good Company Grades and Corresponding Numerical Scores

A +	=	7 or higher	C+	=	1
A	=	6	C	=	0
A−	=	5	C−	=	−1
B+	=	4	D+	=	−2
B	=	3	D	=	−3
B−	=	2	F	=	−4 or lower

Note: data was not available for some categories for some companies; those cases were treated as zeroes for scoring purposes.

GOOD EMPLOYER

In order to calculate a score for a given company, we begin by measuring how good an employer it is. Using companies that have at least 25 employee reviews as of April 2010, we get a starting number based on the octile into which a company falls in Glassdoor.com's overall ratings, relative to other Fortune 100 companies.

Octile	# of points assigned
1st	2
2nd	1
3rd	0
4th	0
5th	0
6th	0
7th	−1
8th	−2

Take the number assigned from table at left → ___

If company is included on *Fortune*'s 100 Best Companies to Work For list, +1   + ___

GOOD EMPLOYER score (maximum +2 total) = ___

GOOD SELLER

The GOOD SELLER score is calculated based on the octile into which a company falls (relative to the entire wRatings company database) in a custom rating calculated by wRatings using customer evaluations of *quality*, *fair price*, and *trust*.

Octile	# of points assigned
1st	2
2nd	1
3rd	0
4th	0
5th	0
6th	0
7th	−1
8th	−2

Take the GOOD EMPLOYER score   → ___

Take the number assigned from table at left. This is the GOOD SELLER score   ± ___

Combined scores of GOOD EMPLOYER and GOOD SELLER   = ___

GOOD STEWARD

To calculate the GOOD STEWARD score, we used six different measures in four categories.

Environment

Octile	# of points assigned
1st	1
2nd	1
3rd	0
4th	0
5th	0
6th	0
7th	−1
8th	−1

Take the combined scores of GOOD EMPLOYER and GOOD SELLER   → ___

Add/subtract points from Green Rankings table at left (as rated by *Newsweek*)   ± ___

If company is included in Dow Jones Sustainability Index, +1   + ___

= ___

Penalties/Fines

If company paid fines between $1 million and $100 million, −1   − ___

If company paid fines of more than $100 million, −2   − ___

= ___

Restraint

CEO COMPENSATION

If its executive compensation is among the 5 highest on either the *New York Times* report or AFL-CIO database, −1   − ___

= ___

TAX HAVENS

If company had subsidiaries in any country with all 3 "tax haven/financial privacy jurisdiction" criteria listed in the GAO's report, −1   − ___

= ___

Contribution

If company demonstrates the use of a core capability to contribute to society/community in some way, +1   + ___

If company has a systematic process (as opposed to a one-time project) for using its core capability to make a contribution to society/community in some way, +1   + ___

Overall good company score   = ___

Sources

GOOD EMPLOYER

Compiled by authors, April 2010, from www.glassdoor.com and *Fortune*'s 2010 list of
100 Best Companies to Work For

GOOD SELLER

Custom rating (2008–2009 data) provided to authors by wRatings (www.wratings.com)

GOOD STEWARD

Environment   www.sustainability-index.com, as of April 2010; and http://green
rankings2009.newsweek.com

Penalties and Fines   Compiled by authors, 2010, through systematic review of 2005
to 2009 penalties and fines listed on U.S. Government agency Web resources plus
review of major European Union fines/penalties during the same period.

Restraint: CEO Compensation   *New York Times* report on executive compensation,
April 2010, http://projects.nytimes.com/executive_compensation and AFL-CIO
executive compensation database, April 2010, http://www.aflcio.org/corporate
watch/paywatch/ceou/database.cfm (Different methodologies used; each source
had multiple missing data points.)

Restraint: Tax Havens   U.S. Government Accountability Office, *International
Taxation: Large U.S. Corporations and Federal Contractors with Subsidiaries Listed
as Tax Havens or Financial Privacy Jurisdictions*, December 2008, http://www.gao
.gov/new.items/d09157.pdf

Contribution   Compiled by authors, 2010, based on (a) direct requests to companies
for information on their activities , and (b) systematic review of available social
responsibility (or similar) sections of their Web sites for relevant information

SELECTED WORKS FOR FURTHER READING

Bassi, Laurie, and Daniel McMurrer. "Does Employee Engagement Really Drive Business Results?" *Talent Management* (March 2010).

———. "Maximizing Your Return on People." *Harvard Business Review* 85, no. 3 (2007).

Bassi, Laurie, Rob Carpenter, and Dan McMurrer. *HR Analytics Handbook: Report of the State of Knowledge.* Amsterdam: Reed Business, 2010.

Bogle, John J. *The Battle for the Soul of Capitalism.* New Haven: Yale University Press, 2005.

Bok, Derek. *The Politics of Happiness: What Government Can Learn from the New Research on Well-Being.* Princeton, N.J.: Princeton University Press, 2010.

Boudreau, John, and Peter Ramstad. *Beyond HR: The New Science of Human Capital.* Boston: Harvard Business Press, 2007.

Bragdon, Joseph J., Jagdish Bhagwati, and Alan S. Blinder. *Offshoring of American Jobs: What Response from U.S. Economic Policy?* Cambridge: MIT Press, 2009.

Callan, Scott J., and Janet M. Thomas. "Corporate Financial Performance and Corporate Social Performance: An Update and Reinvestigation." *Corporate Social Responsibility and Environmental Management* 16, no. 2 (2009): 61–78.

Cappelli, Peter, Harbir Singh, Jitendra V. Singh, and Michael Useem. "Leadership Lessons from India." *Harvard Business Review* (2010).

Cascio, Wayne. *Responsible Restructuring: Creative and Profitable*

Alternatives to Layoffs. San Francisco: Berrett-Koehler Publishers, 2002.

Cascio, Wayne, and John Boudreau. *Investing in People: Financial Impact of Human Resource Initiatives.* Upper Saddle River, N.J.: FT Press, 2008.

CedarCrestone. *CedarCrestone 2009–2010 HR Systems Survey: HR Technologies, Deployment Approaches, Value and Metrics.* Alpharetta: CedarCrestone, 2009.

Collins, Jim. *Good to Great: Why Some Companies Make the Leap . . . and Others Don't.* New York: HarperCollins Publishers, 2001.

———. *How the Mighty Fall: And Why Some Companies Never Give In.* New York: HarperCollins Publishers, 2009.

Davenport, Thomas, and Jeanne G. Harris. *Competing on Analytics.* Boston: Harvard Business School Press, 2007.

Davenport, Thomas, Jeanne Harris, and Jeremy Shapiro. "Competing on Talent Analytics." *Harvard Business Review* (2010): 2–6.

Davenport, Thomas, Robert Morison, and Jeanne Harris. *Analytics at Work: Smarter Decisions, Better Results.* Boston: Harvard Business Press, 2010.

de Geus, Arie. *The Living Company.* Boston: Harvard Business School Press, 1997.

Falletta, Salvatore. "HR Intelligence: Advancing People Research and Analytics." *IHRIM Journal* 12, no. 3 (2008): 21–31.

Frauenheim, Ed. "Commitment Issues." *Workforce Management* (November 2009).

———. "Making the Call for Themselves." *Workforce Management* (August 2010).

———. "The Too-Fast Track." *Workforce Management* (March 2007).

Friedman, Thomas L. *The Worlds Is Flat: A Brief History of the Twenty-first Century.* New York: Farrar, Straus and Giroux, 2005.

Gibbons, John, and Christopher Woock. "Evidence-Based Human Resources: A Primer and Summary of Current Literature." *The Conference Board.* Ref# E-0015-07-RR (2007).

Hollender, Jeffrey, and Bill Breen. *The Responsibility Revolution: How the Next Generation of Businesses Will Win.* San Francisco: Jossey-Bass, 2010.

Kanter, Rosabeth M. *Supercorp: How Vanguard Companies Create Innovation, Profits, Growth, and Social Good.* New York: The Crown Publishing Group, 2009.

Logan, Dave, John King, and Halee Fischer-Wright. *Tribal Leadership: Leveraging Natural Groups to Build a Thriving Organization.* New York: Harper Business, 2008.

Miller, Danny, and Isabelle Le Breton-Miller. *Managing for the Long Run: Lessons in Competitive Advantage from Great Family Businesses.* Boston: Harvard Business Press, 2005.

Nayar, Vineet. *Employees First, Customers Second.* Boston: Harvard Business Press, 2010.

O'Toole, James, and Edward Lawler III. *The New American Workplace.* New York: Palgrave Macmillan, 2006.

Pew Research Center. *Millennials: A Portrait of Generation Next. Confident. Connected. Open to Change.* Washington, D.C.: Pew Research Center, 2010.

Pfeffer, Jeffrey, and Robert Sutton. *Hard Facts, Dangerous Half-Truths and Total Nonsense: Profiting from Evidence-Based Management.* Boston: Harvard Business Press, 2006.

Pink, Daniel H. *Drive: The Surprising Truth about What Motivates Us.* New York: Riverhead Books, 2009.

Porter, Michael E., and Mark R. Kramer. "Strategy and Society: The Link Between Competitive Advantage and Corporate Social Responsibility." *Harvard Business Review* (2006).

Posner, Richard A. *A Failure of Capitalism: The Crisis of '08 and the Descent into Depression.* Boston: Harvard University Press, 2009.

Senge, Peter. *The Necessary Revolution: How Individuals and Organizations Are Working Together to Create a Sustainable World.* New York: Doubleday, 2008.

Sisodia, Taj, Jag Sheth, and David B. Wolfe. *Firms of Endearment: How World-Class Companies Profit from Passion and Purpose.* Upper Saddle River, N.J.: Pearson Prentice Hall, 2007.

Uchitelle, Louis. *The Disposable American: Layoffs and Their Consequences*. New York: Knopf, 2006.

United Nations Global Compact and Accenture. *A New Era of Sustainability: UN Global Compact-Accenture CEO Study 2010*. Washington, D.C.: United Nations, 2010.

Watson Wyatt Worldwide and WorldatWork. *2009/2010 U.S. Strategic Rewards Report*. Watson Wyatt Worldwide, 2010.

ACKNOWLEDGMENTS

This book has been many years in the making. In the long and winding journey to its completion, we have benefited from many acts of kindness, generosity, and goodwill from people who believed in the book's message (even before we were able to articulate it with any coherence).

We are indebted to the many writers, thinkers, and doers around the globe who share our vision that the world *can and will* be made a better place through the decisions and choices that are made every day in work and commerce. These leaders—and they exist at every level in organizations around the globe—have served as our inspiration and teachers.

We gratefully acknowledge the insights that we gained from over 200 people interviewed in the years leading up to this book—people ranging from front-line employees to CEOs and academics. And we would especially like to thank Accenture, Aflac, American Express, Bechtel, Beth Israel Deaconess Medical Center, Camden Property Trust, Caterpillar, ConAgra Foods, the Container Store, EMC Corporation, FedEx, HCL Technologies, Herman Miller, Infosys Technologies, Intel, Lockheed Martin, McCain Foods, NetApp, PepsiCo, Principal Financial Group, Ritz Carlton, Rollins Corporation, Scotia Bank, Seventh Generation, Sherwin Williams, SRA International, Symphony Services, Ultimate Software, Umpqua Holdings, Unilever, Valero Energy Company, WOW!, Zappos.com, and Zillow.com for participating in the interview process.

A handful of colleagues deserve our special thanks. Throughout much of this long process, Rick Frazier provided us with encouragement as well as access to his considerable network and knowledge base. Gary Williams was extremely generous in sharing wRatings's customer ratings for the Fortune 100. And the great work that Rich Barton, Robert Hohman, and their colleagues are doing at Glassdoor.com provided us with an unmatched capability to see inside of organizations. In addition, numerous friends and colleagues read and provided helpful comments on chapter drafts and title ideas.

We also thank Rob Carpenter, Meghan Healy, Mike Powers, Michael Roberts, and Deborah Sanders, who served as research assistants in this work.

We are indebted to the wonderful Berrett-Koehler publishing community, which contributed in so many ways to the creation of this book, and most especially to Neal Maillet and Jeevan Sivasubramaniam for their expert guidance, enthusiastic support, and encouragement.

We reserve our final thanks for our families, who listened patiently to our endless musings, endured our late nights and weekend absences, contributed their insights, and believed in the worthiness of what we were doing.

NOTES

We have relied heavily on Web sites as sources of the facts and figures that we cite throughout the book and have made every possible effort to ensure that we have cited only high-quality sources.

CHAPTER 1. THE WORTHINESS IMPERATIVE

1. In contrast to Nardelli's 2005 base salary of $2.16 million, Blake was given base pay of $975,000 when he took over. And Blake's contract had no guaranteed bonuses and no massive severance package. See Patti Bond, "No Golden Net for New Depot Chief," *Atlanta Journal-Constitution*, January 25, 2007.

2. Ibid.

3. The Home Depot, "The Home Depot Presents 2007 Key Priorities and Financial Outlook," news release, February 28, 2007, accessed December 17, 2010, http://ir.homedepot.com/phoenix .zhtml?c=63646&p=irolnewsArticle &ID=1267173&highlight.

4. Scott Burns, "Is Home Depot Shafting Shoppers?" *MSN Money*, March 7, 2007, accessed December 17, 2010, http://articles.moneycentral.msn.com/ Investing/Extra/HomeDepotShaftingShoppers.aspx.

5. See Messages 1–4714, "Is Home Depot Abusing Its Customers?" *MSN Money Message Boards*, March 13, 2007, accessed December 17, 2010. The comments are no longer available online because *MSN Money*'s message board has been retired.

6. Message #3832, Ibid., March 12, 2007. This comment is no longer available online because *MSN Money*'s message board has been retired.

7. Frank Blake, "Home Depot CEO: Sorry We Let You Down," *MSN Money,* March 13, 2007, accessed May 3, 2011, http://articles.moneycentral .msn.com/Investing/Extra/HomeDepotCEOWeLetYouDown.aspx.

8. Edelman, "Despite Prolonged Global Recession, an Increasing Number

of People Are Spending on Brands That Have Social Purpose," news release, October 21, 2009, accessed December 17, 2010, http://www.edelman.com/news/ShowOne.asp?ID=222.

9. Ibid.

10. Gretchen Morgenson and Louise Story, "Banks Bundled Bad Debt, Bet Against It and Won," *New York Times*, December 23, 2009, accessed December 18, 2010, http://www.nytimes.com/2009/12/24/business/24trading.html.

11. Peter Coy, Michelle Conlin, and Moira Herbst, "The Disposable Worker," *Bloomberg Businessweek*, January 7, 2010, accessed December 18, 2010, http://www.businessweek.com/magazine/content/10_03/b4163032935448.htm.

12. Edelman, *2011 Edelman Trust Barometer Executive Summary*, 2, accessed January 26, 2011, http://www.scribd.com/doc/47515988/2011-Edelman-Trust-Barometer-Executive-Summary#. Edelman's study surveyed people ages 25 to 64 who are "informed publics," defined as people who are college-educated, have a household income in the top quartile for their age in their country, read or watch business/news media at least several times a week, and follow public policy issues in the news at least several times a week.

13. Packaged Facts, "Despite Recession, the Market for 'Ethical' Consumer Products Remains Healthy," news release, October 5, 2009, accessed December 19, 2010, http://www.packaged facts.com/about/release.asp?id=1476.

14. Edelman, "Role of Citizen Consumer to Tackle Social Issues Rises, as Expectation of Government to Lead Declines," news release, November 4, 2010, accessed January 25, 2011, http://www.edelman.com/news/2010/EdelmangoodpurposeUSpressrelease.pdf.

15. Ibid.

16. Accenture, *Mobility Takes Center Stage: The 2010 Accenture Consumer Products and Services Usage Report*, 15–16, accessed December 19, 2010, https://microsite.accenture.com/landing _pages/consumertechnologyusage/Documents/AccentureConsumerTech2010.pdf.

17. Edelman, "Mutually Beneficial Marketing Takes Flight," 2009, accessed January 20, 2011, www.goodpurposecommunity.com/Documents/2009goodpurposedeck.pdf.

18. The Conference Board Inc., "U.S. Job Satisfaction at Lowest Level in Two Decades," news release, January 5, 2010, accessed December 19, 2010, http://www.conference-board.org/press/press detail.cfm?pressid=3820.

19. Association of Executive Search Consultants, "Senior Executives

Dissatisfied Following Recession," news release, March 17, 2010, accessed December 19, 2010, http://www.aesc.org/eweb/Dynamicpage.aspx?webcode =PressRelease&wps_key=b65e90a6-5d6f-4c71-87f6-970ddfad0004.

20. Francois Vetri, head of communications for research and investment firm Sustainable Asset Management, e-mail message to Ed Frauenheim, January 23, 2010. Sustainable Asset Management (SAM) does the analysis that underpins the Dow Jones Sustainability Indexes.

21. Laurie Bassi and Daniel McMurrer, "The Impact of U.S. Firms' Investments in Human Capital on Stock Prices," McBassi & Company, June 2004, accessed January 10, 2011, http://www.bassi-investments.com/downloads/ ResearchPaper_June2004.pdf; and Laurie Bassi and Daniel McMurrer, "Maximizing Your Return on People," *Harvard Business Review,* March 2007, accessed January 10, 2011, https://archive.harvardbusiness.org/cla/web/pl/ product.seam?c=8385&i=8387&cs=63637a444784d5307f8c562ffa2635fd.

22. "Financial Results," Great Place to Work Institute Inc., accessed December 20, 2010, http://www.greatplacetowork.com/what_we_believe/ graphs.php.

23. TerraChoice Environmental Marketing, "Greenwashing Affects 98% of Products Including Toys, Baby Products and Cosmetics," news release, April 15, 2009, http://www.terrachoice.com/images/Seven%20Sins%20of %20Greenwashing%20Release%20-%20April%2015%202009%20-%20US .pdf.

24. BP, "BP Parent Company Name Change Following AGM Approval," news release, May 1, 2001, http://www.bp.com/genericarticle.do?category Id=2012968&contentId=2001578. Immediately prior to the name change, the company had been called BP Amoco. Also, see "BP Brand and Logo," BP, accessed December 21, 2010, http://www.bp.com/sectiongenericarticle.do? categoryId=9014508&contentId=7027677.

25. BP does not break out revenue from its Alternative Energy business, but groups that business into its "Other businesses and corporate" unit. Revenue for that unit in 2009 was $2.8 billion, and total BP revenue was $239.3 billion. BP, *Annual Report and Accounts 2009*, 127, accessed December 21, 2010, http://www.bp.com/assets/bp_internet/globalbp/ globalbp_uk_english/set_branch/STAGING/common_assets/downloads/ pdf/BP_Annual_Report_and_Accounts_2009.pdf; Robert Wine, BP Press Officer, e-mail message to Ed Frauenheim, May 11, 2010. Wine said BP's investments in its Alternative Energy business amounted to about $1.3 billion in 2009. BP's total capital expenditure for 2009 was $20.7 billion. See BP, *Annual Report and Accounts 2009*, 115.

26. PricewaterhouseCoopers and Sustainable Asset Management, *The Sustainability Yearbook 2010*, accessed January 10, 2011, http://www .samgroup.com/htmle/yearbook/downloads/The _Sustainability_Year book_2010_FINAL.pdf?CFID=2716250&CFTOKEN=3c75df4ab40 b4e17-71765 ACC-B74D-DF31-203D32380FE91951.

27. Sustainable Asset Management, *SAM Corporate Sustainability Investment—The Review,* 2009, 2, accessed January 10, 2011, http://www .sam-group.com/yearbook/download/10years_scsa_en.pdf.

28. "Is Home Depot Abusing Its Customers?" *MSN Money Message Boards*, last updated April 14, 2007, accessed December 21, 2010. The comments are no longer available online because *MSN Money*'s message board has been retired.

29. "Scores by Company: Home Depot," American Customer Satisfaction Index, accessed December 21, 2010, http://www.theacsi.org/index .php?option=com_content&task=view&id=149&Itemid =157&c=Home +Depot.

30. Ibid.

31. Blake, "Home Depot CEO: Sorry We Let You Down," *MSN Money*.

32. FedEx Corp., *Everything Is Connected: A Global Citizenship Update for 2009*, 16, accessed January 25, 2011, http://about.fedex.designcdt.com/ files/FedEx_09_GCR_final_boomrk_0415.pdf.

33. Deborah Willig, FedEx spokeswoman, e-mail message to Ed Frauenheim, January 20, 2010.

34. Mitch Jackson, vice president of environmental affairs and sustainability at FedEx, interview by Ed Frauenheim, January 18, 2010.

35. Richard Stengel, "For American Consumers, a Responsibility Revolution," *Time,* September 10, 2009, accessed December 21, 2010, http://www .time.com/time/nation/article/0,8599,1921444,00.html.

36. "Legal Framework," B Lab, accessed December 21, 2010, http://www .bcorporation.net/become/legal.

37. "IBM Response to the Southern Asia Tsunami: Final Report," World Health Organization, WHO Conference on the Health Aspects of the Tsunami Disaster in Asia, Presentation by Brent Woodworth, IBM Crisis Response Team, March 28, 2005, accessed December 21, 2010, http:// www .who.int/hac/events/tsunamiconf/presentations/2_17_private_sector_wood worth_doc.pdf.

38. "Best Companies Lists," Great Place to Work Institute Inc., accessed December 21, 2010, http://www.greatplacetowork.com/what_we_do/ lists-us-bestusa-2010.htm; "Cleaner Vehicles," FedEx, accessed December

21, 2010, http://about.fedex.designcdt.com/corporate_ responsibility/the
_environment/alternative_energy/cleanervehicles.

39. William J. Logue, Executive Vice President, FedEx Express, *Transportation Sector Fuel Efficiency*, testimony before the Committee on Energy & Natural Resources, United States Senate, January 30, 2007, accessed January 25, 2011, http://news.van.fedex.com/files/BillLogueTestimony_energy.pdf.

40. Vinod Khosla, "The Seven That Matter in Clean Technology," *Forbes*, November 22, 2010, accessed January 25, 2011, http://www.forbes.com/forbes/2010/1122/powerful-people-10-vinod-khosla-gillette-chu-clean-technology.html.

41. "Training and development," The Walt Disney Company, 2008 Corporate Responsibility Report, accessed December 21, 2010, http://disney.go.com/crreport/workplaces/disneyoperations/traininganddevelopment.html; "Disney's Enviroport 2007," The Walt Disney Company, accessed December 21, 2010, http://corporate.disney.go.com/environmentality/enviroport/2007/ea/oep.html.

42. Diane Dray, Disney communications manager, e-mail message to Ed Frauenheim, December 9, 2010.

43. "Corporate Responsibility," The Walt Disney Company, accessed December 21, 2010, http://corporate.disney.go.com/responsibility/index.html.

44. Message #3832, "Is Home Depot Abusing Its Customers?" This comment is no longer available online because *MSN Money*'s message board has been retired.

45. "Scores by Company: Home Depot," American Customer Satisfaction Index, accessed December 21, 2010, http://www.theacsi.org/index.php?option=com_content&task=view&id=149&Itemid =157&c=Home+Depot.

46. "LOW Charts," Yahoo Finance, accessed January 25, 2011, http://finance.yahoo.com/echarts?s=low#chart13:symbol=low;range=2y;compare=hd+^gspc;indicator=volume;charttype=line;crosshair=on;ohlcvalues=0;logscale=on.

CHAPTER 2. THE ECONOMIC IMPERATIVE

1. John W. Boudreau and Peter M. Ramstad, *Beyond HR: The New Science of Human Capital* (Boston: Harvard Business School Publishing Corporation, 2007), 54.

2. B. Joseph Pine II & James H. Gilmore, "What Business Are You Really In?" *Chief Executive*, October, 1999, reprinted in "Other Writings," Strategic Horizons, accessed January 4, 2011, http://strategichorizons.com/documents/ChiefExecutive-9910-WhatBusinessAreYouReallyIn.pdf.

3. William M. O'Barr, "A Brief History of Advertising in America," *Advertising & Society Review*, 6, no. 3 (2005), sections 7 and 8, http://muse.jhu.edu/journals/asr/v006/6.3unit02.html.

4. Pine II & Gilmore, "What Business Are You Really In?"

5. Virgin America, "Virgin America Corporate Fact Sheet," accessed January 4, 2011, http://www.virginamerica.com/va/html/virgin-america-corporate-fact-sheet.pdf.

6. Virgin America, "Virgin America Reports Third Quarter 2010 Financial Results," November 9, 2010, accessed January 10, 2011, http://www.virginamerica.com/press-release/2010/virgin-america-reports-third-quarter-2010.html.

7. David Kiley, "Walmart Is Out to Change Its Story with New Ads," *BusinessWeek*, September 13, 2007, accessed January 4, 2011, http://www.businessweek.com/the_thread/brandnewday/archives/2007/09/walmart_is_out.html.

8. Bruce Temkin, "The 6 Laws of Customer Experience," *Customer Experience Matters Blog*, 2008, accessed January 4, 2011, http://experiencematters.files.wordpress.com/2009/05/the-6-laws-of-customer-experience_v8b.pdf.

9. Ibid.

10. John Harrington, "MLK, Michelangelo, Street-Sweepers, & You," *Photo Business News & Forum*, August 6, 2009, accessed January 4, 2011, http://photobusinessforum.blogspot.com/2009/08/mlk-michelangelo-street-sweepers-you.html.

11. The Walt Disney Company, "The Walt Disney Company Reports Earnings for Fiscal Year 2009," news release, November 12, 2009, accessed January 4, 2011, http://corporate.disney.go.com/investors/quarterly_earnings/2009_q4.pdf.

12. The Animation Guild, "The Disney Strike, 1941," accessed January 4, 2011, http://animationguild.org/disney-strike-1941/.

13. Bruce Temkin, "Words of Wisdom: Walt Disney on EBD," *Customer Experience Matters*, November 20, 2007, accessed December 26, 2010, http://experiencematters.wordpress.com/2007/11/20/words-of-wisdom-walt-disney-on-ebd/.

14. Towers Watson, "2010 Global Workforce Study: Supporting Exhibits from the U.S. Research," accessed January 4, 2011, http://www.towerswatson.com/assets/pdf/global-workforce-study/TWGWS_2010_US_Media_Deck.pdf.

15. Watson Wyatt Worldwide, *2009/2010 U.S. Strategic Rewards Report*, 2009. (Watson Wyatt Worldwide later merged with consulting firm Towers Perrin to become Towers Watson.)

16. Ibid.

17. Heidi Shierholz, Economist, Economic Policy Institute, *Implementation of Unemployment Insurance Provisions in the Recovery Act*, testimony before the Committee on Ways and Means Subcommittee on Income Security and Family Support, U.S. House of Representatives, April 23, 2009, accessed January 4, 2011, http://epi.3cdn.net/eb66be7317fe84d185_l6m6ivvsc.pdf, 34.

18. Peter G. Gosselin, "If America Is Richer, Why Are Its Families So Much Less Secure?" *Los Angeles Times,* October 10, 2004, accessed January 4, 2011, http://articles.latimes.com/2004/oct/10/business/fi-riskshift10?pg=3.

19. OECD, "Encouraging Employment—OECD Countries Balance Benefits, Wages and Taxes," December 13, 2007, accessed January 4, 2011, http://www.oecd.org/document/30/0,3343,en _2649_37419_39776222_1 _1_1_1,00.html.

20. Principal Financial Group, "Worker Expectations for Retirement Continue to Fall, Many Anticipate Working Longer," accessed January 4, 2011, http://www.principal.com/about/news/2009/ris_ebrisurvey_041409 .htm.

21. WorldPublicOpinion.org, "Wide Dissatisfaction with Capitalism— Twenty Years after Fall of Berlin Wall," November 9, 2009, accessed January 4, 2011, http://www.worldpublicopinion.org/pipa/articles/btglobalization tradera/644.php.

22. Daniel Gilbert, "What You Don't Know Makes You Nervous," the *New York Times*, May 20, 2009, accessed January 4, 2011, http://opinionator .blogs.nytimes.com/2009/05/20/what-you-dont-know-makes-you-nervous/.

23. Watson Wyatt Worldwide, "Economic Downturn Leading to Decline in Employee Commitment, Morale, Watson Wyatt Worldwide/WorldatWork Survey Finds," September 21, 2009, accessed January 4, 2011, http://www .watsonwyatt.com/news/press.asp?ID=22341.

24. Companies can overemphasize engagement (more on this in Chapter 7). But as discussed in the previous section, motivated employees are crucial to great customer service and company performance generally.

25. The Corporate Executive Board Company, *Rebuilding the Employment Value Proposition*, July 2009.

26. The Corporate Executive Board Company, *Engagement Trends*, October 2010.

27. "The stark reality of iPod's Chinese factories," *MailOnline*, August 18, 2006, accessed January 4, 2011, http://www.mailonsunday.co.uk/news/ article-401234/The-stark-reality-iPods-Chinese-factories.html.

28. Kevin Lane and Florian Poliner, "How to address China's growing

talent shortage," *McKinsey Quarterly,* July 2008, accessed January 19, 2011, http://web.rollins.edu/~tlairson/china/chitalentshort2.pdf.

29. Ibid.

30. Ed Frauenheim, "The Too-Fast Track," *Workforce Management,* March 2007, accessed January 4, 2011, http://www.workforce.com/archive/feature/24/80/98/index.php.

31. Ed Frauenheim, "Dubai's Dark Globalism," *Global Work Watch* (blog), *Workforce Management,* November 12, 2007, accessed January 4, 2011, http://workforce.com/wpmu/globalwork/2007/11/12/dubai_danger/.

32. Tim Connor, "Still Waiting for Nike to Do It," *Global Exchange,* May 2001, accessed January 4, 2011, http://www.globalexchange.org/campaigns/sweatshops/nike/stillwaiting.html.

33. Apple, "Report on iPod Manufacturing," August 17, 2006, accessed January 4, 2011, http://www.apple.com/hotnews/ipodreport/. Apple does not mention its supplier by name in the report. But given that the press controversy centered on Foxconn, it was clear Apple was referring to Foxconn.

34. Apple, "Report on iPod Manufacturing."

35. Stephanie Wong, John Liu, and Tim Culpan, "Foxconn Workers in China Say 'Meaningless' Life Sparks Suicides," *Bloomberg Businessweek,* June 2, 2010, accessed January 19, 2011, http://www.businessweek.com/news/2010-06-02/foxconn-workers-in-china-say-meaningless-life-sparks-suicides.html.

36. Apple, *Supplier Responsibility: 2011 Progress Report,* accessed March 15, 2011, http://images.apple.com/supplierresponsibility/pdf/Apple_SR _2011_Progress_Report.pdf; and Apple, *Supplier Responsibility: 2010 Progress Report,* accessed January 19, 2011, http://images.apple.com/supplier responsibility/pdf/SR_2010_Progress_Report.pdf. Among other things, the 2010 report states: "At 24 facilities, our auditors found that workers had been paid less than minimum wage for regular working hours." The report also details cases of underage workers, falsified records, and wage violations. Apple also discovered that foreign workers recruited to work in supplier facilities had paid illegally high fees to get their jobs.

37. Apple, *Supplier Responsibility: 2011 Progress Report.* Despite Apple's disclosures in its annual supplier reports, some observers say the company can be far more open about problems. In early 2011, a coalition of Chinese environmental groups accused Apple of having the least transparency about pollution issues in its supply chain among 29 technology companies. Friends of Nature, Institute of Public and Environmental Affairs, and Green Beagle, *The Other Side of Apple,* January, 20, 2011, accessed March 16, 2011, http://

www.business-humanrights.org/media/documents/it_report_phase_iv-the
_other_side_of_apple-final.pdf.

38. Billy, "How Long Will It Take for Amazon to Drop the Price of the
New iPod Touches?" *Amazon,* September 8, 2010, accessed January 19, 2011,
http://www.amazon.com/Amazon-drop-price-ipod-touches/forum/-/Tx1I7
L0MZLG0R6W/1/ref=cm_cd_et_md_pl?_encoding=UTF8&cdMsgNo
=17&asin=B001FA1O18&cdSort=oldest&cdMsgID=Mx303IF629GQWN
4#Mx303IF629GQWN4.

39. The stories not only focused on Apple's review of the Foxconn suicides
but also took note of other supplier labor problems. See Aaron Ricadela, "Apple's
Cook Visited Foxconn in 2010 Suicide Response," *Bloomberg,* February 14,
2011, accessed March 16, 2011, http://www.bloomberg.com/news/2011-02-14/
apple-report-says-cook-visited-foxconn-in-2010-suicide-response.html.

40. Apple, "Apple Reports Fourth Quarter Results," October 18, 2010,
accessed January 19, 2011, http://www.apple.com/pr/library/2010/10/18
results.html.

41. Alan S. Blinder, "Offshoring: The Next Industrial Revolution?"
Foreign Affairs 85, no. 2 (March/April 2006): 113–128.

42. Steve Jobs, "You've Got to Find What You Love," *Stanford Report,*
June 14, 2005, accessed January 4, 2011, http://news-service.stanford.edu/
news/2005/june15/jobs-061505.html.

43. Henry Blodget, "Getting Fired at Yahoo: A Twitter Log," *Business
Insider,* February 12, 2008, accessed January 4, 2011, http://www.business
insider.com/s?q=Henry+Blodget %2C+%E2%80%9CGetting+Fired+At
+Yahoo%3A+A+Twitter+&vertical=&author=.

44. Ibid.

45. Ed Frauenheim, "Social Media Begins Forcing the Totally Transparent Layoff," *Workforce Management,* December 16, 2008, accessed January 4,
2011, http://www.workforce.com/section/00/article/26/04/12.php.

46. Yahoo Message Boards, "Buy the Latest iPhone/Gizmo! Consume!!"
2009, accessed January 4, 2011, http://messages.finance.yahoo.com/Stocks
_%28A_to_Z%29/Stocks_A/threadview?m=tm& bn=60&tid=2470583
&mid=2470583&tof=-1&rt=2&frt=2&off=1.

47. Gadget Queen, "BEWARE of the SIGNIFICANT DIFFERENCES
between Kindle 1 and Kindle 2!" *Amazon Customer Reviews,* March 14, 2009,
accessed January 4, 2011, www.amazon.com/review/RV0R3AODMRNJZ.

48. Colby Hall, "Twitter Ban Continues: ESPN Bans Its Reporters from
Sports-Related Social Media," *MEDIAITE,* August 5, 2009, accessed January
4, 2011, http://www.mediaite.com/online/espn-bans-its-reporters-from-sports
-related-twitter-activity.

49. "Kindle Wireless Reading Device (6" Display, U.S. Wireless),"
Amazon.com., accessed January 19, 2011, http://www.amazon.com/gp/
product/B00154JDAI/ref=cm_rdp_product.

50. Ed Frauenheim, "Social Media Begins Forcing the Totally Transparent Layoff," *Workforce Management,* December 16, 2008, accessed January 4,
2011, http://www.workforce.com/section /00/article/26/04/12.php.

CHAPTER 3. THE SOCIAL IMPERATIVE

1. Ea_spouse, "EA: The Human Story," *ea-spouse.livejournal.com,*
November 10, 2004, accessed January 5, 2011, http://ea-spouse.livejournal
.com/274.html.

2. Ed Frauenheim, "For Developers, It's Not All Fun and Games," *ZD
Net,* November 18, 2004, accessed January 5, 2011, http://www.zdnet.com/
news/for-developers-its-not-all-fun-and-games/139833.

3. Ea_spouse, "EA: The Human Story."

4. Facebook, "Statistics," 2011, accessed January 11, 2011, http://www
.facebook.com/press/info.php?statistics.

5. Ea_spouse, "EA: The Human Story."

6. Lev Grossman, "Time's Person of the Year: You," *Time,* December
13, 2006, accessed January 5, 2011, http://www.time.com/time/magazine/
article/0,9171,1569514,00.html.

7. Yelp, "About Us," accessed January 21, 2011, http://www.yelp.com/
about.

8. Edelman Trust Barometer, "2010 Edelman Trust Barometer Executive Summary," 2010, accessed January 5, 2011, http://www.edelman.com/
trust/2010/docs/2010_Trust_Barometer_Executive_Summary.pdf.

9. Anonymous, "White-collar Slavery Is Alive and Well in the Games
Industry," November 10, 2004, comment on ea_spouse, "EA: The Human
Story," accessed January 25, 2011, http://ea-spouse.livejournal.com/274.html
?thread=10514#t10514.

10. Ed Frauenheim, "Overtime Coming to Electronic Arts," *ZD Net,*
March 11, 2005, accessed January 5, 2011, http://news.zdnet.com/2100-9589
_22-141743.html.

11. Ea_spouse, "EA: The Human Story."

12. Anonymous, "Unacceptable," July 9, 2009, comment on ea_spouse,
"EA: The Human Story," accessed January 5, 2011, http://ea-spouse.live
journal.com/274.html?thread=1387794#t1387794.

13. Wikipedia, "Death of Neda Agha-Soltan," accessed January 5, 2011,
http://en.wikipedia.org/wiki/Death_of_Neda_Agha-Soltan.

14. WorldPublicOpinion.Org, "People Who Know Foreigners or

Travel More Likely to See Themselves as Global Citizens: Global Survey," May 18, 2009, accessed January 5, 2011, http://www.worldpublicopinion .org/pipa/articles/views_on_countriesregions_bt/608.php?lb=btvoc&pnt =608&nid=&id=.

15. The Pew Research Center, "Independents Take Center Stage in Obama Era," May 21, 2009, accessed January 5, 2011, http://people-press.org/ report/?pageid=1522; and The Pew Research Center, "Trends in Political Values and Core Attitudes: 1987–2007," March 22, 2007, accessed January 5, 2011, http://people-press.org/reports/pdf/312.pdf.

16. Emmanuel Saez, "Striking It Richer: The Evolution of Top Incomes in the United States," *Pathways Magazine,* August 5, 2009, accessed January 5, 2011, http://elsa.berkeley.edu/~saez/saez-UStopincomes-2007.pdf.

17. Ibid.

18. Fleishman-Hillard Inc. and the National Consumers League, *Rethinking Corporate Social Responsibility*, May 2007, accessed January 5, 2011, http:// fleishmanhillard.com/wp-content/uploads/2007/05/csr_white_paper.pdf.

19. NielsenWire, "Global Shoppers Consider Ethics and Environment," November 21, 2008, accessed January 4, 2011, http://blog.nielsen.com/ nielsenwire/consumer/global-shoppers-consider-ethics-and-environment/.

20. The Pew Research Center, "Independents Take Center Stage in Obama Era," May 21, 2009, accessed January 21, 2011, http://people-press .org/report/?pageid=1517.

21. Corporation for National and Community Service, "Volunteering in America Research Highlights," July 2009, accessed January 5, 2011, http:// www.volunteeringinamerica.gov/assets/resources/VolunteeringInAmerica ResearchHighlights.pdf.

22. Ibid.

23. Corporation for National and Community Service, "Volunteering in America 2010," June 2010, accessed January 11, 2011, http://www .volunteeringinamerica.gov/assets/resources/Issue BriefFINALJune15.pdf.

24. Michael J. Berland, "What America Cares About: Compassion Counts More Than Ever," *Parade,* March 07, 2010, accessed January 5, 2011, http://www.parade.com/news/what-america-cares-about/featured/100307 -compassion-counts-more-than-ever.html.

25. Edelman, "Despite Economic Crisis, Consumers Value Brands' Commitment To Social Purpose, Global Study Finds," news release, November 17, 2008, accessed January 5, 2011, http://www.edelman.com/news/ShowOne .asp?ID=198.

26. Ibid.

27. Martin Fletcher and Greg Hurst, "Oxford's Tribute to Student Neda

Soltan Denounced by Iran," *The Times,* November 11, 2009, accessed January 5, 2011, http://www.timesonline.co.uk/tol/news/uk/article6911629.ece.

28. We Are Neda, "About Us," accessed January 5, 2011, http://neda .webnode.com/about-us/.

29. Lee Scott, CEO of Walmart, "Twenty First Century Leadership," prepared remarks, October 24, 2005, accessed January 5, 2011, http://www .walmartstores.com/download/1965.pdf.

30. Walmart, "Walmart Takes the Lead on Environmental Sustainability," March 1, 2010, accessed January 5, 2011, http://www.walmartstores.com/ download/2392.pdf.

31. Ibid.

32. Carbon Disclosure Project, *Carbon Disclosure Project 2009,* accessed January 5, 2011, https://www.cdproject.net/CDPResults/CDP%202009 %20SandP500%20with%20Industry%20Snapshots.pdf.

33. Scott, "Twenty First Century Leadership."

34. Lydia Saad, "Water Pollution Americans' Top Green Concern," *Gallup,* March 25, 2009, accessed February 12, 2011, http://www.gallup.com/ poll/117079/water-pollution-americans-top-green-concern.aspx.

35. Ibid.

36. WorldPublicOpinion.org, "Multi-Country Poll Reveals That Majority of People Want Action on Climate Change, Even if It Entails Costs," December 3, 2009, accessed January 5, 2011, http://www.worldpublicopinion .org/pipa/articles/btenvironmentra/649.php?lb=bte&pnt=649&nid=&id=.

37. Accenture, "Mobility Takes Center Stage: The 2010 Accenture Consumer Electronics Products and Services Usage Report," 2010, accessed January 5, 2011, https://microsite.accenture.com/landing_pages/consumer technologyusage/Documents/AccentureConsumerTech2010.pdf.

38. Riley E. Dunlap and Angela G. Mertig, *American Environmentalism: The U.S. Environmental Movement, 1970–1990* (Washington, D.C.: Taylor & Francis, 1992).

39. Lydia Saad, "Increased Number Think Global Warming Is Exaggerated," *Gallup,* March 11, 2009, accessed January 5, 2011, http://www.gallup .com/poll/116590/Increased-Number-Think-Global-Warming-Exaggerated .aspx.

40. Jeffrey M. Jones, "Oil Spill Alters Views on Environmental Protection," *Gallup,* May 27, 2010, accessed January 5, 2011, http://www.gallup .com/poll/137882/Oil-Spill-Alters-Views-Environmental-Protection.aspx.

41. See overview of *The Omnivore's Dilemma,* by Michael Pollan, accessed January 5, 2011, http://michaelpollan.com/omnivore.php.

42. Laurie Goodstein, "Evangelical Leaders Join Global Warming Initia-

tive," *New York Times,* February 8, 2006, accessed January 5, 2011, http://www.nytimes.com/2006/02/08/national/08warm.html?pagewanted=all.

43. Gabe Derita, "Envirogelicalism: The Growing Force of Evangelicals in the Climate Change Debate," *OnEarth,* February 17, 2010, accessed January 5, 2011, http://www.onearth.org/blog/envirogelicalism-the-growing-force-of-evangelicals-in-the-climate-change-debate.

44. Climate Solutions, "BLCS member listing," accessed January 5, 2011, http://climatesolutions.org/solutions/initiatives/blcs/search-business-leaders.

45. United Nations, "Overview of the UN Global Compact," November 23, 2010, accessed January 5, 2011, http://www.unglobalcompact.org/AboutTheGC/index.html.

46. Accenture and The United Nations, "A New Era of Sustainability," 2010, accessed January 5, 2011, https://microsite.accenture.com/sustainability/research_and_insights/Pages/A-New-Era-of-Sustainability.aspx.

47. Stacy Mitchell, "Putting Wal-Mart's Green Moves in Context," *Grist,* March 4, 2010, accessed February 12, 2011, http://www.grist.org/article/putting-wal-marts-green-moves-in-context/.

48. Walmart, "Walmart Announces Sustainable Product Index," July 16, 2009, accessed January 5, 2011, http://walmartstores.com/FactsNews/NewsRoom/9277.aspx; and Walmart, "Walmart Announces Goal to Eliminate 20 Million Metric Tons of Greenhouse Gas Emissions from Global Supply Chain," February 25, 2010, accessed January 5, 2011, http://walmartstores.com/FactsNews/NewsRoom/9668.aspx.

49. Walmart, "A Message from Mike Duke," *Walmart 2009 Global Sustainability Report*, accessed January 5, 2011, http://walmartstores.com/sites/sustainabilityreport/2009/letterMikeDuke.html.

50. Hannah Teter, interview by NBC Nightly News with Brian Williams, February 19, 2010, accessed January 21, 2011, http://www.msnbc.msn.com/id/3032619//vp/35259534#35259534.

51. Frank N. Magid Associates, Inc., *American Tapestry: The Millennial Generation*, presentation to the Carnegie-Knight News21 Initiative for the Future of Journalism, December 5, 2008, accessed January 25, 2011, http://www.knightdigitalmediacenter.org/resources/powerpoint/200812Tapestry-Shutte.ppt.

52. Pew Research Center, "The Millennials: Confident. Connected. Open to Change," February 24, 2010, accessed January 5, 2011, http://pewresearch.org/pubs/1501/millennials-new-survey-generational-personality-upbeat-open-new-ideas-technology-bound.

53. Lydia Saad, "Increased Number Think Global Warming Is Exagger-

ated," *Gallup,* March 11, 2009, accessed January 5, 2011, http://www.gallup
.com/poll/116590/increased-number-think-global-warming-exaggerated.aspx.

54. Morley Winograd and Michael D. Hais, "The Republican Party
Ignores Young 'Millennials' at Its Peril," *Los Angeles Times,* May 10, 2009,
accessed February 12, 2011, http://articles.latimes.com/2009/may/10/
opinion/oe-winograd-hais10.

55. Pew Research Center, "The Millennials: Confident. Connected. Open
to Change."

56. Hannah Teter, Twitter message, February 11, 2010, accessed January
5, 2011, http://twitter.com/hannahteter/status/8998019158.

57. Edelman, "Highlights from the Edelman 8095 Global Study and
8095 Live That Demonstrate How Brands Fit into Millennials' Lives,"
accessed January 25, 2011, http://www.edelman.com/insights/special/
8095/8095GlobalOverview.pdf; and Edelman, "New Study Shows That for
Millennials, Taking Action on Behalf of Brands Is a Core Value," accessed
January 25, 2011, http:// www.edelman.com/news/ShowOne.asp?ID=261.

58. Nicole Giuntoli, "Three Millennial Myths . . . Debunked!" *Families
and Work Institute Blog,* July 24, 2009, accessed January 5, 2011, http://
familiesandwork.org/blog/?p=192.

59. Ron Alsop, *The Trophy Kids Grow Up* (San Francisco: Jossey-Bass,
2008), 16.

60. Pew Research Center, "A Pro-Government, Socially Liberal Generation," February 18, 2010, accessed January 5, 2011, http://pewresearch.org/
assets/pdf/1497.pdf.

61. Pew Research Center, "The Millennials: Confident. Connected. Open
to Change."

62. Ibid.

CHAPTER 4. THE POLITICAL IMPERATIVE

1. CNN World Business, "European Commission Fines Computer
Chipmaker Intel $1.45B," May 13, 2009, accessed January 5, 2011, http://edi-
tion.cnn.com/2009/BUSINESS/05/13/europe.intel.anti.trust/.

2. Europa, "Antitrust: Commission Imposes Fine of 1.06 bn Euro on
Intel for Abuse of Dominant Position; Orders Intel to Cease Illegal Practices,"
May 13, 2009, accessed January 5, 2011, http://europa.eu/rapid/pressReleases
Action.do?reference=IP/09/745.

3. Associated Press, "EU Fines Microsoft a Record $1.3 Billion," Febru-
ary 27, 2008, accessed January 17, 2011, http://www.msnbc.msn.com/id/
23366103/ns/business-world_business/.

4. *Forbes,* "100 Most Powerful Women: #53 Neelie Kroes," August 19,

2009, accessed January 5, 2011, http://www.forbes.com/lists/2009/11/power-women-09_Neelie-Kroes_41C2.html.

5. Europa, "Antitrust: Commission imposes fine."

6. Government Equalities Office, "Equality Act of 2010," 2010, accessed January 11, 2011, http://www.equalities.gov.uk/equality_bill.aspx.

7. Government Equalities Office, "Equality Act: Four Decades after the 'Made in Dagenham' Pioneers, Employees Get a New Weapon in the Fight for Equal Pay," news release, October 1, 2010, accessed March 22, 2011, http://www.equalities.gov.uk/media/new_funding_will_help_disabled/equality_act_four_decades_aft.aspx; and Government Equalities Office, "FAQs on the Equality Act 2010: Equal Pay," accessed January 11, 2011, http://www.equalities.gov.uk/equality_act_2010/faqs_on_commencement_of_the_eq/equal_pay.aspx.

8. Government Equalities Office, "Harman: Equality Bill Confirmed in Legislative Programme," news release, December 3, 2008, accessed January 5, 2011, http://www.equalities.gov.uk/media/press_releases/equality_bill_confirmed.aspx.

9. Sheryl Gay Stolberg, "Obama Signs Equal-Pay Legislation," *New York Times,* January 29, 2009, accessed January 5, 2011, http://www.nytimes.com/2009/01/30/us/politics/30ledbetter-web.html.

10. Huma Khan, "In First 100 Days, Obama Flips Bush Admin's Policies," *ABC News,* April 29, 2009, accessed January 5, 2011, http://abcnews.go.com/Politics/Obama100days/story?id=7042171&page=3.

11. U.S. Department of Labor, "Secretary Hilda L. Solis Presents Us Department of Labor Budget Request for Fiscal Year 2011," news release, February 1, 2010, accessed January 25, 2011, http://www.osha.gov/pls/oshaweb/owadisp.show_document?p_table=NEWS_RELEASES&p_id=17139.

12. Ed Frauenheim, "China's Contract Law: Something for Everyone," *Workforce Management,* August 20, 2007, accessed January 5, 2011, http://www.workforce.com/archive/feature/25/09/64/index.php.

13. *People's Daily Online*, "Editorial on Importance of Building Socialist Harmonious Society," October 12, 2006, accessed January 5, 2011, http://english.peopledaily.com.cn/200610/12/eng20061012_311272.html.

14. John M. Broder, "Climate Goal Is Supported by China and India," *New York Times,* March 9, 2010, accessed January 5, 2011, http://www.nytimes.com/2010/03/10/science/earth/10climate.html.

15. Richard A. Posner, "Capitalism in Crisis," *Wall Street Journal,* May 7, 2009, accessed January 5, 2011, http://online.wsj.com/article/SB124165301306893763.html.

16. WorldPublicOpinion.org, "Global Poll Shows Support for Increased

Government Spending and Regulation," September 13, 2009, accessed January 5, 2011, http://www.worldpublicopinion.org/pipa/articles/btglobalization tradera/637.php?lb=btgl&pnt=637&nid=&id=.

17. WorldPublicOpinion.org, "Wide Dissatisfaction with Capitalism—Twenty Years after Fall of Berlin Wall," November 9, 2009, accessed January 5, 2011, http://www.worldpublicopinion.org/pipa/ articles/btglobalization tradera/644.php?lb=btgl&pnt=644&nid=&id=.

18. Harris Interactive, "A Record Number of Americans (88%) Say the Reputation of Corporate America Is 'Not Good' or 'Terrible,' but the Public Rewards Companies That Concentrate on Building Their Reputations with 'Excellent' Reputation Scores," April 28, 2009, accessed January 5, 2011, http://www.harrisinteractive.com/news/pubs/Harris_Interactive _News_2009_04_28.pdf.

19. Frank Newport, "Americans Leery of Too Much Gov't Regulation of Business," *Gallup,* February 2, 2010, accessed January 5, 2011, http://www .gallup.com/poll/125468/americans-leery-govt-regulation-business.aspx.

20. Kenneth P. Vogel, "Court Decision Opens Floodgates for Corporate Cash," *Politico,* January 21, 2010, accessed January 21, 2011, http://www .politico.com/news/stories/0110/31786.html.

21. Peter Cleveland, "Intel Statements on the European Commission Decision," *Intel Blog,* May 13, 2009, accessed January 5, 2011, http://blogs .intel.com/policy/2009/05/intel_statements_on_the_european_commission _decision.php.

22. Office of the Attorney General, "Attorney General Cuomo Files Antitrust Lawsuit Against Intel Corporation, the World's Largest Maker of Microprocessors," November 4, 2009, accessed January 6, 2011, http://www .ag.ny.gov/media_center/2009/nov/nov4a_09.html.

23. Federal Trade Commission, "FTC Challenges Intel's Dominance of Worldwide Microprocessor Markets," news release, December 16, 2009, accessed January 6, 2011, http://www.ftc.gov/opa/2009/12/intel.shtm.

24. Peter Wallsten and Eliza Gray, "Confidence Waning in Obama, U.S. Outlook," *Wall Street Journal,* June 23, 2010, accessed January 6, 2011, http://online.wsj.com/article/SB10001424052748703900004575325263274951230.html.

25. Neelie Kroes, "Neelie Kroes European Commissioner for Competition Policy Five Years of Sector and Antitrust Inquiries Keynote Address at Competition 09 Summit," Brussels, December 3, 2009, http://europa.eu/ rapid/pressReleasesAction.do?reference=SPEECH/09/568&format=HTML &aged=0&language=EN&guiLanguage.

26. Brian Grow, "Home Depot's CEO Cleans Up," *BusinessWeek,* May

23, 2006, accessed January 27, 2011, http://www.businessweek.com/investor/content/may2006/pi20060523_284791.htm; and Brian Grow, "Out at Home Depot," *BusinessWeek,* January 9, 2007, accessed January 6, 2011, http://www.msnbc.msn.com/id/16469224/.

27. Mark Clothier, "Home Depot's Nardelli Ousted after Six-Year Tenure," *Bloomberg,* January 3, 2007, accessed March 17, 2011, http://www.bloomberg.com/apps/news?pid=newsarchive&sid=aLphvT.qIqZI&refer=home; and Grow, "Out at Home Depot."

28. Ibid.

29. The Home Depot, "Proxy Statement Pursuant to Section 14(A) of the Securities Exchange Act of 1934," December 18, 2006, accessed January 6, 2011, http://sec.gov/Archives/edgar/data/354950/000089882206001486/homdepdef14a.txt.

30. Charles Duhigg, "Investor Seeks Review of Home Depot's Management," *New York Times,* December 19, 2006, accessed January 6, 2011, http://www.nytimes.com/2006/12/19/business/19home.html.

31. Grow, "Out at Home Depot."

32. Audit Analytics, "Activist Shareholder Analysis—A Three-Year Trend," May 18, 2009, accessed January 6, 2011, http://www.alacrastore.com/storecontent/Audit_Analytics_Trend_Reports-Activist_Shareholder_Analysis_A_Three_Year_Trend-2033-12.

33. Walden Asset Management, "More Than 50 Companies Voluntarily Adopt 'Say on Pay' as Institutional Investors Continue to Press for an Advisory Vote," news release, March 2, 2010, accessed January 6, 2011, http://www.waldenassetmgmt.com/social/action/SOP_3-2-10.pdf.

34. John Keenan of AFSCME, e-mail message to Ed Frauenheim, March 11, 2010.

35. Walden Asset Management, "More Than 50 Companies Voluntarily Adopt 'Say on Pay'."

36. AFSCME, "More than 50 Companies Voluntarily Adopt 'Say on Pay' as Institutional Investors Continue to Press for an Advisory Vote," March 2, 2010, accessed January 6, 2011, http://www.afscme.org/press/27802.cfm.

37. The Library of Congress, *Dodd-Frank Wall Street Reform and Consumer Protection Act,* 111th Cong., 2d sess., 2010, H.R.4173.

38. People's Solidarity for Participatory Democracy, "PSPD Hold Press Conference on SK Conglomerates Group's Minority Shareholders Movement," news release, January 19, 2004, accessed January 6, 2011, http://blog.peoplepower21.org/English/10653.

39. Robert Goddard, "Germany: 'Say on Pay' Arrives and Other Remuneration Reforms," *Corporate Law and Governance* (blog), September 17,

2009, accessed January 6, 2011, http://corporatelawandgovernance.blogspot
.com/2009/09/germany-say-on-pay-arrives-and-other.html.

40. Rudy Ruitenberg and Fabienne Lissak, "Atos Says Centaurus, Pardus
Should Be Denied Majority," *Bloomberg,* May 16, 2008, accessed January
6, 2011, http://www.bloomberg .com/apps/news?pid=20601085&sid=au
F9EEcUR3xQ&refer=europe; Atos Origin, "Joint Statement between
Atos Origin and Centaurus & Pardus," May 28, 2008, accessed January 6,
2011, www.atosorigin.com/en-us/Newsroom/en-us/Press_Releases/2008/
2008_05_28_01.htm; and Dominique Vidalon, "Atos Origin to Change to
Single Board Structure," *Reuters,* January 2, 2009, accessed January 6, 2011,
http://www.reuters.com/article/idUSL218587320090102.

41. RiskMetrics Group, "Turning Point for Shareholder Activism in
Europe," Description of Webcast to take place June 27, 2008, http://replay
.waybackmachine.org/20090315005400/http://www.riskmetrics.com/
webcasts/2008shareholder_activism_eu.

42. The Home Depot, *Annual Report Pursuant to Section 13 or 15(d) of
The Securities Exchange Act of 1934,* January 29, 2006, accessed January 6,
2011, http://sec.gov/Archives/edgar/data/354950/000104746906004211/
a2168212z10-k.htm.

43. Mark Clothier, "Home Depot's Nardelli Ousted After Six-Year
Tenure," *Bloomberg,* January 3, 2007, accessed January 6, 2011, http://www
.bloomberg.com/apps/news?pid=20601087&sid=aLphvT.qIqZI&refer
=home.

44. Grow, "Out at Home Depot."

45. Ibid.

46. Yonca Ertimur, Fabrizio Ferri, and Volkan Muslu, *Shareholder
Activism and CEO Pay,* August 2009, accessed January 6, 2011, http://center
forpbbefr.rutgers.edu/20thFEA/AccountingPapers/Session5/Ertimur,%20
Ferri,%20and%20Muslu.pdf.

47. Ylan Q. Mui, "Seeing Red Over a Golden Parachute," *The Washington
Post,* January 4, 2007, accessed January 6, 2011, http://www.washingtonpost
.com/wp-dyn/content/article/2007/01/03/AR2007010300553.html.

48. Patti Bond, "No Golden Net for New Depot Chief," *Atlanta Journal-
Constitution,* January 25, 2007.

49. Rachel Tobin Ramos, "Shareholders Mostly Satisfied," *Atlanta
Journal-Constitution,* May 29, 2009.

50. Ibid.

51. Darden Business Publishing, "HCL Technologies: Employees First,

Customers Second," September 29, 2008, accessed January 6, 2011, http://www.hcltech.com/pdf/Darden.pdf.

52. Ibid.

53. Vineet Nayar, *Employees First, Customers Second* (Boston: Harvard Business Press, 2010), 7.

54. Thomas Friedman, *The World Is Flat: A Brief History of the Twenty-first Century* (New York: Farrar, Straus & Giroux, 2005), 178–179.

55. James O'Toole and Edward E. Lawler III, *The New American Workplace* (New York: Macmillan, 2008), 47.

56. Ibid., 50.

57. Ibid., 50.

58. Ibid., 48.

59. Ibid., 49.

60. Ed Frauenheim, "HCL Optimas Award Winner for Innovation," *Workforce Management,* October 2008, accessed January 6, 2011, http://www.workforce.com/archive/feature/25/88/20/index.php.

61. Darden Business Publishing, "HCL Technologies: Employees First, Customers Second."

62. Ibid.

63. O'Toole and Lawler, *The New American Workplace,* 46–47.

64. Ibid., Chapter 11.

65. WorldBlu, "40 Companies Win Worldwide Award for Democracy in the Workplace," news release, April 14, 2009, accessed January 6, 2011, http://www.worldblu.com/wp-content/themes/worldblu/docs/world blu-press-041409-list.pdf.

66. Jena McGregor, "The World's Most Influential Companies," *Business-Week,* December 11, 2008, accessed January 6, 2011, http://images.business week.com/ss/08/12/1211_most_influential/26.htm.

67. David Kirkpatrick, "The World's Most Modern Management—in India," *Fortune,* April 14, 2006, accessed January 6, 2011, http://money.cnn.com/2006/04/13/magazines/fortune/fastforward_fortune/index.htm.

68. Vineet Nayar, *Employees First, Customers Second*, 13.

CHAPTER 5. GOODNESS MATTERS

1. The major advantage of using a firm's stock performance—its appreciation or depreciation over time—as a method of assessing the payoff to "goodness" is that it can be measured comparably across all publicly traded firms. This is especially true when stock performance is measured relative to the firm's competitors (since this controls for variations in performance that

are attributable to the industry in which the firm operates, as opposed to its goodness). Other measures, such as profits, vary considerably with firm size (and industry).

2. Great Place to Work Institute, "Our Model," 2011, accessed January 14, 2011, http://great placetowork.com/what_we_do/model.php. The criteria used to judge companies for the annual *Fortune*'s Best Companies to Work For list overlap closely with our definition of a good employer. The Great Place to Work Institute, which compiles the list for *Fortune*, says a great place to work is one in which you "trust the people you work for, have pride in what you do, and enjoy the people you work with." Trust and camaraderie are natural outgrowths of the caring environment and ethical, collaborative leadership style we see as crucial to goodness as an employer. And pride comes in part from an inspiring purpose, which is central to our vision of worthy companies. Our definition of a good employer, though, extends beyond trust, camaraderie, and pride to include smart use of quantitative data analysis in the way companies marshal and manage workers.

3. Great Place to Work Institute, "Financial Results," 2011, accessed January 14, 2011, http://www.greatplacetowork.com/what_we_believe/ graphs.php. This portfolio (managed by the Russell Investment Group) is reset annually. That is to say, if a firm is removed from *Fortune*'s Best Places to Work For list, it is then removed from the portfolio. Conversely, when a new (publicly traded) company is added to the list, it is added to the portfolio. This portfolio performs substantially better than a portfolio that has not been reset annually, being based instead on the original (1998) Best Places to Work For list (10.30% vs. 6.44%).

4. Alex Edmans, "Does the Stock Market Fully Value Intangibles? Employee Satisfaction and Equity Prices," *Journal of Financial Economics* (forthcoming 2011).

5. Gathering the data necessary to make these investment decisions is an arduous and imperfect process (since the data is not publicly available). So we almost certainly fail to include some high-investing firms that should be included in Portfolio A and incorrectly include other firms (who provide us with unaudited and perhaps incorrect data on their investments in employee education and training). Although the process is imperfect, the resulting portfolio nonetheless has performed impressively in the stock market.

6. There is, of course, a potential chicken-and-egg problem here. It could be that companies that are successful for reasons other than training simply pour more money into training. Dan and Laurie, along with colleagues from the Federal Reserve Board and Georgetown University, tackled this issue in a

2004 paper. It found that training expenditures were not driven by past stock returns, even as it showed a strong link between training expenditures and subsequent stock market performance.

7. KLD Indexes, "KLD400 Performance Statistics," 2010, accessed January 14, 2011, http://www.kld.com/indexes/ds400index/performance.html.

8. SAM, "Sam Corporate Sustainability Assessment—The Review," 2009, accessed January 14, 2011, http://www.sam-group.com/yearbook/download/10years_scsa_en.pdf.

9. ATKearney, "Companies with a Commitment to Sustainability Tend to Outperform Their Peers During the Financial Crisis," news release, February 9, 2009, accessed January 14, 2011, http://www.atkearney.com/index.php/News-media/companies-with-a-commitment-to-sustainability-tend-to-out perform-their-peers-during-the-financial-crisis.html.

10. Scott J. Callan and Janet M. Thomas, "Corporate Financial Performance and Corporate Social Performance: An Update and Reinvestigation," *Corporate Social Responsibility and Environmental Management,* February 24, 2009, accessed January 14, 2011, http://onlinelibrary.wiley.com/doi/10.1002/csr.182/abstract.

11. Arie de Geus, *The Living Company* (Boston: Harvard Business School Press, 1997).

12. Ibid.

13. Ibid.

14. Danny Miller and Isabelle Le Breton-Miller, *Managing for the Long Run: Lessons in Competitive Advantage from Great Family Businesses* (Boston: Harvard Business School Publishing, 2005).

15. Joseph B. Bragdon, *Profit for Life: How Capitalism Excels* (Cambridge: The Society for Organizational Learning, 2006).

16. Ibid.

17. Theresa Welbourne, "Want to Make Money on IPOs? Learn About Companies' HR Management Strategies," *Workforce Management,* September 2010, accessed January 14, 2011, http://www.workforce.com/archive/feature/hr-management/want-make-money-ipos-learn-about-companies-hr/index.php.

18. Theresa Welbourne, interview by Ed Frauenheim, August 21, 2010.

19. Welbourne, "Want to Make Money on IPOs?"

20. Christine Harper, "Goldman Sachs Posts Record Profit, Beating Estimates," *Bloomberg,* July 14, 2009, accessed January 14, 2011, http://www.bloomberg.com/apps/news?pid=newsarchive&sid=a2jo3RK2_Aps.

21. Edelman, "Despite Prolonged Global Recession, an Increasing Number of People Are Spending on Brands That Have Social Purpose," news

release, October 21, 2009, accessed January 25, 2011, http://www.edelman
.com/news/ShowOne.asp?ID=222.

22. Edelman, "Role of Citizen Consumer to Tackle Social Issues Rises,
as Expectation of Government to Lead Declines," news release, November 4,
2010.

23. Edelman, "Despite Prolonged Global Recession, an Increasing
Number of People . . ."

24. Edelman, "Edelman goodpurpose Study 2010," accessed January 10,
2011, http://www.edelman.com/insights/special/GoodPurpose2010global
PPT_WEBversion.pdf.

25. Edelman, "Role of Citizen Consumer to Tackle Social Issues Rises . . ."

26. WPP, "2009 Green Brands Global Survey Published," July 21, 2009,
accessed January 14, 2011, http://www.wpp.com/wpp/press/press/default.htm
?guid=%7Bb983b1a9-ab92-4427-b75f-ab35f2565dad%7D.

27. Ibid.

28. Ibid.

29. Co-operative Bank, "Ten Years of Ethical Consumerism: 1999–2008,"
accessed January 14, 2011, http://www.goodwithmoney.co.uk/assets/Ethical
-Consumerism-Report-2009.pdf.

30. Packaged Facts, "Despite Recession, the Market for Ethical Consumer
Products Remains Healthy," October 5, 2009, accessed January 14, 2011,
http://www.packagedfacts.com/about/release.asp?id=1476.

31. Ibid.

32. Remi Trudel and June Cotte, "Does It Pay to Be Good?" *MIT Sloane
Management Review* 50, no. 2 (2009).

33. Ibid.

34. Fleishman-Hillard/National Consumers League, *Rethinking
Corporate Social Responsibility*, May 2007, accessed January 7, 2011, http://
fleishmanhillard.com/wp-content/uploads/2007/05/csr_white_paper.pdf.

35. Trudel and Cotte, "Does It Pay to Be Good?"

36. Edelman, "Mutually Beneficial Marketing Takes Flight."

37. Randstad, "2009 World of Work," 2009, accessed January 14, 2011,
http://us.randstad.com/content/findcandidates/employer-services/file-index/
2009-World-of-Work.pdf.

38. Representative of SAM, e-mail to Ed Frauenheim, January 23, 2010.
Research and investment firm SAM does the analysis that underpins the Dow
Jones Sustainability Indexes.

39. Richard Stengel, "For American Consumers, a Responsibility Revolution," *Time,* September 10, 2009, accessed January 14, 2011, http://www.time
.com/time/nation/article/0,8599,1921444,00.html.

40. Towers Watson, "Leveraging Your Brand to Create an Engaged Workforce," August 2008, accessed January 14, 2011, http://www.watson wyatt.com/render.asp?id=19667.

41. Ibid.

42. A notorious 2005 memo suggested the company could limit benefit costs by making cashiers do some "cart-gathering" to attract a healthier workforce. Steven Greenhouse and Michael Barbaro, "Wal-Mart Memo Suggests Ways to Cut Employee Benefit Costs," *New York Times,* October 26, 2005, accessed January 14, 2011, http://www.nytimes.com/2005/10/26/business/26walmart.ready.html; and Ed Frauenheim, "Wal-Mart Memo Highlights Health Care Risk," *Workforce Management,* October 27, 2005, accessed January 14, 2011, http://www.workforce.com/section/00/article/24/19/76.php.

43. Ylan Q. Mui, "Wal-Mart Says It Will Improve Health Benefits," *Washington Post,* February 24, 2006, accessed January 14, 2011, http://www.washingtonpost.com/wpdyn/content/article/2006/02/23/AR2006022301857.html; and Ceci Connolly, "At Wal-Mart, a Health-Care Turnaround," *Washington Post,* February 13, 2009, accessed January 14, 2011, http://www.washingtonpost.com/wpdyn/content/article/2009/02/12/AR2009021204096.html?sid=ST2009021300507.

44. WPP, "2009 Green Brands Global Survey Published," July 22, 2009, accessed January 14, 2011, http://www.wpp.com/wpp/press/press/default.htm?guid=%7Bb983b1a9-ab92-4427-b75f-ab35 f2565dad%7D.

45. Harris Interactive, *Annual RQ2008 Summary Report,* 2009.

46. Ibid.

47. Ibid.

48. Ibid.

49. Harris Interactive, *Annual RQ 2009 USA Summary Report,* April 2010.

50. Edelman, "Edelman goodpurpose Study 2010."

51. Richard Stengel, "Doing Well by Doing Good," *Time,* September 10, 2009, accessed January 14, 2011, http://www.time.com/time/magazine/article/0,9171,1921591,00.html.

52. Richard Stengel, "For American Consumers, a Responsibility Revolution," *Time,* September 10, 2009, accessed January 14, 2011, http://www.time.com/time/nation/article/0,8599,1921444,00.html.

CHAPTER 6. RANKING COMPANIES

1. Indeed, there were missing values even for some of the Fortune 100 companies on some of the measures that we selected, thereby reducing the comparability of the final Good Company Index rankings for those companies.

2. We choose wRatings because it was the most comprehensive cross-industry source of information on customer ratings that we could find. Robert McCormack (a partner at Pasadena Angels, a group of private investors) says, "With wRatings, the guesswork is gone. You can immediately see which companies are best positioned to out-maneuver their rivals and build market share."

3. We don't think it's necessarily fair or accurate to label the employers at the low end of the Glassdoor.com rating system "bad" employers. But we do believe that the evidence from the employee surveys available on Glassdoor .com accurately indicates that some substantial segment of employees at these firms find their experience to be unsatisfactory. Hence, we merely note the fact that these firms fall at the bottom of the employee ratings that are available on Glassdoor.com.

4. Glassdoor.com, "Companies & Reviews," accessed January 11, 2011, http://www.glassdoor.com/Reviews/index.htm.

5. The degree of confidence in the representativeness of employees' rating of their employer increases with the number of employees who have responded to the survey. Hence, we choose 25 as the minimum number of responses on which to make our assessment. For the 22 companies that had fewer than 25 responses, we coded this information as missing (with an implicit score of 0) in our overall Good Company ranking system.

6. If there is a "normal distribution" of firms, then firms that are in the top (or bottom) 12.5 percent (one-eighth) of the distribution are one standard deviation above (or below) the mean of the distribution. In large samples, such as wRating's database, this is a statistically significant difference from the average value, and we applied the same standard to the Glassdoor.com data.

7. In order to maintain consistency with other categories in our Good Company Index ranking system, we capped the number of "Good Employer" points at 2. So an organization that appeared on the *Fortune* list of Best Companies to Work For *and* in the top one-eighth of the Glassdoor.com distribution would receive a maximum of 2 points in the Good Employer category.

8. HP Alumni, "The HP Way," accessed January 17, 2011, http://www .hpalumni.org/hp_way.htm.

9. Ed Frauenheim, "HP Fattened up before Latest Trim," *CNET News,*

July 20, 2005, accessed January 17, 2011, http://news.cnet.com/HP-fattened-up-before-latest-trim/2100-1014_3-5797194.html.

10. Eric Jackson, "Mark Hurd's Excesses Were in Plain Sight," *The Street,* August 7, 2010, accessed January 17, 2011, http://www.thestreet.com/story/10830261/1/hurds-excesses-have-been-in-plain-sight.html.

11. Joe Nocera, "Real Reason for Ousting H.P.'s Chief," *New York Times,* August 13, 2010, accessed January 17, 2011, http://www.nytimes.com/2010/08/14/business/14nocera .html?pagewanted=2&_r=1.

12. Hewlett-Packard Company, Form 8-K, Securities and Exchange Commission, August 6, 2010, accessed January 17, 2011, http://sec.gov/Archives/edgar/data/47217/00010474691000 7177/a2199755z8-k.htm; and Ashlee Vance, "Boss's Stumble May Also Trip Hewlett-Packard," *New York Times,* August 8, 2010, accessed January 17, 2011, http://www.nytimes .com/2010/08/09/technology/09hp.html?hp.

13. wRatings incorporates information on the following 17 components: trusted, quality, fair-priced, consistent, simplicity, time-sensitive, precise, connection, stability, useful, availability, safe, competent, variety, unique, cool, leadership.

14. If there is a "normal distribution" of firms, then firms that are in the top (or bottom) 12.5 percent (one-eighth) of the distribution are one standard deviation above (or below) the mean of the distribution. In large samples, such as wRatings's database, this is a statistically significant difference from the average value.

15. Note that because the Fortune 100 are compared to wRatings's larger database, it need not be the case that 25 percent of the Fortune 100 fall into the top (or bottom) 25 percent of wRatings's ranking of over 4,000 firms for which it has ratings.

16. Although CEO pay is reported in corporate filings by publicly traded companies, it can be difficult to compare accurately across firms due to differences in bonus terms, valuation of stock and option awards, and other benefits and perquisites. Therefore, we used the 2010 *New York Times* executive compensation study compiled by compensation research firm Equilar, with the AFL-CIO compensation database serving as a backup source. Full details are available in the Appendix.

17. Systematic information on corporate use of tax havens is difficult to come by. Based on our research, the 2008 GAO report is the most complete source of information available, and we therefore used it as the basis for the inaugural Good Company Index scoring in this area. But we also recognize that some of the specific information in the report may no longer be fully

up-to-date. As noted in more detail below, we also notified each company of the specific elements of their scores and invited their responses. No companies objected to their tax haven scores.

18. Kraft Foods, "Community Involvement," accessed January 17, 2011, http://www.kraftfoodscompany.com/About/community-involvement/community-involvement.aspx.

19. IBM, "IBM Reading Comprehension Grants Improve Literacy Skills," accessed January 17, 2011, http://www.ibm.com/ibm/ibmgives/grant/adult/ReadingCompanion.shtml.

20. It should be noted that our Contribution ratings are based on a systematic and disciplined review and scoring of materials voluntarily made available by companies. It is our hope that more extensive and/or more comparable information will gradually become available in future years, strengthening this element of the scoring process.

21. Government Accountability Office, "International Taxation," December 2008, accessed January 17, 2011, http://www.gao.gov/new.items/d09157.pdf.

22. This finding also is supported by an extensive analysis done jointly by the Investor Responsibility Research Center Institute and PROXY Governance Incorporated. Investor Responsibility Research Center (IRRC) Institute and PROXY Governance Inc., "Executive Compensation Analysis Reveals High CEO Pay for Underperforming Companies," news release, June 24, 2010, accessed January 17, 2011, http://eon.businesswire.com/portal/site/eon/permalink/?ndmViewId=news_view&newsId=20100024005334&newsLang=en.

23. "EU Fines Microsoft a Record $1.3 Billion," *Associated Press*, February 27, 2008, accessed January 17, 2011, http://www.msnbc.msn.com/id/23366103/ns/business-world_business/.

24. Department of Justice, "General Reinsurance Corporation Enters into Agreement Resolving Its Role in Fraudulent Reinsurance Transaction with AIG," January 20, 2010, accessed January 17, 2011, http://www.justice.gov/opa/pr/2010/January/10-crm-053.html.

25. Department of Health and Human Services Office of Inspector General, "OIG Reports More Than $2 Billion in Recoveries from Fighting Fraud, Waste, and Abuse for First-Half FY 2008," June 12, 2008, accessed January 17, 2011, http://oig.hhs.gov/publications/docs/press/2008/semiannual_press_spring2008.pdf.

26. Department of Justice, "U.S. Files Suit Against Johnson & Johnson for Paying Kickbacks to Nation's Largest Nursing Home Pharmacy," January

15, 2010, accessed January 17, 2011, http://www.justice.gov/opa/pr/2010/January/10-civ-042.html.

27.   Natasha Singer and Reed Abelson, "Can Johnson & Johnson Get Its Act Together?" *New York Times*, January 15, 2011, accessed January 22, 2011, http://www.nytimes.com/2011/01/16/business/16johnson-and-johnson.html.

28.   We sent a certified letter to the CEO of each of the 94 companies that we rated in which we provided them an opportunity to comment on their ratings and invited them to be in touch with us should they want to discuss their company's rating.

29.   Stephanie Strom, "Wal-Mart Gives $2 Billion to Fight Hunger," *New York Times,* May 12, 2010, accessed January 17, 2011, http://www.nytimes.com/2010/05/13/us/13gift.html?hp.

30.   Home Depot, "Rebuilding Hope & Homes," accessed January 17, 2011, http://corporate.homedepot.com/wps/portal/!ut/p/c1/04_SB8K8xLLM9MSSzPy8xBz9CP0os3gDdwNHH0sfE3M3AzMPJ8MAfxcDKADKR2LKmxrD5fHr9vPIz03VL8iNKAcATDeEqQ!!/dl2/d1/L2dJQSEvUUt3QS9ZQnB3LzZfMEcwQUw5TDQ3RjA2SEIxUExEMDAwMDAwMDA!/.

31.   S. Permanent Subcommittee on Investigations, Hearing on Wall Street and the Financial Crisis: The Role of Investment Banks, Exhibits, April 27, 2010, accessed December 21, 2010, http://hsgac.senate.gov/public/_files/Financial_Crisis/042710Exhibits.pdf.

32.   Great Place to Work Institute, "Best Companies Lists," 1998, accessed January 17, 2011, http://greatplacetowork.com/what_we_do/lists-us-bestusa-1998.htm.

33.   American Customer Satisfaction Index, "Scores by Company," 2010, accessed January 17, 2011, http://www.theacsi.org/index.php?option=com_content&task=view&id=149&Itemid=157&c=FedEx+.

34.   FedEx, "Disaster Readiness, Relief and Recovery," 2011, accessed January 17, 2011, http://about.fedex.designcdt.com/corporate_responsibility/philanthropy/disaster_relief.

35.   Ed Frauenheim, "FedEx Loses Driver-Classification Legal Skirmishes," *Workforce Management,* April 4, 2008, accessed January 17, 2011, http://www.workforce.com/section/00/article/25/45/95.html; Scott Malone, Andre Grenon, Steve Orlofsky, and Bernard Orr, "UPDATE 2-Drivers Sue Fedex over Contractor Status," *Reuters,* August 17, 2010, accessed January 17, 2011, http://www.reuters.com/article/idUSN1715781720100818; and FedEx Ground/Home Delivery Drivers Nationwide Class-Action Lawsuit, "Fre-

quently Asked Questions," accessed January 17, 2011, http://www.fedexdrivers lawsuit.com/faq.htm.

36. Disney is not, however, without its flaws. In 2010 it was ordered to pay nearly $270 million for using creative accounting to hide profits from, and therefore to reduce the amount it owed to, a partner. Sue Manning, "Disney-Celador Lawsuit Verdict: Disney Ordered to Pay 'Millionaire' Makers $269.2 Million," *The Huffington Post*, July 7, 2010, accessed January 17, 2011, http://www.huffing tonpost.com/2010/07/07/disneycelador-lawsuit-ver_n_638518.html.

37. "2011 Best Places to Work–Employees' Choice Awards," Glassdoor .com, accessed January 25, 2011, http://www.glassdoor.com/Best-Places-to -Work-LST_KQ0,19.htm; and Glassdoor Team, "Glassdoor Reveals Lowest Rated Companies; United Stays Grounded as Gibson Guitar Strikes a Cord [*sic*]With Employees," *glassdoor.com blog*, December 15, 2009, accessed January 25, 2011, http://www.glassdoor.com/blog/glassdoor-reveals-lowest-rated -companies-united-stays-grounded-gibson-guitar-strikes-cord-employees/.

38. Jody Hoffer Gittell, *The Southwest Airlines Way: Using the Power of Relationships to Achieve High Performance* (New York: McGraw Hill, 2005).

39. American Customer Satisfaction Index, "Scores by Industry," 2010, accessed January 17, 2011, http://www.theacsi.org/index.php?option=com _content&task=view&id=147&Itemid=155&i=Airlines.

40. Southwest will give a full refund on "Wanna Get Away" fare tickets if they are cancelled within 24 hours. After that, funds from a cancelled "Wanna Get Away" ticket can be used for travel for up to 12 months from when the ticket was bought. Southwest also sells more expensive fully refundable tickets.

41. Like Southwest, United does provide full refunds on nonrefundable ticket purchases that are cancelled within 24 hours.

42. Atul Gawande, "The Cost Conundrum," *The New Yorker*, June 1, 2009, accessed January 17, 2011, http://www.newyorker.com/reporting/ 2009/06/01/090601fa_fact_gawande?currentPage=all.

43. Karen Mazurkewich, "Open-book Policy Can Boost Bottom Line," *Financial Post*, May 8, 2010, accessed January 22, 2011, http://www.financial post.com/Open+book+policy+boost+bottom+line/3009185/story.html.

44. McAlvain, "Open Book Policy," 2009, accessed January 17, 2011, http://www.mcalvain.com/content/open-book-policy.

45. Torry McAlvain, interview by Laurie Bassi, May 24, 2010.

46. Seventh Generation, *Crossroads: Reinventing the Purpose and Possibility of Business*, 2009, corporate report, accessed January 7, 2011, http://www.svg2008report.org/pdf/2008_SVG_CC_Report.pdf; and CSR Wire, "Seventh Generation Releases 2008 Corporate Consciousness Report," August 12, 2009, accessed January 17, 2011, http://www.csrwire

.com/press_releases/27466-Seventh-Generation-Releases-2008-Corporate
-Consciousness-Report.

47. Seventh Generation, *Crossroads,* 2009.

48. Ibid.

49. Seventh Generation, "Sales and Economic Performance," *Return on Purpose,* corporate report, 2010, accessed January 7, 2011, http://www.7genreport.com/introduction/performance.php.

50. Seventh Generation, *Crossroads,* 2009.

51. By way of full disclosure, Ultimate Software is a client of Laurie Bassi's in her consulting work at McBassi & Company.

52. Ed Frauenheim, "From Dot-Com Bust to SaaS Strength," *Workforce Management,* July 2009, accessed January 17, 2011, http://www.workforce.com/section/software-technology/feature/from-dot-com-bust-saas-strength/index.html.

53. Ultimate Software, "2009 Annual Report," accessed January 17, 2011, http://www.ultimatesoftware.com/annual_report_2009.asp.

54. Beginning in 2009, Ultimate began giving employees restricted stock units instead of stock options. As with stock options, restricted stock units are recognized as an expense in financial statements.

55. Ultimate Software, "2009 Annual Report."

56. Great Place to Work, "Best Companies Lists," 2009, accessed January 17, 2011, http://www.greatplacetowork.com/what_we_do/lists-us-sme-2009.htm; and Great Place to Work, "Best Companies Lists," 2008, accessed January 17, 2011, http://www.greatplacetowork.com/what_we_do/lists-us-sme-2008.htm.

SIDEBAR: Goldman Loses Its Good Name (pages 118–119)

57. "100 Best Companies to Work For 2009," *Fortune,* accessed December 21, 2010, http://money.cnn.com/magazines/fortune/bestcompanies/2009/index.html; Dow Jones Sustainability Indexes, "DJSI United States 2009/2010," as of December 31, 2009; see, for example, "World's Most Admired Companies," *Fortune,* accessed December 21, 2010, http://money.cnn.com/magazines/fortune/mostadmired/2009/full_list/, "America's Most Admired Companies 2008," *Fortune,* accessed December 21, 2010, http://money.cnn.com/magazines/fortune/mostadmired/2008/index.html, and "America's Most Admired Companies 2007," *Fortune,* accessed December 21, 2010, http://money.cnn.com/magazines/fortune/mostadmired/2007/top20/index.html.

58. See, for example, Phillip Inman, "Goldman to Make Record Bonus Payout," *Guardian.co.uk,* June 21, 2009, accessed December 22, 2010, http://www.guardian.co.uk/business/2009/jun/21/goldman-sachs-bonus-payments.

59. United States Securities and Exchange Commission, "SEC Charges Goldman Sachs with Fraud in Structuring and Marketing of CDO Tied to Subprime Mortgages," news release, April 16, 2010, http://www.sec.gov/news/press/2010/2010-59.htm.

60. S. Permanent Subcommittee on Investigations, Hearing on Wall Street and the Financial Crisis: The Role of Investment Banks, Exhibits, April 27, 2010, accessed December 21, 2010, http://hsgac.senate.gov/public /_files/Financial _Crisis/042710Exhibits.pdf; Morgenson and Story, "Banks Bundled Bad Debt, Bet Against It and Won."

61. S. Permanent Subcommittee on Investigations, Hearing on Wall Street and the Financial Crisis: The Role of Investment Banks, Exhibits, April 27, 2010.

62. Morgenson and Story, "Banks Bundled Bad Debt, Bet Against It and Won."

63. United States Securities and Exchange Commission, "SEC Charges Goldman Sachs with Fraud."

64. Goldman Sachs Group Inc., "Prepared Remarks by Lloyd C. Blankfein, Chairman and Chief Executive Officer," April 27, 2010, accessed December 22, 2010, http://www2.goldman sachs.com/our-firm/on-the-issues/psi-folder/lloyd-blankfein-testimony.html.

65. United States Securities and Exchange Commission, "Goldman Sachs to Pay Record $550 Million to Settle SEC Charges Related to Subprime Mortgage CDO," news release, July 15, 2010, accessed December 22, 2010, http://www.sec.gov/news/press/2010/2010-123.htm.

66. Goldman Sachs Group Inc., "Goldman Sachs Reports Earnings per Common Share of $22.13 for 2009," news release, January 21, 2010, accessed December 22, 2010, http://www2.goldmansachs.com/our-firm/press/press-releases/current/pdfs/2009-q4-earnings.pdf.

67. Harris Interactive, *Annual RQ 2009 USA Summary Report*, April 2010.

68. Goldman Sachs Group Inc., *Report of the Business Standards Committee*, accessed January 25, 2011, http://www2.goldmansachs.com/our-firm/business-standards-committee/report.pdf.

69. Goldman Sachs Group Inc., "Goldman Sachs Reports Earnings per Common Share of $13.18 for 2010," news release, January 19, 2011, accessed January 25, 2011, http://www2.goldmansachs.com/our-firm/press/press-releases/current/pdfs/2010-q4-earnings.pdf.

70. Goldman Sachs Group Inc., "Prepared Remarks by Lloyd C. Blankfein, Chairman and Chief Executive Officer," April 27, 2010.

CHAPTER 7. THE GOOD EMPLOYER

1. In the *U.S. News & World Report* 2010–11 list of Best Hospitals, 152 of nearly 5,000 hospitals studied made the publication's rankings in at least one specialty. Beth Israel earned a ranking in seven categories. "Beth Israel Deaconess Medical Center," *U.S. News & World Report*, accessed January 18, 2011, http://health.usnews.com/best-hospitals/beth -israel-deaconess-medical-center-6140013.

2. Paul Levy, "Overview," Beth Israel Deaconess Medical Center, accessed January 18, 2011, http://www.bidmc.org/AboutBIDMC/Overview.aspx. Levy's words are no longer on the site, and he resigned from the hospital in 2011.

3. Insights from interviews with the following executives were helpful in guiding us as we wrote this chapter: Tony Hsieh (CEO of Zappos.com), Paul Levy (former CEO of Beth Israel Deaconess Hospital), Mali Mahalingam (Executive Vice President & Chief People Officer at Symphony Services Corporation), Polly Pearson (former VP of Employee Branding at EMC), Kip Tindell (CEO of the Container Store), and Shami Khorana (president of HCL America).

4. Laurie Bassi and Daniel McMurrer, "Maximizing Your Return on People," *Harvard Business Review* 85 (2007).

5. Ed Frauenheim, "Downturn Tests HCL's Pledge to Employees," *Workforce Management,* November 16, 2009, accessed January 18, 2011, http://www.workforce.com/archive/feature/hr-management/downturn-tests -hcls-pledge-employees/index.php.

6. Heather Timmons, "Inquiry Faults Management at BP in Blast That Killed 15," *New York Times,* January 17, 2007, accessed January 18, 2011, http://www.nytimes.com/2007/01/17/ business/worldbusiness/17baker.html ?scp=15&sq=texas+city+refinery&st=nyt.

7. Louisa Lim, interview by Guy Raz, February 7, 2010, accessed January 18, 2011, http://www.npr.org/templates/story/story.php?storyId=123472217.

8. Fred Smith, "Minimizing Job Losses and Protecting FedEx for the Long-Term," *Team Member Stories*, December 18, 2008, accessed January 25, 2011, http://blog.fedex.designcdt.com/node/551.

9. "Our Culture: People-Service-Profit," FedEx Corp., accessed January 25, 2011, http://fedex.com/bm/about/careers/ourculture.html.

10. Smith, "Minimizing Job Losses and Protecting FedEx for the Long-Term."

11. Kimberely Howell Jones, April 12, 2010, comment on Smith, "Minimizing Job Losses and Protecting FedEx for the Long-Term."

12. FedEx Corp., "FedEx Corp. Reports Higher Fourth Quarter and Full Year Earnings," news release, June 16, 2010, accessed January 25, 2011, http://ir.fedex.com/releasedetail.cfm? ReleaseID= 479710.

13. Jim Collins, *How the Mighty Fall: And Why Some Companies Never Give In* (New York: HarperCollins Publishers, 2009).

14. Lim, interview by Guy Raz, February 7, 2010.

15. Margaret L. Williams, Michael A. McDaniel, and Nhung T. Nguyen, "A Meta-Analysis of the Antecedents and Consequences of Pay Level Satisfaction," *Journal of Applied Psychology* 91, no. 2 (2006): 392–413.

16. Aliosha Alexandrov, Emin Babakus, and Ugur Yavas, "The Effects of Perceived Management Concern for Frontline Employees and Customers on Turnover Intentions," *Journal of Service Research* 9 (2007): 356–371.

17. Jack K. Ito and Céleste M. Brotheridge, *Does Supporting Employees' Career Adaptability Lead to Commitment, Turnover, or Both?* (Hoboken: John Wiley & Sons, Inc., 2005).

18. Guy Paré and Michel Tremblay, "The Influence of High-Involvement Human Resources Practices, Procedural Justice, Organizational Commitment, and Citizenship Behaviors on Information Technology Professionals' Turnover Intentions," *Group Organization Management* 32, no. 3 (2007): 326–357.

19. Pearson left EMC in mid-2010 to become an independent communications advisor.

20. Saul Hansell, "Google Answer to Filling Jobs Is an Algorithm," *New York Times,* January 3, 2007, accessed January 18, 2011, http://www.nytimes.com/2007/01/03/technology/03google.html?_r=2&pagewanted=all.

21. Scott Morrison, "Google Searches for Staffing Answers," *The Wall Street Journal,* May 19, 2009, accessed January 18, 2011, http://online.wsj.com/article/SB124269038041932531.html.

22. IBM, "What Does It Mean to Be Smarter?" accessed January 18, 2011, http://www.ibm.com/smarterplanet/us/en/overview/ideas/index.html?ca=v_now&re=ussph2.2.

23. FedEx Corp., *Everything Is Connected: A Global Citizenship Update for 2009,* 16, accessed January 25, 2011, http://about.fedex.designcdt.com/files/FedEx_09_GCR_final_boomrk_0415.pdf.

24. Hilton Worldwide, "About Us," 2010, accessed January 18, 2011, http://www.hiltonworldwide.com/aboutus/index.htm.

25. Richard L. Daft and Dorothy Marcic, *Understanding Management* (Florence: South-Western College Publishing, 2008); and Geoff Colvin, "The 100 Best Companies to Work For 2006," *Fortune,* January 11, 2006,

accessed January 25, 2011, http://money.cnn.com/magazines/fortune/fortune
_archive/2006/01/23/8366990/index.htm.

26. Dave Logan, John King, and Halee Fischer-Wright, *Tribal Leadership: Leveraging Natural Groups to Build a Thriving Organization* (New York: HarperCollins Publishers, 2008), 25, 241.

27. Ibid.

28. Daniel H. Pink, *Drive: The Surprising Truth about What Motivates Us* (New York: Riverhead Books, 2009).

29. Ed Frauenheim, "Commitment Issues—Restoring Employee Engagement," *Workforce Management,* November 16, 2009, accessed January 18, 2011, http://www.workforce.com/section/hr-management/feature/commitment-issues-restoring-employee-engagement/.

30. Christine McConville, "Beth Israel Board Fines CEO Paul Levy $50G for 'Lapse,'" *Boston Herald,* May 3, 2010, accessed January 18, 2011, http://www.bostonherald.com/business/healthcare/view/20100503beth_israel_board_fines_ceo_paul_levy_50g_for_lapse/srvc=home&position=recent.

31. Liz Kowalczyk, "AG Urges Beth Israel to Rethink CEO's Fitness," *The Boston Globe,* September 2, 2010, accessed January 18, 2011, http://www.boston.com/news/local/massachusetts/articles/2010/09 /02/ag_urges_beth_israel_to_rethink_ceos_ fitness/.

32. Ibid.

33. Liz Kowalczyk, "Beth Israel Deaconess Chief Paul Levy Resigns," *The Boston Globe*, January 7, 2011, accessed March 16, 2011, http://www.boston.com/news/health/blog/2011/01/beth_israel_chi.html.

34. Kowalczyk, "AG Urges Beth Israel to Rethink CEO's Fitness," *The Boston Globe.*

35. Christine McConville, "Flush Hospitals Dole out Staff Bonuses," *Boston Herald,* October 5, 2010, accessed January 18, 2011, http://www.bostonherald.com/news/regional/view.bg?articleid=1286583.

36. Glassdoor.com, "Beth Israel Deaconess Medical Center Employee Review," 2011, accessed January 18, 2011, http://www.glassdoor.com/Reviews/Employee-Review-Beth-Israel-Deaconess-Medical-Center-RVW596631.htm.

CHAPTER 8. THE GOOD SELLER

1. Ed Frauenheim, "Making the Call for Themselves," *Workforce Management,* August 2010, accessed January 6, 2011, http://www.workforce.com/section/training-development/feature/making-call-themselves/.

2. Department of Justice, "Justice Department Sues American Express, Mastercard and Visa to Eliminate Rules Restricting Price Competition; Reaches Settlement with Visa and Mastercard," news release, October 4, 2010, accessed January 6, 2011, http://www.justice.gov/opa/pr/2010/October/ 10-at-1115.html.

3. J. D. Power and Associates, "Overall Customer Satisfaction with Credit Cards Rebounds Slightly from 2009, but Loyalty Continues to Decline," news release, August 19, 2010, accessed January 6, 2011, http://businesscenter .jdpower.com/news/pressrelease.aspx?ID=2010159.

4. National Highway Traffic Safety Administration, "Statement from U.S. Transportation Secretary Ray LaHood on Toyota's Agreement to Pay Maximum Civil Penalty," news release, April 19, 2010, accessed January 6, 2011, http://www.nhtsa.gov/PR/DOT-71-10.

5. Mattel, *Playing Responsibly: 2009 Global Citizenship Report*, accessed January 6, 2011, http://corporate.mattel.com/about-us/2009GCReport.pdf.

6. Jennifer C. Kerr, "Mattel Fined $2.3M for Lead Paint on Toys," *USA TODAY,* June 5, 2009, accessed January 6, 2011, http://www.ustoday.com/ money/industries/retail/2009-06-05-mattel-fine_N.htm.

7. Mattel, *Playing Responsibly*.

8. *BusinessWeek*, "Secrets, Lies, and Sweatshops," November 27, 2006, accessed January 6, 2011, http://www.businessweek.com/magazine/content/ 06_48/b4011001.htm.

9. Louise Story and David Barboza, "Mattel Recalls 19 Million Toys Sent from China," *New York Times,* August 15, 2007, accessed January 6, 2011, http://www.nytimes.com/2007/08/15/business/worldbusiness/15imports .html.

10. Mattel, "Consumer Relations Support Center: Product Recall/Advisory," accessed January 6, 2011, http://service.mattel.com/us/recall.asp.

11. Heather Green, "How Amazon Aims to Keep You Clicking," *BusinessWeek,* February 19, 2009, accessed January 6, 2011, http://www .businessweek.com/magazine/content/09_09/b412103 4637296.htm; and *BusinessWeek*, "The Customer Service Champs," February 19, 2009, accessed January 6, 2011, http://www.businessweek.com/interactive_reports/customer _service_2009.html.

12. *BusinessWeek*, "The Customer Service Champs."

13. By the time of the 2010 report, *BusinessWeek* had been purchased by *Bloomberg*. *Bloomberg Businessweek*, "Standouts in Customer Service," February 18, 2010, accessed January 6, 2011, http://bwnt.businessweek.com/ interactive_reports/customer_service_2010/?chan=magazine+channel _special+report.

14. Zappos, "Twitter Posts," accessed January 6, 2011, http://twitter.zappos.com/employee_tweets.

15. Microsoft, "Microsoft Investor Relations," accessed January 6, 2011, http://www.microsoft .com/msft/ic/Default.aspx.

16. Clive Thompson, "The See-Through CEO," *Wired,* March 2007, accessed January 6, 2011, http://www.wired.com/wired/archive/15.04/wired40_ceo.html.

17. Amazon.com, "Kindle Wireless Reading Device, Wi-Fi, Graphite, 6" Display with New E Ink Pearl Technology," 2010, accessed January 11, 2011, http://www.amazon.com/Kindle-Wireless-ReaderWifi Graphite/dp/B002Y27P3M/ref=amb_link_354880722_2?pf_rd_m =ATVPDKIKX0DER&pf_rd_s =center1&pf_rd_r=08F4RCKTZN2 BSD4JJADC&pf_rd_t=101&pf_rd_p=1286053422&pf_rd_i=507846.

18. *New York Times*, "Video of Earthquake Damage in Chile," February 28, 2010, accessed January 6, 2011, http://community.nytimes.com/comments/thelede.blogs.nytimes.com/2010/02 /28/video-of-earthquake-damage-in-chile/#postComment; and *Washington Post*, "Your Photos: Political Signs," January 3, 2011, accessed January 6, 2011, http://www.washington post.com/wpdyn/content/gallery/2010/08/23/GA2010082303447.html.

19. Clive Thompson, "The See-Through CEO," *Wired*.

20. Morgenson and Story, "Banks Bundled Bad Debt, Bet Against It and Won."

21. *The Wall Street Journal*, "Tech: What They Know," accessed January 6, 2011, http://online.wsj.com/public/page/what-they-know-digital-privacy .html.

22. Julia Angwin, "The Web's New Gold Mine: Your Secrets," *Wall Street Journal*, July 30, 2010, accessed January 6, 2011, http://online.wsj.com/article/ SB10001424052748703940090457539507 3512989404.html.

23. Jessica E. Vascellaro, "Google Agonizes on Privacy as Ad World Vaults Ahead," *Wall Street Journal,* August 10, 2010, accessed January 6, 2011, http://online.wsj.com/article/SB100014240527487033097045754135385 1854026.html?mod=WSJ_article_RecentColumns_WhatTheyKnow; and Preston Gralla, "How to Protect Yourself against Google Ad Snooping," *ComputerWorld,* March 13, 2010, accessed January 6, 2011, http://blogs.computer world.com/how_to_protect_yourself _against_google_ad_snooping.

24. Miguel Helft and Tanzina Vega, "Retargeting Ads Follow Surfers to Other Sites," *New York Times,* August 29, 2010, accessed January 6, 2011, http://www.nytimes.com/2010/08/30/technology/30adstalk.html.

25. Ibid.

26. Department of Justice, "Justice Department Sues American Express, Mastercard and Visa."

27. Kenneth I. Chenault, "Why Amex Is Fighting Justice's Bad Deal for Credit Card Holders," op-ed in *Washington Post,* October 8, 2010, accessed January 6, 2011, http://about.americanexpress .com/news/pr/2010/wp-op-ed .aspx.

28. J. D. Power and Associates, "Fees and Rates Drive Decline in Overall Credit Card Customer Satisfaction," news release, September 1, 2009, accessed January 6, 2011, http://businesscenter.jdpower.com/news/press release.aspx?ID=2009162.

29. American Express, "American Express Reports Second Quarter EPS of $0.84, Up Significantly from a Year Ago," news release, July 22, 2010, accessed January 6, 2011, http://www.business wire.com/news/home/20100722006778/en/American-Express-Reports-Quarter-EPS-0.84-Significantly.

30. Great Place to Work Institute, "2011 *Fortune*'s 100 Best Companies to Work For," accessed March 12, 2011, http://www.greatplacetowork .com/what_we_do/lists-us-bestusa.htm?PHPSESSID=326d9b50147ffa 75f749b806da35e989.

31. BrightScope, "American Express Company," accessed January 6, 2011, http://www.brightscope.com/401k-rating/54898/American-Express -Company/55755/American-Express-Retirement-Savings-Plan.

32. Ed Frauenheim, "Making the Call for Themselves," *Workforce Management,* August 2010, accessed January 6, 2011, http://www.workforce.com/section/training-development/feature/making-call-themselves/.

33. *Newsweek,* "Green Rankings 2010," accessed January 6, 2011, http://greenrankings.newsweek.com/companies/view/american-express.

34. *Newsweek,* "Green Rankings: The 2009 List," accessed January 25, 2011, http://greenrankings2009.newsweek.com/companies/view/american-express.

35. E-mail message from American Express to Ed Frauenheim, January 5, 2010.

36. E-mail message from American Express to Ed Frauenheim, December 20, 2010.

37. E-mail message from American Express to Ed Frauenheim, July 21, 2010.

38. Ed Frauenheim, "Making the Call for Themselves," *Workforce Management,* August 2010.

39. American Express, "Corporate Responsibility: Community Service," accessed January 6, 2011, http://about.americanexpress.com/csr/comm_serv .aspx.

40. American Express, "Corporate Responsibility: Leadership," accessed January 6, 2011, http://about.americanexpress.com/csr/leadership.aspx.

41. American Customer Satisfaction Index, "National Quarterly Scores," accessed January 6, 2011, http://www.theacsi.org/index.php?option=com _content&task=view&id=31&Itemid=35.

42. American Express, *Recognizing Responsibility*, November 2007, accessed January 6, 2011, http://about.americanexpress.com/csr/docs/cresp .pdf.

CHAPTER 9. THE GOOD STEWARD

1. Seventh Generation, *Crossroads: Reinventing the Purpose and Possibility of Business,* 2009, corporate report, accessed January 7, 2011, http://www .svg2008report.org/pdf/2008_SVG_CC_Report.pdf.

2. Environmental Protection Agency, "1,4-Dioxane," August 11, 2010, accessed January 7, 2011, http://www.epa.gov/iris/subst/0326.htm; and Seventh Generation, *Crossroads*, 2009.

3. Better World Shopper, "The 20 Best Companies," 2006, http://www .betterworldshopper.org/topten.html.

4. Agency for Toxic Substances & Disease Registry, "Diethyl Phthalate," September 1996, accessed January 7, 2011, http://www.atsdr.cdc.gov/toxfaqs/ tf.asp?id=602&tid=112; Agency for Toxic Substances & Disease Registry, "Di(2-ethylhexyl)phthalate (DEHP)," September 2, 1010, accessed January 7, 2011, http://www.atsdr.cdc.gov/substances/toxsubstance.asp?toxid=65; and European Chemicals Agency, "Evaluation of New Scientific Evidence Concerning the Restrictions Contained in Annex XVII to Regulation (EC) No 1907/2006 (REACH)," July 2010, accessed January 7, 2011, http://echa .europa.eu/doc/reach/restrictions/dnop_echa_review_report_2010_6.pdf.

5. Seventh Generation, *Crossroads*, 2009.

6. Ibid.

7. Seventh Generation, "The 7 Acts of Seventh Generation," accessed January 7, 2011, http://www.seventhgeneration.com/7-acts-seventh-generation.

8. Fleishman-Hillard/National Consumers League, *Rethinking Corporate Social Responsibility*, May 2007, accessed January 7, 2011, http://fleishman hillard.com/wpcontent/uploads/2007/05/csr_white_paper.pdf.

9. Fleishman-Hillard/National Consumers League, *Rethinking Corporate Social Responsibility*.

10. Towers Watson, "From Recession to Recovery: How Far, How Fast, How Well Prepared?" April 2010, accessed January 7, 2011, http://www .towerswatson.com/research/1551.

11. Ryan Tate, "Jann Wenner's Heartless Christmas Layoffs," accessed

January 7, 2011, http://gawker.com/5117514/jann-wenners-heartless
-christmas-layoffs; Gannett Blog, "Tally Hits 863 as Gannett's Mass Layoff
Spreads; Second Big Wave to Slam Papers on Wednesday; Thousands More
Employees Are Still Vulnerable," December 3, 2008, accessed January
7, 2011, http://gannettblog.blogspot.com/2008/12/breaking-gannett-
launches-mass-layoff.html; Erick Schonfeld, "DivX Cuts 21 People from
Payroll," *TechCrunch,* December 11, 2008, accessed January 7, 2011, http://
techcrunch.com/2008/12/11/divx-cuts-21-people-from-payroll/; and Ed
Frauenheim, "The Rueff Truth on 'Abusive' Employers and the Talent Flight
Ahead," *Global Work Watch* (blog), *Workforce Management,* November 23,
2009, accessed January 7, 2011, http://workforce.com/wpmu/globalwork/
2009/11/23/rueff-truth_on_abusive_employers/.

12. Ed Frauenheim, "SuccessFactors, Inventor of the Blame-Shifting
Layoff?" *Global Work Watch* (blog), *Workforce Management,* September
15, 2008, http://workforce.com/wpmu/globalwork /2008/09/15/blame
_shifting_layoff/.

13. Wayne F. Cascio, *Employment Downsizing and Its Alternatives*, report
for the SHRM Foundation, 2009, accessed January 7, 2011, http://www.shrm
.org/about/foundation/products/Documents/Downsizing%20EPG-%20
Final.pdf.

14. Fleishman-Hillard, "Agency News: Expert Panel to Discuss 2007
Survey on Corporate Social Responsibility," news release, May 9, 2007,
accessed January 7, 2011, http://fleishmanhillard .com/2007/05/09/
expert-panel-to-discuss-2007-survey-on-corporate-social-responsibility/.

15. Edelman, "Edelman goodpurpose Study 2010."

16. Procter & Gamble, "Always and Tampax: Protecting the Futures of
Girls," accessed January 7, 2011, http://www.pg.com/en_US/sustainability/
social_responsibility/protecting_futures.shtml.

17. Michael E. Porter and Mark R. Kramer, *Strategy and Society: The Link
Between Competitive Advantage and Corporate Social Responsibility* (Boston,
MA: Harvard Business Review, 2006).

18. Naomi Klein, *No Logo: No Space, No Choice, No Jobs,* (Great Britain:
Flamingo, 2000).

19. Naomi Klein, "Frequently Asked Questions about No Logo," accessed
January 7, 2011, http://www.naomiklein.org/no-logo/faq.

20. Sarah Anderson, Chuck Collins, Sam Pizzigati, and Kevin Shih,
"CEO Pay and the Great Recession," Institute for Policy Studies, September 2,
2010, accessed January 7, 2011, www.ips-dc.org/files/2433/EE-2010-web.pdf.

21. Jane G. Gravelle, "Tax Havens: International Tax Avoidance and Eva-

sion," Congressional Research Service, July 9, 2009, accessed January 7, 2011, http://assets.opencrs.com/rpts/ R40623_20090709.pdf.

22. U.S. Environmental Protection Agency, "ExxonMobil Petroleum Refinery Settlement," December 17, 2008, accessed January 25, 2011, http://www.epa.gov/compliance/resources/cases/civil/caa/exxonmobil05caa.html.

23. Larry West, "It's Official: BP Gusher in Gulf Is Biggest Oil Spill Ever," *About.com,* August 3, 2010, accessed January 7, 2011, http://environment.about.com/b/2010/08/03/its-official-bp-gusher-in-gulf-is-biggest-oil-spill-ever.htm.

24. Ben Casselman and Russell Gold, "BP Decisions Set Stage for Disaster," *Wall Street Journal,* May 27, 2010, accessed January 7, 2011, http://online.wsj.com/article/SB10001424052748704026204575266560930780190.html; and 60 Minutes, "Blowout: The Deepwater Horizon Disaster," *CBS News.com,* August 22, 2010, accessed January 7, 2011, http://www.cbsnews.com/stories/2010/08/19/60minutes/main6787685.shtml.

25. National Commission on the BP Deepwater Horizon Oil Spill and Offshore Drilling, "Deep Water: The Gulf Oil Disaster and the Future of Offshore Drilling," report to the president, January 2011, vii, accessed January 23, 2011, https://s3.amazonaws.com/pdf_final/1_OSC_Intro.pdf.

26. The 2007 Fleishman-Hillard/National Consumers League study found that consumers ranked going beyond the law to protect the environment as the second-highest priority among seven behaviors related to corporate social responsibility. Only treating or paying employees well ranked higher. See *Rethinking Corporate Social Responsibility*, A Fleishman-Hillard/National Consumers League Study, 2007.

27. Water quality is another area where government standards have become dangerously outdated. Water Americans drink can pose what scientists say are serious health risks yet still be legal. A wide array of drugs—including antibiotics, mood stabilizers, and sex hormones—has been found in the drinking water supplies of tens of millions of Americans. Although the concentrations are low, the presence of the pharmaceuticals raises concerns among scientists about the long-term effects on human health. Charles Duhigg, "That Tap Water Is Legal but May Be Unhealthy," *New York Times,* December 16, 2009, accessed January 7, 2011, http://www.nytimes.com/2009/12/17/us/17water.html?_r=1; and Jeff Donn, Martha Mendoza, and Justin Pritchard, "Drugs Found in Drinking Water," *Associated Press,* September 12, 2008, accessed January 7, 2011, http://www.usatoday.com/news/nation/2008-03-10-drugs-tap-water_N.htm.

28. Carbon Disclosure Project, "What We Do," an overview, accessed

January 7, 2011, https://www.cdproject.net/en-US/WhatWeDo/Pages/overview.aspx.

29. Ibid.

30. SAM Research, *Corporate Sustainability Assessment Questionnaire*, 2009.

31. TerraChoice, "Greenwashing Affects 98% of Products Including Toys, Baby Products and Cosmetics," news release, April 15, 2009, accessed January 7, 2011, http://www.terrachoice.com/images/Seven%20Sins%20of%20Greenwashing%20Release%20%20April%2015%202009%20-%20US.pdf.

32. Bill Breen & Jeffrey Hollender, *The Responsibility Revolution: How the Next Generation of Businesses Will Win* (San Francisco: Jossey-Bass 2010).

33. *Newsweek*, "Green Rankings 2010," accessed January 7, 2011, http://greenrankings.newsweek.com/companies/view/hewlett-packard.

34. Traci Purdum, "Manufacturers Are Seeing Bottom-Line Benefits of Designing for the Environment," *Industry Week,* August 1, 2006, accessed January 7, 2011, http://www.industryweek.com/articles/manufacturers_are_seeing_bottomline_benefits_of_designing_for_the_environment_12310.aspx?ShowAll=1.

35. Hewlett-Packard Development Co., "HP Planet Partners Recycling Program," accessed January 25, 2011, http://www.hp.com/hpinfo/globalcitizenship/environment/recycling/product-recycling.html.

36. Hewlett-Packard Development Co., "Product Return and Recycling," accessed January 25, 2011, http://www.hp.com/hpinfo/globalcitizenship/environment/recycling/unwanted-hardware.html.

37. Walmart, "Walmart Announces Sustainable Product Index," news release, July 16, 2009, accessed January 7, 2011, http://walmartstores.com/pressroom/news/9277.aspx.

38. Ibid.

39. Rosabeth Moss Kanter, "Wal-Mart's Environmental Game-Changer," *Harvard Business Review,* July 16, 2009, accessed January 7, 2011, http://blogs.hbr.org/kanter/2009/07/walmarts-environmental-gamecha.html.

40. Seventh Generation, "Executive Summary," *Return on Purpose,* 2010, accessed January 7, 2011, http://www.7genreport.com/introduction/execsummary.php#3.

41. Robin, "The Precautionary Principle," *Articles,* February 8, 2008, accessed January 7, 2011, http://www.seventhgeneration.com/learn/news/precautionary-principle-0.

42. Traci Purdum, "Manufacturers Are Seeing Bottom-Line Benefits of Designing for the Environment," *Industry Week,* August 1, 2006.

43. Seventh Generation, "Improved Products," *Return on Purpose,* 2010,

accessed January 7, 2011, http://www.7genreport.com/products/improved
.php.

44. Seventh Generation, "Sales and Economic Performance," *Return on
Purpose,* 2010, accessed January 7, 2011, http://www.7genreport.com/intro-
duction/performance.php.

45. Carolyn Said, "Green MBA Degrees Sprout up on Campuses,"
SFGate.com, April 21, 2010, accessed January 7, 2011, http://articles.sfgate
.com/2010-04-21/business/20858394_1_mba-programs-business-administra-
tion-programs-greenhouse.

46. SKS Microfinance, "Our People," accessed January 23, 2011, http://
www.sksindia.com/our_people.php.

47. John Tozzi, "What a Good Company Looks Like," *The New
Entrepreneur* (blog), *Bloomberg Businessweek,* March 15, 2010, http://www
.businessweek.com/smallbiz/running_small_business/archives/2010/03/
what_a_good_com.html.

48. Bruce Edwards, "New Law Keeps with Vt.'s Social Conscience," *Vermont Today,* June 13, 2010, accessed January 11, 2011, http://www.vermont
today.com/apps/pbcs.dll/article?AID=/RH/20100613/BUSINESS/10061
9977/-1/VBJ.

49. John Tozzi, "Maryland Passes 'Benefit Corp.' Law for Social Entre-
preneurs," *The New Entrepreneur* (blog), *Bloomberg Businessweek*, April 13,
2010, accessed March 12, 2011, http://www.businessweek.com/smallbiz/
running_small_business/archives/2010/04/benefit_corp_bi.html.

50. B Lab, "Legal Framework," 2011, accessed January 7, 2011, http://
www.bcorporation.net/become/legal.

51. B Lab, "B Community," 2011, accessed January 11, 2011, http://www
.bcorporation.net/community.

52. As an employer, for example, Seventh Generation has strived to hire
people who share its values—which makes for a more inspired workforce. It
also has sought to create an environment where employees can "summon all
their individuality and creativity" as well as speak their mind. And, as of early
2010, employees owned close to 20 percent of the company. As a seller, Seventh
Generation has worked to provide nontoxic home-cleaning products. It also has
been transparent about problems. For example, it conceded in its 2009 Corporate Consciousness Report that it reduced the number of baby wipes in packages
without changing the size of the package, which made the product less green:
"Unacceptably, we did not adequately inform our consumers of this change,
a serious departure from the authenticity we aspire to." Seventh Generation,
Crossroads, 2009, 60; Jeffrey Hollender, "Giving Up the CEO Seat: How I Did

It," *Harvard Business Review*, March 2010; and Seventh Generation, "Executive Summary," *Return on Purpose*, corporate report, 2010, accessed January 25, 2011, http://www.7genreport.com/introduction/execsummary.php.

53. Evidence of the positive effects of employee worthiness on stewardship can be seen by the pride Seventh Generation employees show in pursuing sustainability. Tim Fowler, the company's vice president of research and development, details the bumpy quest to get rid of 1,4-dioxane in hand dishwashing soap in the company's 2009 Corporate Consciousness Report. An expected breakthrough failed, but employees stuck with the effort until it succeeded. And as a seller that communicates extensively with customers—a feature of good sellers—Seventh Generation is helping to change consumer habits to make them more eco-friendly. The number of Seventh Generation "followers" on social media sites such as Facebook, Twitter, and LinkedIn jumped from fewer than 1,800 at the beginning of 2009 to nearly 44,900 a year later. Seventh Generation, "Improved Products," *Return on Purpose*, 2010, accessed January 25, 2011, http://www.7gen report.com/introduction/execsummary .php; and Seventh Generation, "Conversations with our Consumers," *Return on Purpose*, 2010, accessed January 25, 2011, http://www.7genreport.com/ engagement/index.php.

54. Jeffrey Hollender, "Big Changes at Seventh Generation," *7GenBlog*, June 1, 2009, accessed January 7, 2011, http://www.seventhgeneration.com/ learn/blog/big-changes-seventh-generation.

55. Peter Graham, Seventh Generation Chairman, letter to friends and shareholders of Seventh Generation, October 26, 2010, cited in Marc Gunther, "Seventh Generation Sweeps out Its Founder," *Marc Gunther* (blog), November 1, 2010, accessed January 25, 2011, http://www.marcgunther .com/2010/11/01/seventh-generation-sweeps-out-its-founder/. (Graham's letter to shareholders was confirmed as authentic by company spokeswoman Chrystie Heimert via e-mail message to Ed Frauenheim, January 14, 2011.)

56. Ariel Schwartz, "Seventh Generation Co-Founder Jeffrey Hollender Fired by Company Board," *Fast Company*, November 2, 2010, accessed January 7, 2011, http://www.fastcompany.com/1699654/ seventh-generation-co-founder-jeffrey-hollender-fired-by-company-board.

57. In a letter to shareholders, for example, Board Chairman Peter Graham wrote: "To a large extent, present circumstances mirror those at many other companies whose founders have made the decision to turn over the reins to someone else. As organizations grow, so do their managerial requirements. Eventually these increasing layers of complexity demand the recruitment of experienced professional leadership whose abilities and experiences are required to move forward. This is the crossroads at which Seventh Generation

now stands." Graham, letter to friends and shareholders of Seventh Generation, cited in Gunther, "Seventh Generation Sweeps out Its Founder."

58. Dave Rapaport, Seventh Generation Director of Corporate Consciousness, interview by Ed Frauenheim, January 12, 2011.

CHAPTER 10. THE WORTHINESS ERA

1. Ed Frauenheim, "Special Report on HR Technology: Tracking the Contingents," *Workforce Management,* April 2010, accessed January 14, 2011, https://www.workforce.com/section/software-technology/feature/special -report-hr-technology-tracking-contingents/index.html.

2. "The Flexible Labor Force," *Bloomberg Businessweek*, accessed January 14, 2011, http://www.businessweek.com/magazine/content/10_03/b4163036 939047.htm.

3. Watson Wyatt Worldwide, *Effect of the Economic Crisis on HR Programs—Update: 2009*, accessed January 14, 2011, http://www.watsonwyatt .com/news/pdfs/WT-2009-13301.pdf, figure 8.

4. Rob Gray, "Can Outsourcing Really Deliver Cost Savings?" *HR Magazine,* November 1, 2010, accessed January 14, 2011, http://www.hrmagazine. co.uk/news/1037089/outsourcing-really-deliver-cost-savings/; and Jessica Marquez, "Special Report: HR Outsourcing—Back to Basics," *Workforce Magazine,* March 16, 2010, accessed January 14, 2011, http://www.workforce .com/section/hr-management/feature/special-report-hr-outsourcing-back basics/index.html.

5. Cascio, *Employment Downsizing and Its Alternatives*; see also Wayne F. Cascio, *Responsible Restructuring: Creative and Profitable Alternatives* (San Francisco: Berrett-Koehler Publishers Inc., 2002) and Carlos Bergfeld, "The Hidden Costs of Layoffs," *Portfolio.com,* February 1, 2010, accessed January 14, 2011, http://www.portfolio.com/resources/insight-center/2009/02/01/ The-Hidden-Costs-of-Layoffs/.

6. Ed Frauenheim, "5 Questions for Stephen M.R. Covey, Chief Executive of Consulting Firm CoveyLink," *Workforce Management,* November 20, 2006, accessed January 14, 2011, http://www.workforce.com/archive/ feature/24/60/08/index.php.

7. William D. Brosey, Richard E. Neal, and Douglas Marks, *Grand Challenges of Enterprise Integration*, paper for the 8th IEEE International Conference on Emerging Technologies and Factory Automation, April 2001, accessed January 14, 2011, http://www1.y12.doe.gov/search/library/ documents/pdf/ydw-1851.pdf; and Valdis E. Krebs, "Managing the Connected Organization," 2008, accessed January 14, 2011, http://www.orgnet

.com/MCO.html. As the latter essay, by consultant Valdis Krebs, points out, there is power in having "indirect" ties. Those refer to people or organizations that are connected to a person or organization with whom or which you have a direct tie. Having too many direct connections can prove overwhelming to manage. But in order to benefit significantly from indirect ties, people and organizations are wise to have at least some direct, strong ties.

8. Ed Frauenheim, "Client Aids Engagement at Outsourcer," *Workforce Management,* March 2010, accessed January 14, 2011, http://www.workforce .com/archive/feature/hr-management/client-aids-engagement-outsourcer/ index.php; and Rob Gray, "Can Outsourcing Really Deliver Cost Savings?" *HR Magazine,* November 1, 2010, accessed January 14, 2011, http://www.hr magazine.co.uk/news/1037089/outsourcing-really-deliver-cost-savings/.

9. Deborah Willig, FedEx spokeswoman, e-mail to Ed Frauenheim, January 20, 2011.

10. Apple, *Apple Supplier Responsibility: 2011 Progress Report,* accessed March 15, 2011, http://images.apple.com/supplierresponsibility/pdf/Apple _SR_2011_Progress_Report.pdf; and Apple, *Supplier Responsibility: 2010 Progress Report*, accessed January 19, 2011, http://images.apple.com/supplier responsibility/pdf/SR_2010_Progress_Report.pdf.

11. Ed Frauenheim, "Special Report on HR Outsourcing: Why You Should Care about Engagement in Your Outsourcer's Workforce," *Workforce Management,* March 2010, accessed January 14, 2011, http://www.workforce .com/section/hr-management/feature/special-report-hr-outsourcing-why -should-care-about-/.

12. International Monetary Fund, "World Economic Outlook Database," April 2010, accessed January 26, 2011, http://www.imf.org/external/pubs/ft/ weo/2010/01/weodata/weoselgr.aspx.

13. Human Rights Watch, "Vietnam: End Crackdown on Labor Activists," May 4, 2010, accessed January 14, 2011, http://www.hrw.org/en/news/ 2009/05/03/vietnam-end-crackdown-labor-activists; and Human Rights Watch, "China," 2009, accessed January 14, 2011, http://www.hrw.org/en/ node/87491.

14. Kathy Chu and Michelle Yun, "Workers Are Finding Their Voice to Fight for Rights in China," *The China Post*, November 22, 2010, accessed January 23, 2011, http://www.chinapost.com.tw/china/national-news/2010/ 11/22/280826/Workers-are.htm.

15. Ed Frauenheim, "Risk, Reward, and How Angel Yu Got to the 32nd Floor," *Global Work Watch* (blog), *Workforce Management*, March 5, 2007, accessed January 14, 2011, http://workforce.com/wpmu/global work/2007/03/05/risk-reward-and-how-angel-yu-got-to-the-32nd-floor/.

16. Ed Frauenheim, "China to the Rescue?" *Global Work Watch* (blog), *Workforce Management*, March 9, 2007, accessed January 14, 2011, http://workforce.com/wpmu/globalwork/2007/03/09/china-to-the-rescue/.

17. Peter Cappelli, Harbir Singh, Jitendra V. Singh, and Michael Useem, "Leadership Lessons from India," *Harvard Business Review,* March 2010, accessed January 14, 2011, http://hbr.org/2010/03/leadership-lessons-from-india/ar/1.

18. The Nielsen Company, "Consumer Confidence, Concerns, Spending and Attitudes to Recession," consumer report, June 2008, accessed January 14, 2011, http://pt.nielsen.com/documents/tr_0806_GCC_LR_200608.pdf.

19. Richard Payne and Marie Brinkman, "Beyond Compensation—Is It All Just Money?" *Asia Connect* 1, no. 1, (2008), accessed January 14, 2011, http://www.aon.com/thought-leadership/asia-connect/oct-08/beyond-compensation.jsp.

20. Accenture, "Mobility Takes Center Stage: The 2010 Accenture Consumer Electronics Products and Services Usage Report," 2010, accessed January 14, 2011, https://microsite.accenture.com/landing_pages/consumer technologyusage/Documents/AccentureConsumerTech2010.pdf.

21. John Lipsky, First Deputy Managing Director, International Monetary Fund, "Realizing the Potential of Asia's Developing Economies," speech, March 22, 2010, accessed January 14, 2011, http://www.imf.org/external/np/speeches/2010/032210.htm. If nothing is done about climate change, Southeast Asia could lose the equivalent of 6¾ percent of GDP each year by the end of this century, more than twice the global average loss, according to the International Monetary Fund.

22. Jonathan Watts, "Copenhagen destroyed by Danish draft leak, says India's environment minister," *Guardian,* April 12, 2010, accessed January 14, 2011, http://www.guardian.co.uk/environment/2010/apr/12/copenhagen-destroyed-danish-draft-leak.

23. Shailesh M. Bureau, "For PEs, Clean Tech Opens New Investment Frontier," *Economic Times,* March 30, 2010, accessed January 14, 2011, http://economictimes.indiatimes.com/news/news-by-industry/banking/finance/finance/For-PEs-clean-tech-opens-new-investment-frontier/article show/5740643.cms; and Julian Borger and Jonathan Watts, "China Launches Green Power Revolution to Catch up on West," *Guardian,* June 10, 2009, accessed January 14, 2011, http://www.guardian.co.uk/world/2009/jun/09/china-green-energy-solar-wind.

24. Pew Research Center, "G-20 Clean Energy Profile China," accessed January 14, 2011, http://www.pewglobalwarming.org/cleanenergyeconomy/factsheets/China_profile.pdf.

25. Intergovernmental Panel on Climate Change, "Climate Change 2007: Synthesis Report," accessed January 14, 2011, http://www.ipcc.ch/publications_and_data/ar4/syr/en/spms3.html.

26. Ibid.

27. International Labour Organization, "World Day for Safety and Health at Work 2009: FACTS ON Safety and Health at Work," April 2009, accessed January 14, 2011, http://www.ilo.org/wcmsp5/groups/public/---dgreports/---dcomm/documents/publication/wcms_105146.pdf.

28. Ibid.

29. James O'Toole and Edward Lawler III, *The New American Workplace* (New York: Palgrave Macmillan, 2006).

30. Ibid.

31. European Union Consumer Affairs, "3 Minutes to Discover the EU Consumer Policy," October 2008, accessed January 14, 2011, http://ec.europa.eu/consumers/safety/rapex/docs/rapex_annualreport2009_en.pdf. The number of nonfood consumer product safety notifications distributed by the European Commission climbed 16 percent to 1,866 from 2007 to 2008, and in the United States the number of toy-related injuries treated in hospital emergency departments rose 12 percent to 235,300 from 2004 to 2008. Consumer Product Safety Commission, "Toy-Related Deaths and Injuries Calendar Year 2008," accessed January 14, 2011, http://www.cpsc.gov/library/toymemo08.pdf.

32. Consumer Product Safety Commission, "2009 Annual Report to the President and the Congress," 2009, accessed January 14, 2011, http://www.cpsc.gov/cpscpub/pubs/reports/2009rpt.pdf.

33. Paul S. Mead, Laurence Slutsker, Vance Dietz, Linda F. McCaig, Joseph S. Bresee, Craig Shapiro, Patricia M. Griffin, and Robert V. Tauxe, "Food-related Illness and Death in the United States," *Emerging Infectious Diseases*, September–October, 1999; 5(5): 607–25.

34. WorldPublicOpinion.org, "Wide Dissatisfaction with Capitalism— Twenty Years after Fall of Berlin Wall," accessed January 14, 2011, http://www.worldpublicopinion.org/pipa/articles/btglobalizationtradera/644.php?lb=btgl&pnt=644&nid=&id=; and WorldPublicOpinion.org, "Global Poll Shows Support for Increased Government Spending and Regulation."

35. David Barstow, Laura Dodd, James Glanz, Stephanie Saul, and Ian Urbina, "Regulators Failed to Address Risks in Oil Rig Fail-Safe Device," *New York Times*, June 20, 2010, accessed January 14, 2011, http://www.nytimes.com/2010/06/21/us/21blowout.html.

36. David Brooks, "The Larger Struggle," *New York Times*, June 14,

2010, accessed January 14, 2011, http://www.nytimes.com/2010/06/15/ opinion/15brooks.html.

37. Barstow et al., "Regulators Failed to Address Risks in Oil Rig Fail-Safe Device" *New York Times*, June 20, 2010.

38. National Commission on the BP Deepwater Horizon Oil Spill and Offshore Drilling, "Deep Water: The Gulf Oil Disaster and the Future of Offshore Drilling," January 2011, vii, accessed January 23, 2011, https://s3 .amazonaws.com/pdf_final/1_OSC_Intro.pdf.

39. Tuition reimbursement programs may be an example of a particularly effective training investment. Peter Cappelli, "Why Do Employers Pay For College?" accessed January 14, 2011, http://www-management.wharton .upenn.edu/cappelli/documents/WhyDoEmployersPayforCollege.pdf; and Elaine Rigoli, "The Talent-on-Demand Approach with Wharton's Peter Cappelli," *ere.net,* March 12, 2008, accessed January 14, 2011, http://www.ere.net /2008/03/12/the-talent-on-demand-approach-with-whartons-peter-cappelli/.

40. Charlie Cray, "Chartering a New Course: Revoking Corporations' Right to Exist," *Multinational Monitor,* October/November 2002, accessed January 14, 2011, http://www.multinational monitor.org/mm2002/102002/ cray.html.

41. Ibid.

42. *The Corporation*, DVD, a film by Mark Achbar, Jennifer Abbott, and Joel Bakan (Vancouver, BC: Hello Cool World, 2004).

CHAPTER 11. A HOPE*FULLY* IDEALISTIC VISION

1. U.S. Securities and Exchange Commission, "SEC Issues Interpretive Guidance on Disclosure Related to Business or Legal Developments Regarding Climate Change," January 27, 2010, accessed January 14, 2011, http:// www.sec.gov/news/press/2010/2010-15.htm.

2. Ceres, "Case Studies in Sustainability," 2007, accessed January 14, 2011, http://www.ceres.org/Page.aspx?pid=1031#timberland.

3. David Buzzelli, e-mail message to Ed Frauenheim, September 14, 2010.

4. Scott Scherr, interview by Ed Frauenheim, June 8, 2010.

5. The American Customer Satisfaction Index, "National Quarterly Scores," accessed March 18, 2011, http://www.theacsi.org/index.php?option =com_content&task=view&id=31&Itemid=35.

6. Edelman, "Despite Prolonged Global Recession, an Increasing Number of People . . ."

7. Edelman, "Citizens in Emerging Markets Outpace the US and Europe," news release, November 4, 2010, accessed January 26, 2011, http://www .edelman.com/news/ShowOne.asp?ID=262.

8. David Barboza and Keith Bradsher, "In China, Labor Movement Enabled by Technology," *New York Times,* June 16, 2010, accessed January 14, 2011, http://www.nytimes.com/2010 /06/17/business/global/17strike.html.

9. Liza Lin and Yuki Hagiwara, "Honda's Chinese Supplier Strikes Caught Carmaker by Surprise," *Bloomberg Businessweek,* June 16, 2010, accessed January 14, 2011, http://www.businessweek.com/news/2010-06-16/ honda-s-chinese-supplier-strikes-caught-carmaker-by-surprise.html; and David Barboza and Keith Bradsher, "In China, Labor Movement Enabled by Technology," *New York Times,* June 16, 2010, accessed January 14, 2011, http://www.nytimes.com/2010/06/17/business/global/17strike.html.

10. Kathy Chu and Michelle Yun, "Workers Are Finding Their Voice to Fight for Rights in China," *China Post*, November 22, 2010, accessed January 23, 2011, http://www.chinapost.com.tw/china/national-news/2010/ 11/22/280826/Workers-are.htm.

INDEX

ABOUT THE AUTHORS

Dr. Laurie Bassi is the CEO of McBassi & Company, a consulting firm that specializes in human capital analytics. An economist, author, and speaker, Laurie focuses her work on helping companies to identify opportunities to drive better business results through more effective and enlightened management of employees. She has been conducting research on workplaces for over three decades and has consulted with dozens of organizations and governments around the world.

Laurie is also a registered investment advisor and the chair of Bassi Investments (which uses the principles and findings outlined in *Good Company* to manage assets). She has served as the director of research for Saba Software, vice president at the American Society for Training and Development (ASTD), a staff director of two U.S. Government commissions, and a cochair of the Board on Testing and Assessment at the National Academy of Sciences. The early years of Laurie's career were spent as a tenured professor of economics and public policy at Georgetown University.

Laurie has authored over 80 published papers and has given talks throughout the United States, Europe, and Asia. She holds a PhD in economics from Princeton University.

Ed Frauenheim is a journalist with 15 years of experience writing about topics including technology, work, business, and education. He currently is Senior Editor at *Workforce Management* magazine, where he helps lead the magazine's coverage of people management and business strategy. Ed has written extensively about outsourcing, emerging economies, and employee engagement. His stories have earned awards from the Associated Press News Execu-  tive Council of California and Nevada, the American Society of Business Publication Editors, and American Business Media.

Ed has worked at CNET News.com and the *Oakland Tribune* chain of newspapers. He has written freelance stories for publications including *Salon.com*, *Wired* magazine, the *Dallas Morning News*, and *Knowledge@ Wharton*, the online magazine of The Wharton School at the University of Pennsylvania. Ed earned a bachelor's degree in history from Princeton University and a master's degree in education from the University of California at Berkeley.

Dan McMurrer is chief analyst at McBassi & Company and chief research officer at Bassi Investments. Over the past 15 years, Dan and Laurie have worked together, designing and deploying assessment tools for understanding the unique strengths and weaknesses of orga- nizations' work and learning environments, and analyzing how those are linked to business results. Dan is also a registered investment advi-  sor, and works with Laurie to manage Bassi Investments' portfolios.

Prior to cofounding McBassi & Company, Dan worked in research positions at the Urban Institute, Saba Software, the American Society for Training and Development, and the U.S. Department of Labor. He has authored two previous books as well as multiple articles. He holds a bachelor's degree in politics from Princeton University and a master's degree in public policy from Georgetown University.

Larry Costello is an experienced human resource professional, most recently serving as senior vice president for human resources at American Standard Companies. Throughout his career Larry has held senior management positions at the Campbell Soup Company, PepsiCo Inc., North American Van Lines, and Frito Lay.

After American Standard was sold to Ingersoll Rand in 2008, Larry founded The Lawrence Bradford Group, a talent management advisory firm. He consults on a variety of issues and topics, providing human capital expertise in a range of settings.

Larry is a board advisor of LJH Linley Capital, McBassi & Company, Sky-Trax Inc., and Zapoint, and he is chair of the advisory board for the Center for Human Resource Strategy in the School of Management and Labor Relations at Rutgers University. He holds a bachelor's degree in business and finance administration from Rider College (NJ) and attended the Harvard Program for Management Development.

Berrett–Koehler
Publishers

Berrett-Koehler is an independent publisher dedicated to an ambitious mission: *Creating a World That Works for All*.

We believe that to truly create a better world, action is needed at all levels—individual, organizational, and societal. At the individual level, our publications help people align their lives with their values and with their aspirations for a better world. At the organizational level, our publications promote progressive leadership and management practices, socially responsible approaches to business, and humane and effective organizations. At the societal level, our publications advance social and economic justice, shared prosperity, sustainability, and new solutions to national and global issues.

A major theme of our publications is "Opening Up New Space." Berrett-Koehler titles challenge conventional thinking, introduce new ideas, and foster positive change. Their common quest is changing the underlying beliefs, mindsets, institutions, and structures that keep generating the same cycles of problems, no matter who our leaders are or what improvement programs we adopt.

We strive to practice what we preach—to operate our publishing company in line with the ideas in our books. At the core of our approach is stewardship, which we define as a deep sense of responsibility to administer the company for the benefit of all of our "stakeholder" groups: authors, customers, employees, investors, service providers, and the communities and environment around us.

We are grateful to the thousands of readers, authors, and other friends of the company who consider themselves to be part of the "BK Community." We hope that you, too, will join us in our mission.

A BK Business Book

This book is part of our BK Business series. BK Business titles pioneer new and progressive leadership and management practices in all types of public, private, and nonprofit organizations. They promote socially responsible approaches to business, innovative organizational change methods, and more humane and effective organizations.

Berrett–Koehler
Publishers

A community dedicated to creating
a world that works for all

Visit Our Website: www.bkconnection.com

Read book excerpts, see author videos and Internet movies, read our authors' blogs, join discussion groups, download book apps, find out about the BK Affiliate Network, browse subject-area libraries of books, get special discounts, and more!

Subscribe to Our Free E-Newsletter, the *BK Communiqué*

Be the first to hear about new publications, special discount offers, exclusive articles, news about bestsellers, and more! Get on the list for our free e-newsletter by going to **www.bkconnection.com**.

Get Quantity Discounts

Berrett-Koehler books are available at quantity discounts for orders of ten or more copies. Please call us toll-free at (800) 929-2929 or email us at **bkp .orders@aidcvt.com**.

Join the BK Community

BKcommunity.com is a virtual meeting place where people from around the world can engage with kindred spirits to create a world that works for all. BKcommunity.com members may create their own profiles, blog, start and participate in forums and discussion groups, post photos and videos, answer surveys, announce and register for upcoming events, and chat with others online in real time. Please join the conversation!